T0315224

HEALTHCARE PAYMENT SYSTEMS

Prospective Payment Systems

HEALTHCARE PAYMENT SYSTEMS

Prospective Payment Systems

Duane C. Abbey

CRC Press
Taylor & Francis Group
Boca Raton London New York

CRC Press is an imprint of the
Taylor & Francis Group, an **informa** business

A PRODUCTIVITY PRESS BOOK

CRC Press
Taylor & Francis Group
6000 Broken Sound Parkway NW, Suite 300
Boca Raton, FL 33487-2742

First issued in hardback 2018

ISBN 13: 978-1-138-44037-1 (hbk)
ISBN 13: 978-1-4398-7301-4 (pbk)

Library of Congress Cataloging-in-Publication Data

Abbey, Duane C.
    Prospective payment systems / Duane C. Abbey.
      p. ; cm.
    Includes bibliographical references and index.
    ISBN 978-1-4398-7301-4 (pbk. : alk. paper)
    I. Title.
    [DNLM: 1. Prospective Payment System--United States. W 74 AA1]

362.1068'1--dc23

2011050499

Visit the Taylor & Francis Web site at
http://www.taylorandfrancis.com

and the CRC Press Web site at
http://www.crcpress.com

Dedication and Acknowledgments

Everyone who receives a statement from a physician, clinic, hospital, or other healthcare provider and later receives an explanation of benefits from an insurance carrier is often bewildered and befuddled. Attempting to determine what was charged and then how payment was, or was not, made can be convoluted. There may be multiple third-party payers involved, that is, secondary and tertiary payers, which further complicates understanding this critical financial aspect of healthcare.

This text is dedicated to those who want and need to know more about how healthcare services are charged and then paid. While a specific type of payment system is discussed—namely, prospective payment systems—many of the principles and concepts discussed will assist you in better understanding how prospective payment systems work and how these same features may appear in other payment systems, such as fee schedule payment systems.

While this text has been designed to be accessible to a fairly wide audience, including interested laypersons, there is enough technical detail for those who are directly involved in using these payment systems as employees, consultants, advisors, and attorneys to various healthcare providers. Keeping in mind that payment involves two parties, this text is also useful for those on the payer side of the equation. Insurance companies and other third-party payers must also understand and then design the way in which they will make payments for healthcare services.

I wish to acknowledge all the students who have attended my workshops, both in person and through teleconferences. Studying and understanding healthcare payment systems require significant dedication. In today's healthcare environment, another more sinister aspect of healthcare payment is compliance. Most of the prospective payment systems discussed are used by the Medicare program. Because of the complexities of these payment processes, underpayments and overpayments do occur. Thus, simply knowing about a payment system process is not enough; a full understanding is necessary to ensure compliance. A redoubling of efforts is often required for those directly involved in healthcare payment systems in order to ensure compliance.

I also wish to acknowledge the patience and understanding of my family in allowing me the time to prepare this text. Their support and encouragement are greatly appreciated.

Contents

Preface

This is the third text in a series of four books devoted to healthcare payment systems. We address prospective payment systems in this book. References will be made to the other three texts from time to time in our discussions. Here are the titles of the other three books:

- *Introduction to Healthcare Payment Systems*
- *Fee Schedule Payment Systems*
- *Cost-Based, Charge-Based and Contractual Payment Systems*

As feasible, a similar approach and style have been maintained for all four books.

Healthcare payment processes are often quite complicated. At times there can even be political controversy concerning their use. Discussion surrounding various types of healthcare payment processes can become quite confusing unless there is uniformity in terminology and definitions. Unfortunately, one must sometimes glean the meaning of terminology from the context of the discussion.

Because healthcare payment is a statutory issue for the Medicare program and often a contractual issue for private third-party payers, great care must be taken to understand the terminology and the many acronyms that are used in this area. In some cases, healthcare providers file claims to third-party payers with whom the healthcare provider has no relationship. While there should be full payment for the charges made, often the unknown third-party payers will pay on the basis of a predetermined system, including various prospective payment systems (PPSs). Terminology specific to a given third-party payer may seem unorthodox. Always be prepared to ask exactly what certain terms mean.

Many of the adjudication discussions surrounding PPSs can become quite technical. For the Medicare program there are tens of thousands of pages of rules, regulations, bulletins, transmittals, and other documents that are issued. Thus, as a way to make the reading of such materials a little friendlier, I will use *small case studies* to illustrate various concepts as we discuss them.

This text has been prepared to address various complexities by iterating certain concepts. This means that we will address a concept or topic at a high level and then revisit the same or perhaps a similar topic and drill down with more detail. Due to the extreme complexities of prospective payment systems, we are only able to address a few topics at a detailed conceptual level. For this text the goal is to understand many of the features and the way in which prospective payment systems function. When these systems are in use to actually reimburse healthcare providers, they are very dynamic in nature and are constantly changing and evolving

The level of detail provided concerning the PPSs discussed has been balanced with the number of conceptual features that are presented. To fully discuss any one of the PPSs addressed would take a separate book. The intent is to provide a framework to understand and analyze the characteristics of any given PPS.

Comments on Terminology and Notation

Acronyms abound in healthcare for coding, billing, and reimbursement. An acronym listing is provided in Appendix B. As much as possible, when acronyms are first used in a chapter, the meaning is provided. However, you may find times when you need to go to the acronym listing to verify the meanings. We are at a point where there are sometimes *second-order* acronyms; that is, these are acronyms that can be used in different ways. For instance, the acronym *MAC* can refer to monitored anesthesia care or Medicare administrative contractor.

Special notes are provided throughout the text. These notes convey additional information that is an adjunct to the specific discussion. Almost any rule, regulation, or approach to payment will have exceptions and unusual idiosyncrasies. When possible, further references are provided. Also, alerts are made to topics in which change is currently taking place. If healthcare payment systems have any one feature in common, it is that they are in a constant state of change.

Modifiers will be indicated in quotations with a leading hyphen, such as "-LT", *Left*. The description of the modifier will be indicated in italics. This notation is used to indicate that the modifier is used as a suffix that is appended to a CPT® or HCPCS code. This notation is really a follow-over from paper claims. Today, for the most part, modifiers represent data elements that go into a specific location in the electronic format. Thus, the leading hyphen is for human reading purposes, and not for actual claims filing purposes.

We will also generally refer to the *Medicare program* as opposed to CMS (Centers for Medicare and Medicaid Services). CMS is the administrator for the Medicare program. Thus, various rules, regulations, directives, transmittals and the like all emanate from CMS. These various rules and regulations govern the Medicare program and thus the Medicare fee prospective payment systems that we discuss in this book.

We also use abbreviated descriptions for CPT and HCPCS codes as well as for the various modifiers. For full descriptions of codes and modifiers (this can become lengthy), see the respective CPT or HCPCS manual.

Case Study Approach

A series of simple case studies or scenarios are used throughout this book to illustrate the concepts presented. For the most part, these case studies are in the context of a fictitious community, namely, Anywhere, USA. The hospital involved is the Apex Medical Center. When a clinic is needed, we will use the Acme Medical Clinic. Anywhere, USA also has a skilled nursing facility, home health agency, and hospice and other types of healthcare providers. The Maximus Insurance Company is also located in Anywhere, USA.

The individuals that present for various services include

■ Sarah: A feisty lady who has been 87 years old for the past 5 years. While she is actually a nonagenarian, Sarah's most endearing characteristic is her *speed* walker that has a horn, headlight, and racing wheels. She is also tired of signing forms, so she has had a signature stamp fabricated that hangs from the handle on her walker.

- Sam: Sarah's cousin who is an octogenarian, a semi-retired rancher. He also works part-time at the local hardware store.
- Susan: Sarah's daughter who teaches school.
- Sydney and Stephen: Both are elderly Medicare beneficiaries who have a number of chronic health conditions.

While there are other residents that we may use in our case studies, these are the main characters. Keep in mind that this is a fictitious community that exists only in our imaginations. Also, when necessary for a given case study, the specific circumstances involving a healthcare provider may be altered. For instance, the Apex Medical Center may be a regular hospital for a given case study and then changed to be a critical access hospital for another case study.

Anywhere, USA is also home to a regional insurance company, Maximus Insurance Company, that provides health and accident insurance for individuals and companies. As with all third-party payers for healthcare services, Maximus must determine how to pay for healthcare services. We will join them in some of their efforts and thoughts relative to prospective payment systems.

The use of case studies is intended to make the study of sometimes technical material a little more tractable and enjoyable. Note that for a given case study there may be many issues involved even though these are very short in nature and often without appropriately specific detail. Watch for notes that indicate there may be some hidden issues that are not a part of our immediate discussions.

Medicare Orientation

Several Medicare prospective payment systems are discussed in this book. Information about these prospective payment systems is publicly available and quite extensive. Specific information about private third-party payer utilization of prospective payment is not readily available. Also, prospective payment systems are highly variable and may involve unusual features. As a result, we discuss several of the Medicare prospective payment approaches and then address how the concepts and features of the Medicare approaches can be extrapolated to various private third-party payer prospective payment mechanisms.

For healthcare providers and patients alike, the way in which private third-party payer payment systems work can be mysterious and sometimes frustrating. The bottom line for payment systems outside the Medicare program is that variability is the norm. This is the reason why we will concentrate on the relatively well-known, and fully public, Medicare prospective payment processes.

References

References to specific resources are provided on a limited basis. Virtually all the topics addressed are present in the Medicare program in one form or another. The *Federal Register* update process is briefly outlined for the main Medicare PPSs. Other references are to the CMS manuals, *Federal Registers,* or the *Code of Federal Regulations.* The CMS manual system is updated through various transmittals. In some cases, extremely important guidance is made at very informal levels. For instance, there are significant policy statements from CMS through their Question and Answer (Q&A) website. Note that if you are creating policies and associated procedures based on informal guidance, be certain to save a copy of the document or website. Informal guidance can suddenly disappear. Changes to the CMS manuals must go through a more formal process using the transmittals. Thus, there is official notice of the changes so that when changes are made, everyone knows what is being changed and when.

> *Note:* Even with the transmittal process for updating the Medicare manuals, there are times when complete paragraphs are removed from a manual but this may not be reflected in the changes indicated in a given transmittal.

While references to non-Medicare—that is, private third-party payer—would certainly be wonderful, most of these resources depend on very specific implementations, and guidance that is provided through contractual relationships. The specific guidance for coding, billing, and associated payment may actually be adjunct to the actual contract. There are often companion manuals and guidance for providers through the Internet or secure intranets.

Note also that you must constantly update yourself on any given implementation or instantiation of a given prospective payment system. For healthcare payment, change is constant. Thus, this text is oriented toward understanding overall systems and implementation parameters for prospective payment processes. Specific details of exactly how a claim should be developed and then adjudicated must be supplied by the specific third-party payer, and this also includes the Medicare program. There are always gaps in guidance, so questions are always appropriate.

As you read and study the materials in this text, you will probably want to access a number of different resources that are cited. Here is a list of specific resources and an Internet address for each. These are the general resources. You may need to delve further into a particular manual or book to find specific information and concepts referenced.

1. Social Security Act (SSA)—http://www.ssa.gov/OP_Home/ssact/ssact-toc.htm. You will need to know which section in order to reference specific issues. For example, §1861(s)(2)(A) addresses payment to physicians, including "incident-to" language and non-coverage for self-administrable drugs.
2. *Code of Federal Regulations (CFR)*—http://ecfr.gpoaccess.gov/. You will need to know the specific citation, such as 42 CFR §413.65 for the Provider-Based Rule.
3. *Federal Register*—http://www.nara.gov. You will need to know the date or the formal legal citation, such as 74 FR 60315, which refers to page 60315 (and following) of the November 20, 2009, *Federal Register* that discusses physician supervision requirements.
4. CMS Manual System—CMS has a series of very large manuals that provides all the rules and regulations. Go to https://www.cms.gov/manuals/iom/list.asp to start. You will need to know which manual, such as Publication 100-04, "Medicare Claims Processing Manual," and then the chapter and section number within a given manual.
5. CMS Transmittals—CMS uses frequently issued Transmittals to update their manual system. Go to: https://www.cms.gov/transmittals/. You will need to know the number of the transmittal and the manual to which it applies. Typically, if you have the number and date, you will be able to find the correct transmittal.
6. *CPT Manual*—This is published annually by the American Medical Association. Go to http://www.ama-assn.org/ to obtain more information.
7. *HCPCS Manual*—The HCPCS code set is published by CMS and is available at https://www.cms.gov/medhcpcsgeninfo/. This code set is also republished by different healthcare publishing companies. Note that this code set is updated quarterly.
8. AHA Coding Clinic® for ICD-10—Official guidance from the American Hospital Association on ICD-10. See http://www.ahacentraloffice.com/.

9. AHA Coding Clinic® for HCPCS—Official guidance from the American Hospital Association on HCPCS coding. See http://www.ahacentraloffice.com/.

10. UB-04 Data Specifications Manual—See the National Uniform Billing Committee at http://www.nubc.org.

11. 1500 Health Insurance Claim Form Reference Instruction Manual—See the National Uniform Claims Committee at http://www.nucc.org.

12. SNF PPS—The skilled nursing PPS is RUGS. Go to http://www.cms.gov/snfpps/ for additional information.

13. Home Health Agency PPS—Information on the HHA-PPS can be found at https://www.cms.gov/HomeHealthPPS/.

14. Long-Term Care Hospitals—The LTCH-MS-DRGs represent a modification to MS-DRGs for Long-Term Care Hospitals. See http://www.cms.gov/longtermcarehospitalpps/.

15. Inpatient Rehabilitation Facilities—Information for the IRF-PPS can be found at: http://www.cms.gov/InpatientRehabFacPPS/.

16. Inpatient Psychiatric Hospitals—Further information concerning the IPF-PPS can be found at http://www.cms.gov/InpatientPsychFacilPPS/.

17. Hospice—See https://www.cms.gov/Hospice/ for additional information.

18. Pricer Information for all Medicare PPSs—See http://www.cms.gov/PCPricer/.

19. MedPAC—The Medicare Payment Advisory Commission. See http://www.medpac.gov.

20. Medicare Physician Fee Schedule (MPFS)—Go to https://www.cms.gov/PhysicianFeeSched/ to download the large MS Excel spreadsheet that constitutes the MPFS.

21. Medicare Enrollment and CMS-855 Forms—Go to https://www.cms.gov/MedicareProviderSupEnroll for information and the six different forms.

22. Medicare HPSA (Health Personnel Shortage Area) and PSA (Physician Scarcity Area)—Go to https://www.cms.gov/hpsapsaphysicianbonuses/ for additional information.

23. Clinical Laboratory Fee Schedule (CLFS)—Go to https://www.cms.gov/ClinicalLabFeeSched/.

24. Ambulance Fee Schedule (AFS)—Go to https://www.cms.gov/AmbulanceFeeSchedule/.

25. Medicare Secondary Payer (MSP)—Go to https://www.cms.gov/ProviderServices/.

26. *National Correct Coding Initiative (NCCI) Coding Policy Manual*—Go to https://www.cms.gov/NationalCorrectCodInitEd/. In this text, specific references may be to chapter and page numbers along with the version of the policy manual that is referenced.

27. Critical Access Hospitals (CAHs)—See https://www.cms.gov/center/cah.asp. Method II billing is where the hospital bills the professional component for physicians and practitioners on the hospital facility component on the UB-04 claim form.

While the information in the *CFR* is official, it is often rather cryptic. More details can be found in the CMS manual system. The two manuals that are most often referenced relative to payment systems are

■ *The Medicare Claims Processing Manual* (*MCPM*), Publication 100-04
■ *The Medicare Benefit Policy Manual* (*MBPM*), Publication 100-02

For instance, Chapter 3 of the *MCPM* is devoted to Inpatient Hospital Billing. These manuals are updated through rather frequent transmittals, sometimes called change requests (CRs). The transmittals are sometimes only a few pages long while in other cases they can comprise a hundred pages or more.

References to the *Federal Register* and the *Code of Federal Regulations* may also be provided. Generally the date and page number for the *Federal Register* will be provided, along with a notation such as 76 FR 42914. This is Volume 76 page 42914, which was issued on July 19, 2011, and addresses proposed rules for the MS-DRG Pre-Admission Window. A reference such as 42 CFR §413.65 refers to Title 42 of the *CFR* and then Section 413.65. This is the provider-based rule (PBR). For the *CFR*, there are also Volume, Chapter, and Part indicators, but the section numbers appear most commonly.

For the Medicare program there are tens of thousands of pages of manuals, *Federal Register* entries, and less formal guidance that Medicare refers to as *sub-regulatory*. Technically, sub-regulatory refers to guidance that appears below the *CFR* level. The *CFR* actually has force and effect of law and is the equivalent, at the federal level, to state administrative law.

For private third-party payers, specific information about their payment systems is not nearly as readily available. Your healthcare provider may enter into contractual arrangements with a private third-party payer and thus come under several different payment systems for various types of healthcare services. The information on billing, claims adjudication, and payment will probably not be in the contract itself. Most likely there will be companion manuals that go along with the contract. Also, these payment arrangements tend to be individualized to the needs of the payer. And, specific information on these payment arrangements, using various payment methodologies, is not always readily available.

Compliance

Throughout our discussions of the various prospective payment systems, compliance issues will arise. Some of these are straightforward while others can become quite subtle. Because prospective payment involves some sort of classification system at a fairly detailed level, healthcare providers filing claims must use the classification system correctly. This generally involves coding correctly. For some code sets there are modifiers and then there can be extensive edits along with specific coding, billing, and claims filing requirements.

In the text *Healthcare Payment Systems: An Introduction*, various compliance concerns are discussed. Compliance is inherent throughout the overall process of providing services, filling claims, and receiving payments. This process is referred to as the revenue cycle. Because we are interested in claims that are paid through prospective payment systems, the term *reimbursement cycle* is more appropriate. This implies that reimbursement is occurring based upon a filed claim.

From a compliance perspective, what steps in the overall adjudication process could possibly yield any sort of compliance concerns? Here are the generalized steps in the claim adjustment process:

■ Covered individual
■ Covered service or item
■ Ordered by a physician or qualified practitioner
■ Medically necessary
■ Provided by qualified facility and/or healthcare personnel
■ Appropriate written documentation
■ Billing privileges
■ Proper claim filed timely

While each of these steps can create compliance concerns, the main area for prospective payment systems is the proper development and timely filing of the claim for the services provided and/or items dispensed. For instance, while issues such a medical necessity or covered individual are important, the adjudication of claims should not even get to the point of calculating a payment unless these sorts of conditions are satisfied. Because prospective payment systems depend on fairly detailed classification or coding systems, compliance depends on proper coding and then meeting any special claims filing requirements.

There are definitely instances in which the healthcare provider may not properly code services and thus generate incorrect payment. This can occur for a number of reasons, not the least of which is that some claims filing guidance can become confusing and complex. Today the Medicare program uses a number of different audit and recovery programs, the latest of which is the Recovery Audit Contractor (RAC) program. This is a recovery program with regional RACs that are paid a percentage of any incorrect payments, mainly overpayments, made by the Medicare program.

> *Note:* See *The Medicare Recovery Audit Contractor Program: A Survival Guide for Healthcare Providers* published by CRC Press. This book is an adjunct to a more general compliance book for healthcare providers, namely, *Compliance for Coding, Billing & Reimbursement: A Systematic Approach to Developing a Comprehensive Program,* also published by CRC Press.

Enjoy the Technicalities!

This book addresses what most would consider technical, convoluted, and boring. Granted, the *Federal Register* entries from the CMS (Centers for Medicare and Medicaid Services) are not always scintillating, but make the process fun by looking for inconsistencies and obtuse and sometimes misleading language in the various rules and regulations.

Watch for the definitions. Often, words are used and phrases are invented that are never really defined. Discussing any topic without having precise definitions is a misunderstanding waiting to happen. Also watch for words such as *clarification* and *restatement* as opposed to *changes* in rules and regulations.

Look for words such as *believe*. What are people allowed to believe? Basically, anything! This word is often used when an individual does not know something for certain; he or she simply thinks it is true or might be true. Is it not interesting how often this word appears in the *Federal Register*!

About the Author

Duane C. Abbey, Ph.D., is a management consultant and president of Abbey & Abbey Consultants Incorporated. Based in Ames, Iowa, Abbey & Abbey specializes in healthcare consulting and related areas.

He earned his graduate degrees at the University of Notre Dame and Iowa State University and his work in healthcare now spans more than 25 years. Today he spends about half his time developing and teaching workshops (for students who affectionately quip that the *Federal Register* is their favorite reading material) and making presentations to professional organizations. He devotes the other half to consulting work that involves performing chargemaster reviews and compliance reviews, providing litigation support, and conducting reimbursement studies.

Dr. Abbey also uses his mathematical and financial background to perform assessments, develop complex financial models, and conduct various types of statistical work. His studies in the field of neurolinguistic programming have enhanced his ability to provide organizational communication facilitation services for healthcare organizations. He also provides litigation support services for attorneys representing healthcare providers in legal proceedings.

If you wish to contact Dr. Abbey, he can be contacted by e-mail at duane@aaciweb.com. See also our corporate website: http://www.aaciweb.com.

Chapter 1

Introduction to Prospective Payment Systems

Preliminary Comments

Payment for healthcare services is provided through a wide variety of sometimes very different payment systems. For hospital services, skilled nursing facilities, home health agencies, and similar organizations, there are prospective payment systems. In other instances there may be cost-based or charge-based payment systems utilized. For physicians, clinics, and certain other healthcare providers, fee schedule payment systems are used. This book is dedicated to prospective payment systems (PPSs).

PPSs fix in advance the payment rates for healthcare services and items provided. This is where the term *prospective* comes into play. Note that the payment *rate* for services is fixed in advance, generally for the period of a year. PPSs are still fee-for-service type of payment systems. The greater the volume of services, the greater the overall payments will be.

New PPSs are still very much in development, with the Medicare program leading the way. Private third-party payers sometimes adapt the PPSs developed by Medicare. The first major, and thus oldest, PPS is DRG or Diagnosis Related Group. This is a PPS developed for hospital inpatient services. DRGs have become quite complex, with many features that have developed over the years.

> *Note:* In this text we refer to DRGs as a generic term for any and all of the many different DRG payment systems that have been developed. When the context of the discussion needs clarification, we refer to the latest refinement of DRGs by Medicare using MS-DRGs or the Medicare Severity DRGs. If there is a different DRG system, such as the APR-DRGs (All Patient Refined DRGs), we use the full acronym. Whenever studying and investigating a DRG payment system, be certain that you have fixed the context of discussion.

The DRGs developed by Medicare were implemented for 1984, that is, Federal Fiscal Year 1984. This was the first major system for Medicare that moved away from cost-based reimbursement. For Medicare, DRGs use the Federal Fiscal Year of October 1st through September 30th. This PPS was developed in order to contain costs for Medicare hospital inpatient services. Whether this objective was really reached is open to some debate. The next major PPS, at least for Medicare, was implemented on August 1, 2000, and addressed hospital outpatient services. This is the APC or Ambulatory Payment Classification system. Following APCs, Medicare has developed a number of other PPSs addressing home health, skilled nursing, inpatient rehabilitation, long-term care, and the like.

> *Note:* APGs or Ambulatory Patient Groups was a precursor to Medicare's APCs. On a generic basis we refer to APGs to represent all the different variations of APGs, including the specific implementation of Medicare's APCs. When specifically discussing APCs, we use this acronym.

While we discuss the key elements for any prospective payment system, we concentrate on the Medicare DRGs (i.e., MS-DRGs) and APCs as specific examples. Also, as we discuss these two PPSs in some detail, we also discuss alternate approaches for some of the key elements within the given PPS. The architects who design the specific features within PPSs have to make hundreds if not thousands of decisions relative to the way in which services are reported and then how payment is made.

Overview of Healthcare Payment Systems

Many innovative approaches have been developed to pay for healthcare services. The general objective of healthcare payment systems is to reimburse healthcare providers appropriately for services provided. Given the tremendous growth in expenditures for healthcare services, the mechanisms for payment must be designed to properly pay for such services. While healthcare providers complain about inappropriately low payments, conversely healthcare payers claim that there are significant overpayments. Thus, healthcare payment systems must be designed to provide proper payment for necessary services.

Today, most healthcare payment is based on what is termed *fee-for-service*. In other words, the third-party payer reimburses the healthcare provider based on the services provided. Presumptively, the services provided were medically necessary, ordered by a physician, performed by qualified personnel, etc. Note that on a fee-for-service basis, the more services that are provided, the more the third-party payer will pay out for the services.

Healthcare payment based on *capitation* is diametrically the opposite of fee-for-service. With capitation the risk moves to the healthcare provider from the third-party payer. The basic idea is that the healthcare provider receives a fixed payment and then provides whatever services are required. The fixed payment is often on a per-member per-month (PMPM) basis for each covered individual. This payment is made regardless of the number and type of healthcare services required. If more services than anticipated occur, then the healthcare provider will probably incur a loss. If the demand for services is low, then the healthcare provider will make a profit.

The oldest and most fundamental healthcare payment system is cost-based reimbursement. For a third-party payer (e.g., insurance company or Medicare) to reimburse for services on a cost basis, the healthcare provider's costs must be known. This is not an easy task. The Medicare program uses a complicated cost reporting process to determine costs. Obviously there are differences of opinion as to which costs are allowable. Also, there is a significant overhead cost for developing a cost report and then auditing the cost reports to make certain that there is no over-reporting of costs. To fully develop, audit, and settle a cost report takes 3 to 4 years.

One step removed from cost-based payment is charge-based payment. With this approach, the healthcare provider is generally paid a percentage of whatever is charged. Typical percentages range from about 70% on up to 95%. An underlying, often unstated principle is that the charges are presumed to consistently reflect the costs incurred by the healthcare provider.

Fee schedule payment systems tend to use highly delineated classifications of services provided and/or item dispensed. The basic idea is that if you have a code set that describes the various services, then a payment rate can be attached to each of the services in the classification system. Probably the best known, and most complex, fee schedule payment system is the Medicare physician fee schedule (MPFS). This fee schedule payment system uses a combination of CPT® (Current Procedural Terminology) and HCPCS (Healthcare Common Procedure Coding System). Other examples are the ambulance fee schedule (AFS) and a fee schedule for DME (Durable Medical Equipment). See the companion text, *Fee Schedule Payment Systems* for a more detailed discussion.

There are many different approaches to healthcare payment. A few of the major systems have been delineated. In some cases, a third-party payer may contract with a healthcare provider and use a combination of approaches depending upon the specific types of services being provided. Thus, healthcare providers enter into contractual arrangements to provide services and then receive payment. While the nomenclature is not really accurate, these contracts are often referred to as managed care contracts. In some cases the third-party payer does manage care (e.g., medical necessity, frequency limitation, surgery preauthorization), but in other cases these managed care contracts involve primarily payment mechanisms.

Using a fee-for-service approach, a healthcare provider must file a claim for services provided or items supplied. The claim is then adjudicated by the third-party payer and payment is made through a reimbursement process. For prospective payment systems, the two main processes that must occur are claim adjudication and payment calculation.

Claim adjudication can be relatively simple and in other instances a careful analysis of the adjudication logic in use can require lengthy study. Much of the adjudication occurs with a software program called the *grouper*. Prospective payment involves a great deal of bundling of services so that various line-items on a claim will be bundled or grouped together to generate a limited number of categories or groups that will be paid. These groups are then further processed by another, although often integrated, program called the *pricer*. The pricer determines the actual payment amount. The programming logic for the grouper/pricer is very complex. Healthcare providers tend to look at the grouper/pricer as a black box because fully understanding the internal logic would require significant time and effort.

Claims Filing and Payment

As discussed in *Healthcare Payment Systems: An Introduction**, there are many different mechanisms for providing payment to healthcare providers. While the simplest involves having the patient pay directly for the services, very often there is a third party involved. In other words, the third party makes the payment or some portion of the payment. The most typical example of this is with health and accident insurance. However, there are many different types of third-party payers, including liability insurance when accidents are involved or possibly a third-party administrator that makes payment from some sort of trust fund.

When third parties become involved, including cases in which there may be more than one third-party payer, there must be a mechanism to request payment and then a way for the third-party payer to make payment. Requests for payment are made through a claims filing process. There are two main claim forms for healthcare:

1. Professional claims: 1500 or CMS-1500 for the Medicare program
2. Technical claims: UB-04 or CMS-1450 for the Medicare program

The acronym "UB" stands for *Universal Billing* and the "04" refers to the year that the last major update to the form was made, in this case 2004. Professional claims are typically associated with physicians and practitioner services. The technical or facility claims are associated with facilities such as hospitals, nursing facilities, and the like.

While both of these forms exist in paper format, today these claims are typically developed through a more extensive computer-based process. Thus, we have the HIPAA 837-P and 837-I formats. The "P" stands for *professional* and the "I" stands for *institutional*. HIPAA refers to the Health Insurance Portability and Accountability Act of 1997. Within HIPAA was a congressional directive to move healthcare into the realm of electronic data interchange or EDI. From time to time in this book we refer to the HIPAA TSC or Transaction Standard/Standard Code Set rule. Implementation of the HIPAA mandate in this area has resulted in extensive development of forms, formats, and various code sets.

Healthcare providers code and file claims in standardized ways so that various third-party payers can provide payment by adjudicating and processing the claim. This is the point at which healthcare payment systems become involved.

There are literally hundreds of different mechanisms for providing payment for healthcare services. One group of such mechanisms is the prospective payment systems (PPSs), which is the subject this book. Prospective payment is not straightforward. A service is provided and/or an item dispensed, a claim is developed, and the third-party payer receives the claims and then adjudicates the claim using fairly complex logic embedded in the PPS itself.

Of course there are some complicating factors that come into play! First, there must be some uniform way in which to describe the services provided and/or the items dispensed. This raises the need to develop a *classification system* for services and items. Generally this involves developing a set of codes that can be used for services and items. In turn, the code set must have coherence for accurately describing services and items. Thus, we have a coding system that involves the process of coding. For the older PPSs, professional coding staff are necessary to properly code cases.

---

* See *Healthcare Payment Systems: An Introduction*, authored by Dr. Abbey and published by CRC Press, Boca Raton, FL, 2009, ISBN=978-1-4200-9277-6.

For some of the more recent PPSs, the classification of services involves acuity levels that are determined from some sort of patient assessment instrument (PAI). These assessment instruments are lengthy and involved. The information from the PAI is then used to determine a code that represents the acuity level or level of service. Due to the complexity of these forms, the key data are input to a computer program that then determines the proper code.

Second, there must be some way to determine the proper amount to pay for a service provided or items dispensed as described through the code set. Should payment be based on costs? Resources utilized? Skill level? Effort? Risk? Well, the list of ways to determine the payment amounts can become rather extensive.

The third concern can be the most complicated. A basic question that arises is whether or not every service provided or item dispensed should be separately paid. This takes us into the whole area of what we call *adjudication logic*. The logical constructs used in adjudicating claims under prospective payment systems can, and do, become enormously complex. Even simple encounters at a hospital can raise questions about appropriate payment.

Because we use little case studies throughout this book, we will illustrate how decisions must be made relative to separate payment versus bundling payments in various ways.

Consider Case Study 1.1. This is an outpatient hospital encounter. There are two different claims that will be filed: one for the physician or professional component (i.e., 1500 claim) and then one for the hospital, which is the technical component (i.e., UB-04 claim). Technically, this is what is called a *provider-based* situation. The physician claim form will be adjudicated and, most likely, paid under some sort of fee schedule payment system. For the Medicare program, this will be the MPFS. The hospital claim on an outpatient basis and most likely a prospective payment system will be used. For Medicare this will be ambulatory payment classifications (APCs). The claim will involve charges for drugs, routine supplies, the finger splint, laboratory, the x-ray of the finger, the application of the finger splint, and the resources utilized for the examination of the patient by both the physician and nursing staff.

The challenge for APCs in Case Study 1.1 is to sort everything out, bundle as appropriate, and then determine payment. Even for a relatively straightforward case like this, the grouping of the services and eventually calculating the payment is far from easy. Certainly, the drugs and supplies, including the finger splint, will be bundled. But what will they be bundled into? In other words, what is payable under APCs in this case study? The laboratory will be paid separately under the Medicare clinical laboratory fee schedule. The x-ray will be paid separately under APCs. Now what about the examination and the application of the finger splint? The coding for this type of case becomes an issue. For the examination, an E/M (evaluation and

---

CASE STUDY 1.1   EMERGENCY DEPARTMENT VISIT INVOLVING FINGER SPLINT

An individual has presented to a hospital's emergency department after twisting his right index finger. The ER physician performs a general examination to make certain there are no other problems except for the twisted finger. The physician examines the finger. Routine laboratory tests are performed just for safety. Based on x-rays, there is no fracture, only a sprain, and applies a finger splint to protect the finger during the healing process. The patient is discharged home with a supply of analgesics for pain control.

management) code is appropriate, but should there be a separate code for the application of the finger splint?*

As you learn more about APCs and the associated coding processes, you will come to learn that this little case study is filled with some very difficult issues. For proper payment under APCs, this case must be accurately coded according to a multitude of coding guidelines. After the case is coded, then the APC grouper can group the case and then the APC pricer can actually calculate the payment.

If you take this very simple case and extrapolate out to multiple adjudication considerations, the logic involved can become significantly complex even though the overall payment concept is straightforward.

Deductibles and Copayments

Almost all third-party payers, including Medicare, use deductibles and copayments as part of their overall payment process. Generally, deductibles and copayment do not directly enter into the adjudication of claims using a prospective payment system. After the payment amount is calculated, then any deductibles and/or copayments are removed from the payment that is made by the third-party payer. The individual receiving the services is liable for the deductible and any copayments that might apply. In some cases there are special supplemental insurance policies that cover items such as deductibles and copayments.

Note that the terms "coinsurance" and "copayment" may be different, depending on the third-party payer involved. Coinsurance generally refers to the percentage of the payment determined after adjudicating the claim that constitutes the copayment. While this is a little convoluted, the coinsurance is a percentage while the copayment is an actual dollar amount.

In this text, the deductible and copayment concepts are addressed only on a cursory basis. Only if there is something unusual will these processes be raised.

Overview of Medicare Prospective Payment Systems

Prospective payment started in 1984 with the development and implementation of DRGs. DRGs addressed hospital inpatient services. In 2000, APCs were implemented so that hospital outpatient services were brought under prospective payment as well. Since that time, several other PPSs have been developed and implemented by the Medicare program. These include

- Long-term care hospitals
- Skilled nursing facilities
- Home health agencies
- Inpatient rehabilitation facilities
- Inpatient psychiatric facilities

Each of the PPSs developed for these types of services is different. Sometimes they are quite different although each PPS has certain similarities. The two most complex Medicare PPSs are

---

* There is a CPT code for application of the finger splint. Whether this code should be used in this situation may spark a significant discussion with hospital coding and billing staff.

MS-DRGs and APCs, both of which are discussed at some length in separate chapters in this text. The additional PPSs mentioned above are discussed to a lesser extent.

Note that each of these systems, particularly MS-DRGs and APCs, is an extremely complex payment system that changes from year to year. Becoming a true expert at any one of these systems is really a full-time career. For healthcare providers there are service issues, documentation issues, coding issues, billing issues, and reimbursement issues. All of this complexity also leads very directly to compliance concerns. All PPSs use some sort of classification system to sort out and identify the services and/or acuity of services that are being provided. This classification through a grouping process, in turn, drives the payment levels. If services are misclassified, then inappropriate payment will result in both underpayments and overpayments.

Private Third-Party Payer and Prospective Payment Systems

Chapter 6 includes a discussion of private third-party payer use of prospective payment systems. While this should be a rather extensive discussion, due to the extreme variability between hundreds of commercial payers, only generic types of prospective payment systems can be discussed. The Medicare program basically serves as the flagship for an armada of different prospective payment arrangements. The Medicare program has invested many years in the development and implementation of different payment systems, including prospective payment systems.

Often, commercial insurance companies will piggyback on a Medicare PPS. For instance, consider the approach described in Case Study 1.2.

Of course, MIC from Case Study 1.2 must be able to adjudicate claims the same way that Medicare adjudicates claims. Also, do you think there may be some areas of weakness in using this approach? Most likely, some special arrangements for obstetric services may be needed because the Medicare program has been designed and customized for the aged population, not for younger adults and children.

Case Study 1.2 illustrates a very simple approach for piggybacking onto a Medicare payment system. In other cases, a private third-party payer may adopt certain portions of a Medicare payment system and then modify other portions to a greater extent. The variations in this area are significant.

Payment System Interfaces

With the many types of PPSs that we have in place, there are numerous payment system interfaces. During an overall episode of care, an individual may see a physician in a clinic; there may be hospital inpatient services that are then followed by additional recovery in a skilled nursing facility. Once out of the SNF, the patient may come under a home health plan of care. Each of these

---

CASE STUDY 1.2—MEDICARE PLUS A PERCENTAGE

The Maximus Insurance Company (MIC) provides healthcare insurance. Payments must be made for hospital inpatient services. To simplify the process, MIC has decided to simply reimburse hospitals whatever Medicare pays through APCs plus 25%.

services has its own payment system, and there must be some consideration for how these payment systems come together or interface.

In some cases, there may be a choice as to where the given service is provided. Consider a surgical procedure that can be provided in one of the following locations:

1. Hospital outpatient: Paid under APCs
2. Ambulatory surgical center: Paid under hybrid of APCs and MPFS
3. Hospital Inpatient: Paid under MS-DRGs

Note that each of these three providers has different payment systems. Because we are dealing with the same surgical procedure, at least for this discussion, should not the payments for this service be about the same? In other words, there should not be any incentive to use one type of healthcare provider versus another based on the level of payment. The decision as to which provider to use should be based on medical necessity and risk considerations.

Inpatient services are often preceded by other services and also followed by other services. Should any of these pre-admission or post-admission services require some sort of payment adjustments? Payment system interfaces can arise in unexpected ways. A number of different payment interface issues are addressed in our discussions.

Probably the most complex and most utilized payment system interface involves provider-based clinics. These are generally hospital-based clinics. The potential economic advantage of provider-based clinics is that two claim forms are filed: the professional 1500 claim and the technical UB-04 claim. There is a slight reduction in payment for the physician that is more than made up for by reimbursement on the hospital side under APCs. Case Study 1.1 actually involved a provider-based situation through the hospital emergency department. However, there is no payment increase for the ED as there is for provider-based clinics. Hospital EDs are always provider-based.*

The provider-based rule (PBR) governs the whole area of provider-based clinics and associated services. The main tenets of this rule are discussed in order to provide the background necessary to understand this specific payment interface between a fee-schedule payment system (i.e., MPFS) and a prospective payment system (i.e., APCs).

Another more subtle payment system interface occurs with secondary claims. Patients quite often have primary coverage and the secondary coverage is under a different insurance policy or group health plan. The two payers, primary and secondary, may have similar plans or they can be vastly different. For instance, a Medicare beneficiary may be under traditional Medicare and then have one of the specially designed supplemental policies. The supplemental policies are designed to interface to the Medicare payment systems almost seamlessly.

CASE STUDY 1.3 MEDICARE SUPPLEMENTAL INSURANCE

Sydney has been on Medicare for about 10 years. He uses Medicare traditional and then has a supplemental policy. Sydney has been very pleased because when he goes to his primary care physician or even a specialist, he does not have to pay anything out of pocket.

---

* Emergency departments are normally licensed as part of a hospital. There are some states that do allow some variance to this general statement.

CASE STUDY 1.4   SPOUSE WITH GROUP HEALTH PLAN

Stephen is fortunate enough to have a spouse who is still working and he is covered under a group health insurance plan. He has Medicare as secondary. When he goes to the doctor or has services at the hospital, he often receives multiple documents explaining benefits and payments and sometimes he must pay some of the bill.

For Sydney in Case Study 1.3, Medicare is primary and the supplemental policy is secondary so there are very few problems. However, Sydney does not yet realize that there may be certain services that are not covered—for example, eye refractions or the error correction portion of an intraocular lens (IOL).* Also, all the healthcare providers that Sydney uses participate or have provider agreements with Medicare.

Let us consider this secondary claim situation when Medicare is secondary. Take Stephen as an example in Case Study 1.4.

What has happened in Stephen's case is that the claims filed with the primary payer, most likely a commercial payer, are not always developed according to Medicare requirements. Both the commercial insurance company and the Medicare program may each be using a different payment approach for physician and hospital services, but the payment systems have different requirements for claims filing and proper adjudication. In other words, the different payment systems have not been designed to interface smoothly and Stephen ends up paying some of the cost himself.

> ***Note:*** Part of the challenge that Stephen is encountering comes from the fact that different third-party payers have differing requirements for filing claims. The HIPPA Standard Transaction/Standard Code Set rules should allow a standard claim, using standard code sets to be filed for adjudication by all third-party payers. In other words, a healthcare provider should be able to file the same claim for the same service to any third-party payer. Achieving this goal is still very much in the future.

Healthcare Provider Use of Prospective Payment Systems to Set Charges

Fee schedule payment systems provide an easy way for healthcare providers to set charges. For instance, the Medicare Clinical Laboratory Fee Schedule (CLFS) can be used as a relative value system to set charges. A hospital or physician office can simply take the fee schedule and double or triple the payment amount under the fee schedule and use this as a set of charges. This works because fee schedules tend to very finely classify the individual laboratory tests.

One of the hallmarks of prospective payment is that there is a great deal of bundling. Thus, a hospital may have a set of related but different surgical services, all of which have the same payment under a PPS. In other words, the PPS is myopic when it classifies services into the groups within the PPS. As a result, the payment rates for PPSs tend to have little use in setting charges. While the payment levels can provide some general indication as to whether charges are appropriate, the use of PPS payment rates for setting charges is quite limited.

---

* The error-correcting IOLs are usually called New Technology IOLs or NTIOLs. The error-correcting feature in the IOL is not covered although a plain (i.e., non-error-correcting) IOL is covered under Medicare.

Summary and Conclusion

There are numerous prospective payment systems used for hospitals services, both inpatient and outpatient, and for other types of healthcare providers, including skilled nursing and home health. These systems are definitely on the complex side. Each PPS has its own unique characteristics, although there are some common features for all the PPSs in use today. These systems are prospective in the sense that payment is fixed in advance instead of looking back in time (i.e., retrospectively) to see what costs must be covered, such as through a cost-based payment system.

The fact that payment is fixed in advance also creates a payment policy quite different from fee schedule payment systems. Under fee schedule payment, the healthcare provider will be reimbursed the lesser of the amount charged or the fee schedule payment amount. Under a PPS, the fixed payment amount is paid regardless of the charges. In theory, a healthcare provider could charge nothing and still receive the full PPS payment.

Bundling is one of the key features of any PPS. For instance, the Medicare MS-DRG payment system for inpatient services literally bundles virtually everything that is done or provided during a hospital admission into a single payment. This is the ultimate in bundling. Other PPSs such as APCs for hospital outpatient services certainly bundle, but there can be multiple payment groups generated. In theory, this bundling process promotes the development of efficiencies on the part of healthcare providers.

Another feature of PPSs is that there is some sort of grouping that takes place. There must be a classification system of some sort to delineate the services provided or items rendered, but then the results of the classification, often a coding system of some sort, must be grouped into specific categories for payment. MS-DRGs group to only one category. Other PPSs may group to more than one category, depending on how the system is designed.

The payment calculation for PPSs also tends to be fairly complex and is embedded in a computer program called the pricer. Depending on the category or categories that result from the grouping, the payment calculation usually starts with some sort of dollar amount conversion factor. Beyond this there may be adjustments up or down, depending upon circumstances. Among the adjustments for the Medicare program is to adjust payments based on the cost of living in various geographic areas.

The grouper/pricer software that will be discussed for each of the PPSs addressed is important. This computer program is quite complex with convoluted logic. With each update of a PPS, the grouper/pricer must also be reprogrammed. For the older PPSs (i.e., MS-DRGs and APCs), the hospital does not need to have a grouper/pricer. The use of this software is part of the payer's adjudication process. Of course, if a hospital does not have a grouper/pricer, the proper payment that should be received will not be known.

The more recent data-driven PPSs (i.e., home health and skilled nursing) require the provider to at least have the computer program that generates the proper code(s) that goes onto the UB-04 so that the claim can be adjudicated. In Chapter 6, these codes are described as HIPPS, or Health Insurance Prospective Payment codes.

Chapter 2

Healthcare Provider Concepts

Introduction

There are many different types of healthcare providers, ranging from an individual physician or nurse on up to large national chains of hospitals and clinics. The different payment systems must address a wide array of services as well as highly variable organizational structures. In this chapter we briefly discuss some of the main types of healthcare providers and associated organizational structuring. Note that the recognition of certain facilities or organizational structuring often revolves around the Medicare program. There can also be state-level concerns as well as tax complications.

Prospective payment systems generally address certain types of providers and associated organizational structures. While the impetus for certain organizations has evolved from the Medicare program, other private third-party payers may also recognize certain of these different types of providers. For instance, a Sole Community Hospital (SCH) is a Medicare concept. Certain rules and regulations must be met before an SCH can enjoy the special benefits of this designation from the Medicare program.[*] Additionally, other third-party payers will need to pay for services at an SCH, but a given third-party payer may or may not recognize the hospital as being anything more than a duly licensed hospital.

Many of the concepts discussed in this chapter come from the Medicare program. Simply stated, this is due to the fact that the Medicare program has developed extensive organizational structuring requirements for different types of healthcare provider entities. Most private third-party payers do not have separately identifiable organizational structures that are required for payment under the given third-party payer.

> *Note:* As is often the case, terminology must be carefully studied when considering different types of healthcare providers. For the Medicare program, the two words *provider* and *supplier* have formal definitions that are different from common usage.

---

[*] See the Medicare MS-DRG prospective payment system and the special payment processes for SCHs. Note that there are also other designations that provide special reimbursement from the Medicare program.

Billing privileges for Medicare are gained by filing appropriate CMS-855 forms and following the rules generally found at 42 CFR §424. The word *provider* refers to organizations that have provider agreements with Medicare, such as hospitals and skilled nursing facilities. Most other healthcare providers are classified as being *suppliers*. Thus, physicians are classified as suppliers and not providers. This certainly goes against the grain of common usage. Take care to understand the context of any discussion and/or guidance because terminology differences can be significant.

Physicians

For the Medicare program, the word *physician* is used only for two categories

1. MDs or allopathic physicians
2. DOs or osteopathic physicians

So, where does this leave categories such as chiropractors, podiatrists, optometrists, and clinical psychologists? These individuals hold doctorates and are licensed through state laws, but are they considered physicians? The simple answer, at least for Medicare, is no. However, the word *practitioner* may be applied to all of the above. Be careful with physicians; sometimes they may take offence being referred to as a practitioner because this can carry the connotation of something less than a physician.

This may seem an innocuous issue, but the distinction can become important. For instance, under Medicare rules and regulations, physician supervision may be a requirement for certain services. In other cases, hospital services, particularly for payment purposes, must be incident-to a physician's service. Can anyone other than an MD or DO meet the physician supervision requirement and/or incident-to requirement?*

Generally, physicians are paid through fee schedule arrangements for Medicare and most other private third-party payers. This includes chiropractors, podiatrists, optometrists, and clinical psychologists, among others. Over the years the concept of combining physician and hospital reimbursements into a single package, possibly for surgical procedures, has been raised. At this time, physicians and practitioners are generally paid separately from any sort of facilities payment.

Non-Physician Practitioners and Providers

For the very large number of healthcare providers who do not hold doctorates, the general term *non-physician provider* is used. This category includes nurses, medical assistants, radiology technicians, physical therapists—a long list can be developed. Even within the classification of a nurse, there can be many different types of nurses and associated specialty certifications. Some nurses have gained doctorates in nursing, so be careful with the terminology, particularly as it relates to payment for healthcare services.

Important subsets of non-physician providers are the *non-physician practitioners*. Using the word *practitioner* implies that the individual can gain billing privileges from the Medicare program and, theoretically, from other third-party payers. Thus, practitioners can file claims and

---

* Incident-to and physician supervision are Medicare requirements. See the provider-based rule at 42 CFR §413.65 to investigate current rules and regulations. A major issue for physician supervision is qualifying the non-physician practitioner to meet the physician supervision requirement.

> ## CASE STUDY 2.1   CLINICAL NURSE SPECIALIST VERSUS NURSE PRACTITIONER
>
> The Apex Medical Center (AMC) employs a clinical nurse specialist (CNS) who is devoted to oncology services. The CNS works closely with specialty physicians in providing oncology services. Apex has decided not to file professional claims for the CNS. However, there is a nurse practitioner (NP) who works in two different provider-based clinics and Apex has decided to file professional claims for the NP.

separate reimbursement can be gained. As with physicians, non-physician practitioners must be credentialed in order to provide services and also to gain billing privileges.

However, a given practitioner may be employed and the employer may choose not to file claims separately for the practitioner.

The decision in Case Study 2.1 is not related to the two different types of NPPs (non-physician provider/practitioners). The decision is based on the fact that professional billing and filing claims for qualified NPPs is optional. In this case, both the CNS and NP are employed by Apex, a hospital. The difference in choosing to file claims or not will have an effect on the hospital's cost report. For instance, if a professional claim is not filed for the practitioner's services, then the cost of employing the practitioner will be included in the hospital's cost report. The converse is true; that is, if there is professional billing, then the practitioner's cost to the hospital will not be on the cost report.

The listing of qualified NPPs can and does vary, depending on the specific context of various rules and regulations, particularly from the Medicare program. For instance, a listing of qualified NPPs for providing telemedicine services may be different from the NPP listing for those who qualify for separate reimbursement. The most common NPPs who qualify for separate reimbursement include

- Nurse practitioners
- Clinical nurse specialists
- Physician assistants
- Clinical psychologists
- Clinical social workers
- Nurse midwives

On a limited basis this list can be augmented by qualified individuals providing medical nutrition therapy (MNT), diabetes self-management training (DSMT), and kidney disease education (KDE). In the anesthesia area, there are also CRNAs (Certified Registered Nurse Anesthetists) who can be separately paid under certain circumstances.

As with physicians, if qualified NPPs decide to file claims, or have claims filed for them, their payment usually derives from a fee schedule, whether from Medicare or some other third-party payer. While the process for credentialing for billing purposes is well defined in the Medicare program, gaining billing privileges from private third-party payers can be challenging.

Note: When it comes to payment, the world of non-physician practitioners is quite dynamic. Over time, more and more practitioners are moving into the realm of being able to receive reimbursement and file claims, or have claims filed on their behalf, for professional services. For instance, RNFAs, Registered Nurse First Assistants, provide surgical support services. Such support services are separately payable for certain surgeries to other practitioners such as physician assistants and nurse practitioners. In time, RNFAs will probably be recognized for such professional reimbursement.

Clinics

The word *clinic* can be variously interpreted, thus resulting in confusion unless the context of the discussion is well defined. Almost everyone is familiar with the doctor's office where physicians, and possibly qualified NPPs, provide services. The most common example is a physically freestanding office arrangement where patients come to seek services. This is typically an example of a *freestanding clinic*.

Another type of clinic is the *provider-based clinic*. This is a Medicare concept that has significant payment implications. A provider-based clinic is owned and fully integrated into a main provider that is generally a hospital.* For a hospital to have and operate a clinic as provider based, a number of criteria must be achieved as delineated in the Code of Federal Regulations, namely 42 CFR §413.65. The financial advantage for provider-based clinics is that two claim forms are filed:

1. 1500 Claim Form for Professional Services
2. UB-04 Claim Form for Technical Component Services

As we shall see in Chapter 5, Ambulatory Payment Classifications (APCs) are intimately involved with the overall payment process for provider-based clinics. Also in Chapter 4, there is even some involvement of hospital-owned or -operated clinics relative to the MS-DRGs (Medicare Severity Diagnosis Related Groups).

Be careful with the use of the freestanding clinic terminology. This may appear as a physically distinguishing characteristic, but the difference between freestanding and provider based is actually a logical or organizational distinction, not a physical location distinction. Consider the following case study.

In Case Study 2.2, the physician will file, or more probably the hospital will file for the physician, only a 1500 claims form with place of service (POS) as '11' for physician office. Although the

---

CASE STUDY 2.2   FREESTANDING CLINIC INSIDE THE APEX MEDICAL CENTER

A new internal medicine physician has come to Anywhere, USA. The physician wants to start an independent practice. The Apex Medical Center offers to rent space to the new physician, including nursing and clerical staff. A suite of offices and examination rooms are provided on the third floor of the hospital.

---

* Technically, a Medicare provider can establish provider-based facilities such as clinics. Thus, a skilled nursing facility could establish provider-based clinics.

> ### CASE STUDY 2.3 HOSPITAL-OWNED AND -OPERATED CLINICS
>
> The Apex Medical Center has acquired two different family practice clinics, both of which are about 20 miles away in opposite directions. Apex decides to operate one of the clinics as provider-based by filing two different claims, one for the professional and one for the technical component. Due to competitive pressures, the other clinic is operated as a freestanding clinic and files only the 1500 form.

clinic is located inside the hospital, due to the fact that the physician pays rent, this clinic is the physician's office for billing purposes.

For Case Study 2.3, most likely, both of these clinics meet all of the provider-based requirements. However, Apex can choose to operate one of the clinics as freestanding while the other is treated as provider based.

> *Note:* Watch for additional distinctions that CMS may make with freestanding clinics. There have been some hints of differentiating physician-owned freestanding clinics from hospital-owned freestanding clinics.[*] You may also see the phrase *physician clinic*, which would seem to imply physician ownership, but this phrase may simply indicate that only a 1500 claim form is filed.

While the word *clinic* generally implies physician services, various practitioners, if allowed by state law, can establish independent practices. A group of physical therapists may establish an independent physical therapy practice, including radiology services. Nurse practitioners can also establish independent practices although some states require that NPs have a collaborative agreement with a physician. These types of clinics or practices are generally paid through fee schedule arrangements, just as with physicians.

Physicians, practitioners, and clinics are generally reimbursed by fee schedules. For the Medicare program, this is the MPFS or Medicare Physician Fee Schedule. This is a very complex fee schedule with many features that are convoluted.[†] The prospective payment system that becomes the most enmeshed with the MPFS is APCs, which are discussed in Chapter 5.

Hospitals

Hospitals come in a variety of sizes, locations, and specialties. Some are publicly owned, not-for-profit, while others are privately owned and thus are for-profit. In some cases, physicians will own a hospital, and this type of business arrangement has raised issues within the Medicare program relative to the referral of patients to such a physician-owned hospital. With increasing frequency we are also seeing hospitals devoted to specialty services such as orthopedics or cardiology. These types of specialty hospitals are often owned wholly or partially by physicians.

---

[*] See CMS Transmittal 73, dated May 2, 2008, to CMS Publication 100-02, *Medicare Benefits Policy Manual.* This transmittal has been withdrawn, but it does provide some insight into clinic issues.

[†] See the second book in this series, namely *Healthcare Payment Systems: Fee Schedule Payment Systems,* 2010, CRC Press, Boca Raton, FL.

CASE STUDY 2.4   ORTHOPEDIC SPECIALTY HOSPITAL

The Apex Medical Center is a general short-term, acute care hospital. Two years ago, a specialty hospital addressing only certain types of orthopedic surgeries was established about 2 miles down the road. The specialty hospital does not have an emergency department (ED). Apex views the specialty hospital as siphoning off the more common orthopedic services such as knee replacements and hip repairs that are being performed at the specialty hospital.

Case Study 2.4 illustrates the fact that hospitals can and sometimes do become competitors. Other interesting questions can also arise with circumstances such as those in Case Study 2.4. For instance, if an individual was brought to the Apex Medical Center's ED with a severe orthopedic issue, can Apex transfer the patient to the orthopedic specialty hospital even though the specialty hospital does not have an ED? Interestingly enough, under EMTALA (Emergency Medical Treatment And Labor Act), the answer to this question is "yes."[*]

Hospitals are generally licensed at the state level, and their business structuring is based on a combination of state rules and regulations along with significant considerations for tax issues. Layered on top of this are national payment systems such as those from Medicare that generate special hospital designations, which then further complicate the payment systems in use. For instance, consider the following special Medicare designations for hospitals:

- Critical Access Hospital (CAH)
- Sole Community Hospital (SCH)
- Medicare Dependent Hospital (MDH)
- Disproportionate Share Hospital (DSH)
- Rural Referral Center (RRC)

With the exception of the CAHs, all these hospitals are paid through the Medicare inpatient prospective payment system, MS-DRGs, and the outpatient prospective payment system, APCs.

Critical Access Hospitals are reimbursed on a cost basis and thus do not generally use prospective payment from the Medicare program. Keep in mind that being a CAH is a Medicare concept relative to certain conditions of participation (CoPs) and then payment. Outside of Medicare, these hospitals are just hospitals and most likely will be paid on the basis of a variety of payment systems used by various third-party payers. Note that for CAHs there are some further special payment processes in terms of integrating physician/practitioner payment for outpatient services into the payment of the CAH.[†]

The SCHs are generally isolated hospitals that are at least 35 miles from another hospital. This requirement is generally shared by CAHs as well. For Medicare, SCHs do use the PPSs for inpatient and outpatient services, but there are some additional benefits particularly relative to MS-DRGs. For instance, SCHs are not subject to the DRG post-acute care transfer rule[‡] that can reduce MS-DRG payment if the patient is transferred to home health or skilled nursing under certain circumstances. MDHs and SCHs also enjoy certain payment enhancements under MS-DRGs. Rural Referral

---

[*] See EMTALA. See 42 CFR and 489.24 and CMS Publication 100-07, State Operations Manual, Appendix V.

[†] See the Method II billing and payment process for CAHs discussed in the companion text, *Healthcare Payment Systems: Cost-Based, Charge-Based and Contractual Payment Systems*, 2012, CRC Press, Boca Raton, FL.

[‡] While not common, the acronym PACT is sometimes used.

CASE STUDY 2.5   PER-DIEM PAYMENT FOR INPATIENT SERVICES

The Apex Medical Center is reviewing a contract with a private insurance company. The payment methodology for inpatient services is quite simple. There is a per-diem payment rate for medical cases and another higher payment rate for surgical cases.

Centers (RRCs) are larger hospitals that serve a number of smaller, generally rural hospitals. Again, there are certain additional payments that are made under the MS-DRG PPS.

Most often, hospitals are reimbursed for services through prospective payment for both inpatient and outpatient services. This is particularly true for the Medicare program with the MS-DRG and APCs. For private third-party payers, PPSs are also used although there can be a much wider variety of payment systems, particularly for inpatient services.

When payment systems are simple, as in Case Study 2.5, there are typically a number of other questions that arise. In this case study, the insurance company is going to be concerned about the medical necessity of the patient being in the hospital for a given period of time. Apex will probably be worried about extensive surgeries for which there may not be a corresponding in-hospital recovery period.

Hospitals can become quite creative in the way in which they are organized. For instance, we have the concept of a *hospital-within-a-hospital*. As the terminology implies, there is a hospital inside of another hospital. An example of this kind of arrangement would be to have a specialty hospital located inside a general acute care hospital. The specialty hospital might occupy two floors of the main hospital. What advantage is there to such an arrangement? The primary purpose for such an arrangement is to take advantage of economy of scales. The specialty hospital can piggyback on the main hospital for facilities, utilities, maintenance, nursing staff, and the like. Otherwise, the specialty hospital would have to develop the entire support infrastructure separately.

From a payment system perspective, would a hospital-within-a-hospital require special attention? The answer is most likely yes. For the Medicare program, there would be concern about appropriate cost-sharing arrangements through formal rental agreements. Without specific guidelines in place, the cost report preparation for the two hospitals could be inappropriately skewed.

Special Hospitals with Specialized Prospective Payment Systems

In recent years, the Medicare program has developed several PPSs for certain types of hospitals that have special needs outside the short-term, acute care hospital PPS, that is, MS-DRGs. These hospitals are

- Long-Term Care Hospitals (LTCHs)
- Inpatient Rehabilitation Facilities (IRFs)
- Inpatient Psychiatric Facilities (IPFs)

The special DRG payment systems that have been developed for these hospitals are discussed in Chapter 6. As can be recognized from the descriptions, LTCHs address patients who are in the hospital for an average of 25 days or more. IRFs specialize in long-term rehabilitation. The IPFs

---

CASE STUDY 2.6   LTCH INSIDE A SHORT-TERM ACUTE CARE HOSPITAL

A large metropolitan hospital has discovered that it has numerous long-term patients, some staying for up to 2 months or even longer in some cases. Better reimbursement as an LTCH appears to offer a solution. As a result, the hospital is reorganizing one floor of the hospital to accommodate a hospital-within-a-hospital. The new hospital will be an LTCH actually inside the short-term, acute care hospital.

---

specialize in psychiatric services. Note that for both IRFs and IPFs, the term *facilities* is used in a dual capacity. These can be separate hospitals, or they can be distinct-part units in another hospital.

Whether or not the strategy illustrated in Case Study 2.6 will bear fruition is an interesting question. However, this case study does illustrate the organizational complexity that can evolve in lieu of different kinds of payment mechanisms for hospitals.

Hospitals and Integrated Delivery Systems

Over the past several decades, there has been significant movement to consolidate various types of healthcare providers into seamless delivery systems. Even smaller hospitals may have clinics, a skilled nursing facility, a home health agency, and also provide durable medical equipment. As you might imagine, integrated delivery systems (IDSs) are paid through a variety of payment systems, including various prospective payment and fee schedules.

Hospitals often provide the core element in IDSs. Additionally, hospitals also form systems, and associated with each hospital there may also be a separate IDS. Or the hospital system may decide to have a system of home health agencies that are associated with the hospitals in the system, but the organizational structuring and reporting are separate for the hospitals from the home health agencies.

In other words, in the real world of healthcare, there can be many different types of organizational structuring. The way in which payment systems accommodate these various organization structures can become quite complicated.

The basic information given in Case Study 2.7 would suggest that Apex is joining a rather loosely organized IDS. It appears that the IDS may actually function as a management services organization (MSO) that provides various administrative functions for the various member providers of the IDS.

In other cases, an IDS or system of hospitals may be hierarchically structured with tight ownership and highly structured management. Regardless of the specifics of the IDS, there

---

CASE STUDY 2.7   APOGEE HEALTHCARE SYSTEM

The Apex Medical Center has been invited to join the Apogee Healthcare System. Currently, Apogee has three hospitals in the region along with half a dozen skilled nursing facilities, eight home health agencies, two dozen physician clinics, and a reference laboratory. One of the attractions of joining Apogee is that there are sophisticated billing processes that can be used by Apex.

---

will be many different payment systems used, including prospective payment and various fee schedules.

With the enactment of the Affordable Care Act of 2010, a new type of organization is now being developed. These are Accountable Care Organizations (ACOs). Generally, these organizations will be integrated delivery systems that will be allowed to possibly share in savings generated from more efficient delivery of healthcare under the Medicare program. The payment systems for the individual parts of the ACO may not really change, but the accounting for services will certainly need to be changed in order to identify savings that could possibly be shared.

Special Provider Organizations

There are a number of provider organizational structures that provide limited services and/or products. Various types of payment systems are used for these special organizations.

DME Suppliers

Durable medical equipment or, using the full acronym, DMEPOS for DME, prosthetics, orthotics, and supplies, represents a major area for healthcare.* The range of products is extensive, including crutches, canes, walkers, commodes, braces, diabetic shoes, and the list can go on extensively. While there are many compliance issues surrounding DME, particularly medical necessity, the payment process can also become complicated.

Most communities have stand-alone DME suppliers along with providers such as hospitals that also have DME companies. Medicare has an extensive DME fee schedule through which the DME for Medicare beneficiaries is paid. Many private third-party payers also use a fee schedule or some modified form of a fee schedule. Additionally, some DME is provided by physicians, hospitals, home health, and even skilled nursing facilities.

DME is different from other aspects of healthcare, even those aspects providing some sort of a product or supply item. DME can be new, used, rented, or rent-to own. Thus, the ability of a fee schedule to provide payment must be quite adaptable to these different ways of dispensing DME.

While there are many variations on the theme illustrated in Case Study 2.8, being a DME supplier attracts many organizations. For hospitals, compliance issues can complicate the ways in which DME is supplied to hospital patients.

CASE STUDY 2.8   COMPETING DME SUPPLIERS

Anywhere, USA has the distinction of having nearly a dozen DME suppliers in the immediate area. The Apex Medical Center has attempted to use selected DME suppliers but the competition is so fierce that Apex has decided to become a DME supplier itself in order to avoid complaints from local suppliers.

---

* DME is also an area with significant compliance concerns and including fraudulent activities.

Note: While a technicality, the whole concept of implantable DME or, more correctly, implantable devices is an issue for both APCs and MS-DRGs relative to the cost-reporting process. Generally, when referring to DME, reusable DME such as crutches, canes, walkers, wheelchairs, and the like is being discussed.

Skilled Nursing Facilities

SNFs are abundant in most communities. They may be freestanding SNFs, or they may be integrated into a hospital setting. For small, generally rural hospitals, we have the concept of swing-beds in which a hospital bed can be used for inpatient care and then transferred over to providing skilled nursing care.

While SNF payments, at least under Medicare, use a prospective payment system, fee schedules are still used by the physicians and practitioners providing the services. Also, there are nursing facilities (i.e., not at the skilled level), assisted living, and other arrangements that provide varying degrees of less acute care.

As with many payment aspects for healthcare providers, situations can become complex relative to coverage and then associated payment processes. Consider Case Study 2.9.

Under the Medicare program, PEN therapy at an SNF is a part of the overall payment, while at the nursing facility PEN therapy is considered a prosthetic and is paid through the DME fee schedule. Thus, this service can fall under a prospective payment system or a fee schedule payment system, depending on the circumstances.

Home Health Agencies

Home health agencies (HHAs) are used extensively with the Medicare population and to a more limited extent with the population covered by private insurance. While physicians and practitioners must order and substantiate medical necessity for home health services, the payment system used for these services is a special HHA prospective payment system. Also, home health services are often provided after an inpatient discharge so there can be a payment interface between MS-DRGs for the hospital and the PPS used by HHAs.

Case Study 2.10 illustrates some of the frustrations that healthcare providers encounter when they are actually trying to provide needed services. Qualifying for home health services under Medicare can be an involved process. For example, there is the issue of being homebound. What, exactly, does it mean to be homebound? Also, when a healthcare provider provides services to a Medicare patient, there is generally an expectation that the healthcare provider will bill the Medicare program. In this case study, there are individuals requesting the services on a private contract basis. Do you think this might present some special challenges?

CASE STUDY 2.9   PEN THERAPY AT A NURSING FACILITY

Anywhere, USA has a nursing facility that provides skilled nursing and also lower acuity level nursing services. There are several patients who need PEN (parenteral enteral nutrition) therapy. All of these patients are Medicare patients. Most of them are in skilled nursing but two of them are simply in nursing beds.

CASE STUDY 2.10   PRIVATE PAY HOME HEALTH SERVICES

The Apex Medical Center has established a home health service as a part of its integrated services strategy. Most of the patients are Medicare beneficiaries, and payment is made through the Medicare home health PPS. However, there is increasing difficulty in qualifying patients for these services under the Medicare program. As a result, there are requests for these services on a private basis with direct payment from the patients.

Independent Diagnostic Testing Facilities

IDTFs generally provide a limited range of mainly radiology diagnostic tests. This is a provider entity that is recognized by the Medicare program, and payment is made through the Medicare Physician Fee Schedule. There are special supervision requirements mandated by the Medicare program for diagnostic tests. Also, the MPFS has a mechanism to separate the radiological services into a technical component, a professional component, and the total component. Thus, MPFSs can accommodate different arrangements by different providers.

IDTFs are paid through the Medicare physician fee schedule. For the circumstances delineated in Case Study 2.11, a fee schedule payment system must be able to pay for the professional only, the technical component only, and then the combined total of both the professional and technical components.

> *Note:* In the above discussion, the technical component and the professional component are separate but both of them can be billed on the 1500 professional claim form. Typically, the technical component is billed on the UB-04 and the professional on the 1500 form. See Case Study 2.12 below.

CASE STUDY 2.11   IDTF BILLING FOR RADIOLOGY SERVICES

Anywhere, USA has an IDTF across town from the Apex Medical Center. Due to its location, many patients and physicians find that it is convenient to use. In some cases, physicians near the IDTF simply use it as a place to have radiology services provided. The ordering physician may elect to bill for the professional interpretation while the IDTF bills only for the technical component. In other cases, a radiologist at the IDTF interprets the test so that the IDTF bills for the total component, that is, both the professional and technical components.

CASE STUDY 2.12   IDTF ACQUIRED BY APEX AND CONVERTED TO PROVIDER BASED

The Apex Medical Center has decided to purchase the IDTF that is located across town. (See Case Study 2.11.) The hospital takes the necessary steps to convert this into a hospital-based facility. This means that the radiology services are now provided as an extension of the radiology department of the hospital.

For non-Medicare patients, you may find that what is recognized by Medicare as an IDTF for a limited range of diagnostic services may provide a much wider range of services delimited only by state, local, or professional guidelines. Payment processes for these expanded IDTFs can become quite complex.

When a change like that described in Case Study 2.12 occurs, the entire billing and payment process may change. In this case with the change to provider based, the payment system will switch from MPFS over to the outpatient prospective payment system, namely APCs. Of course this is for Medicare. How will such a change be addressed by other third-party payers? The answer to this question can be quite variable, depending on the type of payment system used by a given third-party payer.

Comprehensive Outpatient Rehabilitation Facilities

As the name implies, CORFs provide outpatient rehabilitation services. These are generally freestanding facilities, although hospitals can establish CORFs. For hospital-based CORFs, the provider-based rule does not directly apply because the same fee schedule payment is made as with freestanding CORFs. Payment for services comes from the MPFS utilizing the non-facility RVUs. Various services such as physical and occupational therapy are provided utilizing a comprehensive multidisciplinary approach.

Clinical Laboratories

Laboratory services abound in many different settings. Hospitals and clinics typically have clinical laboratories, although the range of tests may be more delimited for a physician office laboratory. There are freestanding laboratories, some of which may be used as reference laboratories for other healthcare providers who do not perform certain tests. Generally, payment for clinical laboratory services is made by fee schedule arrangements, both for Medicare and non-Medicare.

Ambulatory Surgical Centers

ASCs are a Medicare concept, although hospitals, physicians, and joint ventures of hospitals and physicians also develop and use the ASC concept for non-Medicare patients. ASCs are generally physically freestanding entities although often they are located relatively close to a hospital. In some cases, ASCs are right on the campus of a hospital. Also, while unusual, an ASC could literally be located inside a hospital through some sort of rental agreement.

As the name implies, ambulatory or outpatient surgeries are provided in this setting. For the Medicare program, outpatient surgical services are divided into three categories:

1. Surgeries that must be provided in a hospital setting
2. Surgeries that can be performed in an ASC
3. Surgeries that can be performed in a physician's clinic

Clearly, any outpatient surgical procedure can be performed in a hospital and certainly any medical office procedures can also be performed in an ASC. These three categories are hierarchical. For ASC Medicare payment, there is a complicated payment formula that is a hybrid of MPFS and APCs.

CASE STUDY 2.13   ASC ACROSS THE STREET

A group of surgeons has decided to establish an ASC right across the street from the Apex Medical Center. A wide variety of less complicated surgical services are provided at the ASC. The ASC opens at 6:00 a.m., 6 days a week, and closes promptly at 5:00 p.m. each day.

Even if not organizationally connected, why would an ASC be physically located next to a hospital? Keep in mind that the ASC closes at 5:00 p.m. What happens if there is a patient at the ASC who is not fully recovered?

If you look around your community, assuming that you are someplace close to a metropolitan area, you may start recognizing ASCs that may be highly specialized.

If you take a little time to think about the arrangements in Case Study 2.14, you will probably realize that there are some complicating factors. At this ASC, only the cataract surgical procedure is performed. What happens if there are complications following the surgery? One approach is to have the community physicians and the Apex Medical Center address any follow-up care. For the overall payment processes, this type of situation makes demands on being able to address separate payment for post-operative services (i.e., the follow-up care) versus the actual operation (i.e., intra-operative care).

Note that as for IDTFs, for non-Medicare patients, ASCs may perform significantly increased numbers and types of surgical services. The main delimitations are at the state level and then also within professional guidelines developed by different specialty societies at the national level. In some cases, patients may even be kept overnight.

Summary and Conclusion

There are many different types of healthcare providers and suppliers. Different organizational structures have been developed through the Medicare program and involve different payment mechanisms. While organizational structuring is technically in the area of business structuring and addressing tax considerations, organizational structures used by healthcare providers are often driven by the Medicare program through the use of different payment mechanisms.

Prospective payment systems, along with other forms of payment, are used for these healthcare providers. There is an enormous range in the organizational complexity of healthcare providers. At the simplest level is the solo physician who, most likely, is organized as a sole

---

CASE STUDY 2.14   CATARACT SURGERY ASC

Anywhere, USA has the distinction of having a specialized ASC in the community. While this is not a metropolitan area, there are a sizeable number of retirees on Medicare. This ASC specializes in one, and only one, surgery, namely cataract surgery with IOL (intraocular lens) implantation. While there is a single ophthalmologist, there are three operating bays that have plate glass windows so that friends and relatives of the patient can observe the operation. Also, the ASC has several small buses that will go out, pick up, and then return the patients after the surgery.

proprietor. Even modest-sized hospitals will typically be an integrated delivery system by combining several types of providers together. Large academic medical centers have even more complex business arrangements. There are also national chains of hospitals, nursing homes, and home health agencies. One of the reasons that healthcare payment systems change and evolve is to address these various organizational structures. Hospitals and other healthcare providers develop different service strategies to better service their communities while attempting to receive appropriate payments.

Chapter 3

Anatomy of a Prospective Payment System

Introduction

Prospective payment systems (PPSs) have been developed for various types of health services. While there are numerous variations with different PPSs, there are also some distinctly common features for any given PPS. The common features include

- Payment is fixed in advance, generally on an annual basis.
- A classification system is used to sort and categorize services provided and items rendered.
- A unit of service is predefined to identify services for which grouping to the categories occurs and payment is made.
- Significant bundling occurs within the given categorization process.
- A payment rate is determined for each of the categories in the classification.
- Payment for a bundle of services incentivizes healthcare providers to be more efficient in providing services.

While PPSs utilize a fee-for-service approach—that is, payment is made on the basis of services provided—the significant amount of bundling does enhance a third-party payer's ability to control overall payments. Within a given classification, the healthcare provider will attempt to provide services and/or dispense items that are truly needed in order to reduce the provider's costs relative to the payment for the given category.

The general sequence of steps for determining payment under a PPS is as follows:

1. Service is provided/items are dispensed.
2. Services are documented.
3. Services are classified.

4. Classified services are categorized or grouped.
5. Payment is calculated.

Each of these characteristics requires further definition. For instance, the use of the phrase *on an annual basis* can refer to one of several different types of years:

■ Calendar Year: January 1st through December 31st
■ Federal Fiscal Year: October 1st through September 30th
■ State Fiscal Year: July 1st through June 30th

Additionally, the phrase *rate year* (RY) can also be used. Generally, a rate year is one of the above.

As we will discuss, the classification system used in any PPS is highly variable and generally relates to the type of healthcare services being provided. The unit of service for which grouping occurs can also vary significantly. Consider three examples:

1. Hospital outpatient services: an encounter
2. Hospital inpatient services: a length-of-stay,* that is, admission to discharge
3. Home health: 60-day period

There are other variations as well. Even with these brief descriptions, we still have challenges. For instance, just what is an *encounter*? This may seem simple. Consider an individual going to a healthcare provider, receiving services, and then leaving. Typically, this description entails a brief time period over which the encounter occurs. If you are visiting a hospital clinic, this may be true. But what if you are going to the hospital for outpatient surgery? You may be there for hours, or even overnight in some cases. An individual may go to a hospital emergency department and then be placed under observation for several days. Thus, an outpatient encounter can span a significant time period. Thus, some hospital outpatient PPSs use a window-of-service, which may be a given date of service or even a three-day window.

In addition to the unit of service, you may also encounter the unit of payment. In many cases, these two concepts are the same. In some cases, several units of service may be amalgamated into a single payment so that the unit of payment is different from the unit of service. For instance, in home health services, there are typically a series of visits, including nursing visits and home health aide visits. Each of these visits may be a unit of service that will be amalgamated into a 60-day period that forms the unit of payment.

> ***Note:*** In healthcare payment systems, always anticipate that terminology is rarely uni-formly accepted or consistently utilized. Always check for the specific context of usage.

The true hallmark of PPSs is that significant bundling occurs. For a hospital inpatient PPS, virtually everything that is done during the length of stay is bundled into a single payment under the inpatient PPS. There are always exceptions to bundling everything, but these exceptions are limited for inpatient PPSs. For instance, a patient may have been in the hospital for 10 days and is just about ready to be discharged home. The patient needs a piece of durable medical equipment

---

* You may also see the phrase "episode of care" or "spell of illness." This phraseology is more general; that is, there could be a sequence of outpatient visits addressing the episode of care for an illness or accident, so be certain to check the context of usage.

CASE STUDY 3.1   PAYMENTS LESS THAN COSTS

A financial analyst at the Apex Medical Center has been analyzing the payments received for inpatient services under a specific PPS. Apparently there are several categories that pay significantly below the associated costs for the services. This is occurring with several different types of ophthalmic surgical services.

(DME). While this DME might be bundled into the hospital payment because it was provided while the patient was in the hospital, a more logical approach is to pay for the DME item outside the hospital payment.

A payment rate must be determined for each category or group within the given PPS. Again, there are various different ways to approach this process. In some cases, a dollar amount is determined for each category. In other cases, there are complex statistical analyses that determine a weight or relative value for each category and then assign a conversion factor that is multiplied by the given weight for the category. This is not dissimilar to the conversion factors used in fee schedule payment systems.*

Through the classification system followed by grouping into categories and then using associated payments for each category, payment is fixed in advance for a given time period, generally a year. Why is this significant? The reason is that PPSs were developed as an alternative to cost-based reimbursement, which is retrospective. To determine the costs, we must look back in time. Note that the final payment calculation can be altered at different levels. The classification system may change, the groups or categories may change, and the payment rate for the groups can change.†

Because of the bundling and the predetermined payment amounts, third-party payers utilizing PPSs are better enabled to project their potential costs. Of course the payer must have actuarial projections for utilization because these are still fee-for-service payment systems. If there is an increase in utilization, there will still be an increase in payments to the healthcare provider.

Because of the bundling used in PPSs, for the healthcare provider there is an incentive for greater efficiency in providing services at the lowest cost available. In some cases the payment may be above the provider's costs, while in other cases the costs may be above the payment.

For Case Study 3.1, Apex will have to study this situation more closely. Could the PPS be underpaying for these services? Can Apex reduce its costs for these services? Should these services

CASE STUDY 3.2   NEW TECHNOLOGY PACEMAKERS

The Apex Medical Center has had the good fortune of having two specialized cardiologists join the medical staff. Both of these physicians are now scheduling significant numbers of pacemaker implantations. Most of these services are performed outpatient. A major third-party payer makes a single, bundled payment for both the surgical service and the pacemaker device itself. Unfortunately, new high-tech pacemakers are being used that cost well above the outpatient prospective payment system payment.

---

* See the companion text in the Healthcare Payment Systems series, *Fee Schedule Payment Systems*, published by CRC Press, 2011, ISBN=978-1-4398-4023-8.
† Recalibration is the process for adjusting the groups, and rebasing is the process for adjusting the payment rate.

be de-emphasized? Is the categorization of the surgical services being correctly assigned to the given groupings with the PPS?

Once a prospective payment system is established, changing the payment rates and/or keeping up with technology, which is generally more expensive, becomes an issue. For Apex, in Case Study 3.2, this issue could become quite onerous, with significant surgery losses incurred relative to the cost of the pacemakers. Thus, the given prospective payment system will need to have some sort of features so that new technology can be addressed.

More generally, a mechanism is needed to address unusually expensive services, devices, or drugs that may group to a payment rate that is well below the costs of the services and/or associated devices or drugs. Basically there are two approaches:

1. Develop some sort of outlier payment that can be made for unusually costly services, devices, or drugs
2. Carve out the expensive services, devices, or drugs and pay on a cost basis

Determining payment rates for PPSs is generally a complex mathematical and statistical process. To some degree the process for determining payment rates must be based on the costs incurred by the healthcare provider for providing a given service and/or dispensing various associated items. Because of the bundling process, payments are made on an averaged basis, which, for a particular service, may or may not cover the costs for the specific service. The basic idea is that it will all average out in the end with some payments above costs and other payments below costs.

While there are various methods of determining the costs to healthcare providers under a given PPS, additional features are often integrated into the payment determination. One of the most common is to geographically adjust the payments. In rural areas, the general cost of living is lower and thus payment should be reduced. On the other hand, in major metropolitan areas, the cost of living is higher and healthcare providers should receive an increased payment rate.

PPSs provide financial incentives to the healthcare providers for efficiency in providing services. This incentive can be very specific to a given procedure or much more general relating to overall operating costs. Here are some examples.

The process illustrated in Case Study 3.3 can be carried to the extreme in some cases. For instance, a physician or group of physicians may establish an Ambulatory Surgical Center (ASC) to provide a limited number of outpatient surgical procedures. By limiting the types of procedures to just a few, operational efficiencies can be gained. This concept can also be applied to specialty hospitals that provide a limited range of both outpatient and inpatient surgical procedures.

CASE STUDY 3.3—CATARACT SURGERY

There is an ophthalmologist who is on the medical staff of the Apex Medical Center. The ophthalmologist is working with the surgical staff at Apex in order to dedicate 2 days a week for only cataract surgeries. A time period of 20 minutes is allotted for each surgery and four different operating suites will be required. This way there will be quick throughput of the patients and thus both the ophthalmologist and the hospital will be more efficient and thus increase the reimbursement amounts received.

CASE STUDY 3.4   NURSING STAFF LEVELS

The Summit Nursing Facility is located in Anywhere, USA, down the street from the Apex Medical Center. To optimize reimbursement by lowering costs, Summit is considering reducing the number of registered nurses and using less-expensive medical workers.

Both Case Studies 3.3 and 3.4 illustrate that if a payment system encourages efficiency, then the efficiency may be made at the sacrifice of quality of care. Less expensive devices may be used, fewer supply items are required, there is a lower level of medical personnel, and the list can go on. Thus, especially through the Medicare program, there is significant emphasis on the quality of care, meeting standards of care, and conditions of participation. Making a rather long story short, efficiencies in the provision of healthcare are encouraged by PPSs, but the efficiencies must not sacrifice the quality of care.

Necessary Elements

To establish a prospective payment system, we need to have certain elements or features in place. Given the extreme variability in PPSs, we discuss these features at a general level. In later chapters we look at specific examples.

1. Define the healthcare services that are included in the PPS.
2. Define the unit of service for which payment will be made.
3. Establish the classification system.
4. Develop the categories or groups using the classification system.
5. Develop the payments or payment mechanisms for the categories or groups.
6. Identify exceptional circumstances and exceptional payment mechanisms.
7. Include special incentives and/or constraints through the given PPS.

We now take a brief look at each of these elements. In succeeding chapters we discuss various elements for several different PPSs. As is always the case with healthcare payment systems, variability in features and approaches is the norm.

View the above seven steps as general. Some PPSs have extensive coding systems for classification of services; other PPSs have limited classifications that are almost the same as the groups. In some PPSs, the complicated process is the payment calculation, with the classification and grouping being limited.

PPS Coverage

For any payment system, one of the first questions involves what is covered by the specific implementation of the given type of payment system. Coverage issues can generally be divided into

1. Broad categories of services that are not covered
2. Specific services or items that are not covered

For instance, an outpatient prospective payment system might not cover services such as physical therapy (PT) and occupational therapy (OT) services. The PT/OT services would then be paid through a different payment process. On the inpatient side, a PPS may be established but labor and delivery services might be carved out and paid through some sort of flat fee arrangement.

At a more specific level, a PPS for skilled nursing services might not pay for services such as hyperbaric oxygen therapy or certain types of wound care services. Another outpatient PPS might not pay for corrective lenses but will pay for intraocular lenses used in cataract surgery.

Be careful when using the word *non-covered*. While insurance coverage may extend to services and items not included in a given specific payment system, the insurance policy may still cover the given service or item but payment may be made through other processes. In some cases, the insurance coverage may never pay for the given service or item. Also, as a part of the adjudication process for claims, there is always the question of *medical necessity*. A given service provided or item dispensed may be deemed not medically necessary and thus not covered.

Self-administrable drugs for outpatients under the Medicare program are statutorily not covered as least as far as payment to hospitals and physicians are concerned. Separate pharmacy coverage may apply. See Casey Study 3.5.

The basic facts in Case Study 3.6 seem very straightforward. The patients will go over to the hospital to receive the HBO treatments. Medical necessity would not appear to be an issue, the physicians will certainly order the services so that the hospital will bill for the HBO services, and everyone will be pleased with the care being provided. However, under the Medicare SNF PPS, such HBO services are included and paid as a part of the SNF payment; payment is not separately made to the hospital. Further complications in this case study might include the need to transport the SNF patient by ambulance to and from the hospital. Is this covered? If so, how is the ambulance service billed and paid for? In Case Study 3.6, the ambulance services will be part of the SNF PPS payment.

Healthcare providers as well as insurance enrollees should carefully study what is generally covered and what is not. Beyond that, healthcare providers must fully understand just how covered services are paid through different payment systems. When a third-party payer uses different

---

CASE STUDY 3.5   SELF-ADMINISTRABLE DRUGS

Two weeks ago, Sarah went to the Apex Medical Center's Emergency Department late in the evening with a headache and significant nasal congestion. While she was diagnosed with sinusitis, she was given a decongestant and a pain medication, both in tablet form, along with prescriptions for additional pharmacy items. Today, Sarah has received a bill from the hospital for the self-administrable drugs. Apparently, she must pay for the tablets she took at the hospital.

CASE STUDY 3.6   HBO THERAPY

The Summit Nursing Facility has a number of elderly residents who are Medicare beneficiaries. The Apex Medical Center is now offering hyperbaric oxygen therapy treatments. Several of the nursing facility patients need HBO to address some rather severe wounds and their physicians are prescribing such services.

> **CASE STUDY 3.7   SPLINTING SERVICES**
>
> Sam, an elderly retired rancher, has presented to the Apex Medical Center's ED with a badly sprained right elbow. The ED is unusually busy with several accident cases. The ER physician calls physical therapy to have a PT come to the ED to fabricate and apply a splint for Sam.

payment systems, there can be significant *payment system interface issues*. Just how the given payment systems fit together, or don't fit together, can create significant concerns, including what is covered and/or exactly which payment system pays for a given service.

As with many situations, Case Study 3.7 appears very straightforward and the care provided to Sam is appropriate. The current Medicare outpatient PPS does not cover physical therapy services, as such. PT services are paid through a separate fee schedule arrangement. So for this case study, which payment system covers the splinting service and, thus, how should the claim be filed? In this circumstance, the splinting service is not under a physical therapy plan of care so that the outpatient PPS will cover and pay for this service.

For coverage purposes, we must always know

- What services are covered
- What services are not ever covered
- What services might be covered under certain circumstances
- How coverage issues interface to each other, depending upon different payment systems in use by a given insurance policy or third-party payer

Another mechanism that can be used to delimit coverage relates to the type of healthcare provider. For instance, under the Medicare program there are special hospital designations that can remove certain types of hospitals from the standard PPSs used by Medicare. For example, critical access hospitals (CAHs) are not covered under Medicare's inpatient prospective payment system. While services are certainly covered for CAHs, the payment mechanism is cost based. Similar circumstances apply to children's hospitals and cancer hospitals, at least for the Medicare program.

PPS Unit of Service

Under a prospective payment system, a decision must be made concerning the units of service that will be used under the given PPS. The unit of service generally correlates with the types of services being provided although there can be significant variability. In some cases, the unit of service may be slightly different from the unit of payment.

For hospital outpatient services, the unit of service is typically an *encounter*. For physician services, fee schedule payment systems are most typical and they also use the concept of an encounter. Now the typical definition of an encounter may or may not bear much resemblance to a prospective payment system definition of an encounter. A simplistic definition of an encounter is that an individual goes to a healthcare provider (e.g., physician or hospital), receives services, and then leaves. Virtually everyone has gone to the doctor, had an examination, and then left. Another example would be going to the hospital to have a radiological examination. Conceptually, encounters are relatively brief, that is, counted in minutes or possibly an hour or so.

CASE STUDY 3.8   TWO ED VISITS ON THE SAME DAY

Sam has been having a difficult day. In the morning he presents to the Apex Medical Center's ED complaining of abdominal pain. A diagnosis of indigestion is made and medication prescribed, after which he goes home. While at home he has a slight fall and in the afternoon comes back to the ED with a minor laceration.

For hospital outpatient prospective payment system purposes, the definition of an encounter is less intuitive. A similar concept is a *window-of-service*. A given hospital outpatient PPS may define the encounter as a 1-day window-of-service. In other words, all the services provided on a given date of service are considered part of the encounter and thus the PPS will pay for the encounter as the unit of service. This means that all the services provided will be classified and then grouping will consider all the services as a single encounter.

Another PPS may determine that a 3-day moving window-of-service should be considered as an encounter. Yet another PPS may determine that there can be more than one encounter per date of service. This is why the definition of an encounter is so important for an outpatient PPS.

In Case Study 3.8, both of these services have occurred on the same date of service. Are these two separate encounters, or should these two instances be combined into a single encounter for PPS payment purposes? Another approach would be to treat these two presentations as separate encounters because they are not related even though occurring within a 1-day window-of-service. If the two presentations were related, then they would be combined into a single encounter for payment purposes. Of course, this means that there must be a definition of the concept *related services*. Developing such definitions can become quite complicated. However, such definitions must be precise so that their application can effectively be operationalized through the claims filing and claims adjudication processes.

> *Note:* For hospital outpatient PPSs, it is vitally important to have a very precise definition of what constitutes an encounter if that is the unit of service being used. For instance, if an elective outpatient surgical procedure is being performed, does everything done on the date of the surgical procedure become part of the encounter? Are pre-surgical services and post-surgical services performed on different dates of service (i.e., separate encounters) included in the surgical encounter?

For both inpatient and outpatient PPSs, the question concerning this pre-surgery clinic is whether or not these services are included in the payment for the surgery itself. For the outpatient situation, the payment system may prescribe that the pre-surgery clinic services are included in the overall encounter for the surgery. The same situation applies for surgical procedures performed on an inpatient basis, except the unit of service is generally a length-of-stay.

In Case Study 3.9, the pre-surgery clinic may be considered a separate unit of service under an outpatient PPS. However, if there is some sort of global package payment for the surgery, this pre-surgery clinic visit may be included in the payment for the outpatient surgery. If the surgery turns out to be an inpatient procedure, the inpatient PPS may also bundle the pre-surgery clinic visit for payment purposes.

One of the key elements in any PPS is that there is significant bundling of services. Thus, understanding exactly what is included in the unit of service for which payment is being made is

CASE STUDY 3.9   PRE-SURGERY CLINIC

The Apex Medical Center has established a clinic to handle assessments for patients who are scheduled for surgery, both inpatient and outpatient. From the day before surgery on out to 2 weeks prior to surgery, patients come to the clinic and are assessed by a nurse, laboratory and radiology tests are provided, a pre-surgery history and physical are made by a practitioner if not already performed, and an anesthesiologist makes an assessment as well.

crucial in understanding how payments are being made. For instance, in Case Study 3.9, consider an outpatient surgical procedure. The patient comes to the pre-surgery clinic 3 days before the surgery, but then the surgery itself is moved to a different hospital. Normally, payment for the pre-surgery clinic visit would be bundled into the payment for the surgery. However, in this instance, there is no surgical payment to the hospital providing the presurgery services into which to bundle the payment. Thus, the given PPS would have to have a separate process by which to pay for the pre-surgery clinic services.

PPS Classification Systems

Some sort of method must be established to classify services provided and items dispensed. There is enormous variability in the classification systems that can be and is being used. Coding systems are commonly used although the basis for the development of a given code set may be quite different. For instance, for hospital outpatient services, a procedure coding system such as the AMA's CPT (Common Procedural Terminology) may be used, possibly augmented by the CMS HCPCS (Healthcare Common Procedure Coding System) code set. ICD-10 diagnosis and procedure coding is also available, and this code set is typically used for inpatient services.

> *Note:* ICD-10 diagnosis coding is used by many payment systems to establish *medical necessity* for a given service. Medical necessity is a key element in the claim adjudication process. Some payment systems, including PPSs, also use ICD-10 diagnosis coding for classification purposes. Also note that the ICD-10-PCS, that is, the ICD-10 Procedure Coding System, which is a part of ICD-10, can be used to classify services at the procedure level.

For some services, an extensive questionnaire or patient assessment form can be completed into order to classify services. For instance, a PPS for skilled nursing or home health may include establishing the functional status of the patient. There are different ways to approach this, including filling out an extensive form categorizing different aspects of functional status or using a functional status code set.

The results of Case Study 3.10 are not at all atypical. Inexpensive pharmacy items, supply items, anesthesia, and associated non-operating room charges will all be coalesced into the payment for the surgeries. The surgical payment is typically driven by CPT codes. Note that this is a hospital outpatient claim. The anesthesia charge is for the technical component of anesthesia. The anesthesiologist will have a separate professional billing, as will the surgeon.

Figure 3.1 illustrates the overall process that is used to take the services provided and items dispensed that are then eventually converted into a single group or, for some PPSs, multiple groups

CASE STUDY 3.10   OUTPATIENT SURGERY CLAIM

Sylvia is auditing a claim that has been developed for an outpatient surgical case. This claim will be paid under a hospital outpatient PPS and she is checking to see how this will group. Here are the main charges on the claim:

- 14 Pharmaceutical items
- Surgical room charge/code for first procedure
- Surgical room charge/code for second procedure
- Pre-surgical room charge
- Recovery charge
- Post-recovery room charge
- Anesthesia
- 27 Supply items

The grouping process shows that there are only two payable categories. The pricer software indicates that the more extensive surgery is paid at 100% but the lesser surgery is paid at only 75%.

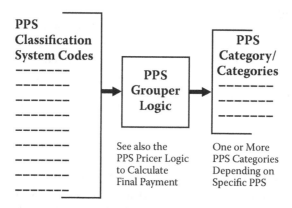

Figure 3.1   General prospective payment grouping process.

that are then paid. This overall process can become quite complicated. The application of the grouping logic is generally performed by computer software referred to as the *grouper*. The logic used by different groupers rapidly becomes a programming challenge. Healthcare providers being reimbursed through a PPS must be extremely careful to verify that correct payment is being received and that the grouper/pricer logic is correct.

Developing Categories or Groups

The establishment of categories or groups is generally based on clinical similarity and resource utilization that is also similar. While the classification system used to report the services or conditions relative to the care provided may result in a listing of various codes or other classifications, the listing is then taken and categorized into one, or possibly more, groups to generate

CASE STUDY 3.11   SEPARATELY PAID FLUOROSCOPY

One of the private third-party payers for the Apex Medical Center uses a PPS for hospital outpatient services. A question has arisen concerning the way that fluoroscopy services are being bundled. For some cases there is separate payment for the fluoroscopy and in other cases the payment is bundled into some other service. The billing personnel at AMC have not been able to determine the logic for bundling (or not) the fluoroscopy services.

the payment. Thus, the architects who design prospective payment systems must develop the bundled categories or groups. Because of the bundling features of PPSs, the number of groups is generally delimited. For broad systems such as those covering inpatient services, several hundred groups may be necessary. Hospital outpatient service PPSs also tend to have several hundred groups. For service areas such as skilled nursing or home health, the number of groups may be less than a hundred.

Grouper/pricer software must be frequently updated, generally on a quarterly basis with major annual updates. As we discuss the architectural design of PPSs, keep in mind that the various features must be programmed into the grouper software. Such programming can be a challenge both for the third-party payer as well as for the healthcare provider. Many healthcare providers simply view the grouper/pricer software as a *black box*.* Using a black box, only the data input and the output data are known. The actual internal logic is not fully known; the use of this type of software is to determine how a given case will group and be paid. With complex grouping PPSs, always be prepared for the unexpected when grouping a case.

The fluoroscopy bundling described in Case Study 3.11 is one of literally thousands of grouping logic decisions that must be determined and then programmed into the grouper. The circumstances described in this case study suggest that the third-party payer is using logic that bundles the fluoroscopy when certain other services are provided (i.e., procedures for which fluoroscopy is normally a part), while in other circumstances the fluoroscopy is paid separately.

> *Note:* Hospitals, and other healthcare providers for that matter, may be receiving payment through dozens of different PPSs, even delimiting consideration to hospital outpatient services. The ability of hospital financial personnel to understand and verify that correct grouping logic has been applied is a major challenge.

Determining Payment Amounts

Overall, payment under PPSs attempts to correlate the payments based on costs or resource utilization. The Medicare program, at least for the Hospital Inpatient Prospective Payment System (i.e., MS-DRGs) and the Hospital Outpatient Prospective Payment System (i.e., APCs), uses a complicated statistical process based on costs. For other PPSs there can be a wide variety of methodologies for determining the payment for the groups within the given PPS.

Typically, Medicare conducts special studies to determine resource utilization and then costs associated with the groups that are part of a PPS. A base year study may be conducted and then

---

* This is a computer engineering concept. You cannot see inside a black box. The opposite is a white box in which you know how, that is, you can see how the logic and programming work.

> **CASE STUDY 3.12   PREPONDERANCE OF COMPLICATED CASES**
>
> A large regional hospital has the good fortune of having several well-recognized specialists in urology and nephrology. As a result, there are many cystoscopy procedures performed at the hospital. However, a significant preponderance of the cases is complex and takes longer than usual. Because of the larger number of complex cases, the averaged payment under one of the PPSs being used is generating payments that are well below the costs of providing the services.

several years later, additional studies may be conducted. In those years in which there is no special study, the payment rate is increased by a predetermined cost-of-living or inflation factor.

As already discussed, a great deal of bundling occurs for PPSs in general. Thus, for a given set of services or items that are categorized through the classification system and then eventually result in one or, for some PPSs, more than one group, the payment for a given group is very much an averaged payment. Healthcare providers receiving payment through PPSs often complain that the payment for certain services does not even cover the costs of providing the services. The logic on the part of the third-party payer is that the payment for some of the services in the group may be below costs while payment for other services in the same group is above costs. The idea is that in the end it all averages out for an appropriate payment for the given group.

Case Study 3.12 illustrates a possible weakness in this averaging approach. If, for the given group within the PPS, a hospital or other healthcare provider performs a full range of services, then the averaged payment will be appropriate. However, if the frequency of services within the group is skewed either toward the more costly or toward the less costly, then the services will generate a loss or a profit, respectively. For instance, at a smaller hospital, the main cystoscopies performed may be routine and thus take less time, which results in lower costs. The averaged payment will then be above the averaged costs and a profit is generated.

One of the main concerns for prospective payment systems is that the groupings that generate the payments may include too many different services that have significantly different costs. In other words, the given group represents too much variability in the costs of providing the services and/or resources utilized to provide the services. Thus, a single averaged payment cannot adequately meet the variability within the group. When there is too much variability, the PPS will typically be modified so that the egregious group is split into two or more new groupings so that the payment amounts are more aligned with costs or resources utilized. Alternatively, the groupings can be adjusted by modifying the grouping logic relative to which services from the classification system are mapped or grouped into the different groupings.

Later is this chapter we develop a very simple PPS with five different categories and we can then revisit this issue (see Relative Weights).

Unusual Circumstances for Additional Payments

As noted in the discussion in the preceding section, appropriate payment for the categories resulting from the grouping process is developed on a statistically averaged basis. In some cases, a given case may require significantly less resources and thus costs, while other services cost significantly more than the payment for the given group of services. When designing PPSs, this kind of situation may (or sometimes may not) be addressed through mechanisms reducing the payment or increasing the payment, depending on the circumstances.

For example, consider an inpatient prospective payment system that has developed both an inlier and outlier payment process. Because the services covered are inpatient services, the length-of-stay (LOS) can be calculated in days. Based on past experience, the average LOS for all the different cases grouping into a given category can be calculated. Let us assume that the historical LOS is 4.0 days. The given PPS may have a feature that if the LOS for a given case is less than 50% of the LOS, then an inlier (i.e., a decreased payment) payment is generated. If the LOS for a given case is more than 200% of the LOS, then an outlier payment is generated. Of course, we must have a formula. For instance, the outlier (i.e., an increased payment) payment may be generated by taking the number of days above the 200% threshold and then making an extra payment consisting of the group payment divided by the average LOS for each day. If the actual LOS is 12 days, 200% of 4.0 days is 8 days. The difference between the 12 and 8 days is 4 days so the extra, outlier, payment would be 4 times the group payment divided by 4.0 (i.e., the average LOS). This means there is an extra per diem payment for an average 4-day period.

Another, more general approach is to establish *cost inliers* and *outliers*. If for a given case the cost of the case is significantly below or above the payment level for a given group within the PPS, then payment is reduced (inlier) or extra payment is provided (outlier). Of course, to generate a formula for calculating the reduction or additional payment will require knowing when the cost has fallen below a preestablished threshold or when the cost has risen above a preestablished threshold.

Another approach is to pay separately for certain items based directly on their cost. This means that certain items are carved out of the PPS itself and cost-based reimbursement is provided. For instance, consider an outpatient service involving the implantation of a pacemaker. While the surgical procedure for implantation can vary to a certain extent, the cost of the surgical service can be dwarfed by the cost of the pacemaker device. The cost of the surgical procedure may be significantly less than the cost of the pacemaker device. Thus, in a given hospital outpatient PPS, only the pacemaker insertion procedure is categorized into a group for payment. The pacemaker itself is broken out and paid on a cost basis, perhaps 10% or 15% above acquisition cost.

The need for PPSs to provide additional payment in unusual circumstances results from the high degree of bundling that is found in PPSs. If, for a given group, the averaged payment is close to the actual cost of providing services—that is, there is not too much variability in the costs for providing the services—then healthcare providers can accommodate the use of such averaged payment. If the payment provided is well below the healthcare provider's costs, then there is always the possibility that provision of the given services may be discontinued, which can then result in limitation on access for patients.

Special Incentives/Constraints

This is the final element of the necessary elements that we will discuss. Usually, special incentives and/or constraints are add-on or take-away in nature and generally financially oriented. The Medicare program is justifiably interested in making certain that rural areas are appropriately served by healthcare providers. Thus, payment incentives are integrated into or added on to the given PPS. For hospitals, Medicare has a number of special designations for rural hospitals that provide for increased payment incentives.

Generally, third-party payers, including the Medicare program, are also interested in promoting quality of care and increased use of electronic health record (EHR) systems. Thus, there may be add-on payments or perhaps the annual update to the payments rates are increased if certain activities are undertaken by the healthcare providers under certain types of PPSs.

These special incentives and/or constraints are not normally a standard part of any given PPS but there are numerous areas where a third-party payer can adjust the payment rates. Given the use of dollar conversion factors makes it all too easy to make slight adjustments that can impact overall reimbursement to certain classes of healthcare providers. As we discuss the features of certain PPSs in more detail, some information will be included concerning this type of special incentive or constraint.

Coding for PPSs

For virtually each and every PPS, accurate and complete coding is essential in gaining proper reimbursement. Of course, any coding can be only as good as the underlying documentation. We are using the word *coding* in a very general sense. The two main PPSs we discuss have the following code sets that are used in generating the group or groups that are processed by the grouper.

■ Medicare Severity DRGs: ICD-10-CM Diagnosis and ICD-10 Procedure Codes
■ Medicare APCs: CPT and HCPCS Procedure Codes

There are many variations in both the Medicare DRGs and Medicare APCs. One variation in APCs is a general system called APGs, which stands for Ambulatory Patient Groups. Historically, APGs were developed first and then the CMS modified the APGs into APCs. In APGs, the grouping process includes not only CPT codes and HCPCS codes, but also can include ICD-10-CM diagnosis codes.

Some PPSs use data-driven information to map or group to a category or possibly categories. For instance, for home health services, the Medicare HH-PPS uses an extensive data collection form that nursing staff use relative to the status and needs of the patient. This is the OASIS or the Outcome and Assessment Information Set. While this is not really coding in the classical sense, it is a process that is used before the grouping and resulting payment calculations can be made. This variable approach to establishing classifications is another example of how PPSs vary. For healthcare payment systems, *variability* seems to be the keyword.

Whenever studying any given specific implementation of a PPS, be certain to carefully study the coding process that is used to develop the input data to the PPS grouper, which then generates the category or sometimes categories, which then generate the payment for the given healthcare services. This generalized coding process is the basis for compliance concerns relative to what is termed *upcoding*. Upcoding is a general concept that involves using higher-level codes and/or data to generate a higher-level group and thus increased payment. This compliance concern applies to all third-party payers with heightened sensitivity for the statutory programs such as Medicare and Medicaid.

For the two major Medicare PPSs (i.e., MS-DRGs and APCs), there are thousands of pages of coding guidelines to assist coding staff in translating the documentation into the appropriate codes, which then drive proper payment under the given PPS. Most recently, the Medicare program has developed the Recovery Audit Contractor (RAC) program to monitor proper coding for both MS-DRGs and APCs[*]. Thus, for any PPS, the code sets, coding process, and supporting documentation are critical elements for proper payment under the given PPS.

---

[*] Actually, the RACs address all Medicare fee-for-service payment systems and that includes the Medicare physician fee schedule as well as other fee schedules.

As we delve into some of the details of several different PPSs, we will also comment on compliance issues that are created by the way in which the given PPS has been designed and then the many implementation parameters that must be established for the given system to work.

Cost Reports

Cost reports are typically developed by hospitals for the Medicare program and to some extent for Medicaid programs. The cost reporting process also includes information on hospital-based skilled nursing services and home health agencies.

The Medicare cost report allows only for reporting *allowed* costs as defined under the Medicare program. The cost report is a complex form[*] and requires significant accounting of costs and associated charges that are made by hospitals. For larger hospitals and hospital systems, dedicated staff work only on the cost report.

A natural question is why the cost reporting process is even used with PPSs. One of the major characteristics of PPSs is to move away from cost-based reimbursement. Historically, the cost report was extremely important when payment for healthcare services was based on costs. As we will see, the cost report is still used, at least by the Medicare program, with the major PPSs. What is used from the cost reports are the cost-to-charge ratios or CCRs.

> *Note:* Cost-based reimbursement is still used for certain healthcare providers, such as Critical Access Hospitals (CAHs), Rural Health Clinics (RHCs), Federally Qualified Health Centers (FQHCs), and certain special hospitals that are not under the Medicare inpatient prospective payment system.

To calculate the CCRs, both the costs and charges must be known within some sort of accounting classification. For example, in a hospital setting, recovery services have a CCR. Thus, in the cost reporting process, all the allowable costs must be determined and then compared to the charges. This generates a ratio, the cost-to-charge ratio. The actual ratios vary significantly, depending on the overall charge structure at the given hospital. See the chargemaster discussion below.

> *Note:* CCRs are an example of a special type of number, namely *index numbers*. Index numbers have no units. Many numbers have units such as pounds- or miles-per hour, or feet and inches. Index numbers have little meaning in and of themselves. They do have meaning when comparing series of index numbers. A good example is the CPI, or consumer price index.

An example of a CCR for recovery services might be 0.54360. This means that the costs for recovery are, on the average, 54.36% of the charges—or, for each dollar charged, the associated costs are 54.36¢. Conceptually, this is not complicated; however, in practice, there can be some challenges. Keeping in mind that the cost report is a highly complex form that must be developed using convoluted rules that are sometimes less than logical, the resulting CCRs can be skewed.[†] Consider Case Study 3.13 below.

---

[*] See the form CMS-2552-10.

[†] A good comparison is to consider the cost report as a very complicated series of tax forms that must be completed following rather strange calculations and a multitude of directives.

CASE STUDY 3.13   SKEWED CCRS

The Chief Financial Officer (CFO) at the Apex Medical Center is reviewing the CCRs from the current cost report and it is noted that some of the CCRs are rather strange. Here is a small sample of the CCRs:

Operating Room	0.65374
Recovery Room	1.10045
Delivery & Labor Room	0.92834
Ultrasound	0.55641
Laboratory	0.66730
IV Therapy	0.88452
Respiratory Therapy	0.45885
Physical Therapy	0.87043
Observation	0.34650
Emergency Room	1.05478

What concerns do you think the CFO has concerning these CCRs? One question that should be raised is: How can a CCR be greater than 1? This would mean that the costs are greater than the charges. In Case Study 3.13, there are two lines where the costs, on average, exceed the charges, namely recovery and the ER. Surely, this cannot be correct! The charge structures at most hospitals are certainly not that low. Second, the CCRs are all quite different; that is, they vary from a low of 0.34650 for observation up to a high of 1.10045 for recovery. Should not the CCRs be a little more uniform?

Cost reporting personnel, when challenged with these types of questions, will simply point out that is just the way the cost report turned out. Everything was done correctly according to all the directives for completing the cost report. Obviously, there is more to such stories. For recovery, there may be a charging problem in that the charges are not appropriately high enough or there may be extra costs being allocated to recovery.

> *Note:* For hospital personnel, the cost reporting personnel or those who gather all the accounting data for the cost report can be excellent sources of information for what is happening at the hospital or in the hospital system. Cost reporting personnel must know everything that is occurring in order to properly complete the cost report.

Hospital Chargemasters

The chargemaster* is simply a listing of all the hospital's charges. Hospital chargemasters have gained some notoriety in recent years as the public becomes more sensitive to hospital charges

---

* Other terminology, such as the Charge Description Master (CDM) or Service Master, may also be used.

as well as charges from other healthcare providers. Typically, the charge structures at hospitals have increased over the years to cost-shift to private third-party payers because of decreased reimbursement from the Medicare program. The ability of Medicare, or any other payers, to reduce reimbursement is attributable to prospective payment and fee schedule payment arrangements.

The cost reports, discussed in the previous section, delineate to sometimes different levels of detail the costs incurred in providing healthcare services. Another piece of basic accounting is how much is charged for providing healthcare services. The ultimate goal is the ability to compare costs relative to charges. This is a special ratio called the ***cost-to-charge ratio,*** or CCR. For the major PPSs, this CCR is used to translate a hospital's charges, as found on claims, into costs, from which statistical calculations are used to determine payments.

Hospital chargemasters are typically very detailed listings of charges made for services, supplies, equipment, procedures, and associated cost items. The listing can be quite long, sometimes ranging into 100,000 line-items or more. The chargemaster is a large file that is part of a hospital's billing system. Generally, these are simple databases consisting of line-items that contain information about the service or products, a description, revenue codes, procedure codes with modifiers as needed, and, of course, a charge. The revenue codes are a special code set that categorizes how the charges that generate the overall revenues should be categorized. For instance, Revenue Code 0450 is for the Emergency Department, Revenue Code 0710 is for recovery services, 0360 is for surgery, and 0762 is for observation services.*

The degree of detail in a chargemaster may vary quite significantly, depending on the specific hospital and types of services provided. The way in which the charges are structured can, and do, vary significantly. Let us join the chargemaster coordinator at the fictitious Apex Medical Center to see what kind of decisions have been made relative to line-item charges that appear in the chargemaster.

- Supply items: Only supply items that cost more than $25.00 are included in the chargemaster, and the markup ranges from 4.0 times the cost to 1.2 times the cost, with the lower markup factor applied to more expensive supply items.
- Surgical services: Charging is by 15-minute time increments, along with a base charge for the level of operating room being used.
- Recovery room: Charges are made by the hour. There are two levels of recovery: regular recovery and extended recovery.
- Medical/surgical rooms: A daily charge is made, depending on the level of care and number of occupants per room.
- Pharmacy items: Cost plus a percentage markup using the same range of markups as with supply items.
- Emergency department: There are five levels of charges corresponding to CPT codes 99281 through 99285. All surgical and medical services are individually priced in the chargemaster.

As you can quickly surmise, this listing is just the beginning of hundreds, if not thousands, of decisions that must be made in establishing and then maintaining the full list of charges. Where services are provided or items dispensed, the charges are accumulated and eventually appear on a claim form.

---

* See the National Uniform Billing Committee (NUBC) for a complete listing of the revenue codes. See http://www.nubc.org.

To understand certain PPSs, our goal is to establish precise cost-to-charge ratios (CCRs) for a given hospital in order to translate charges back into costs. Note that virtually every hospital will have a different chargemaster and thus different CCRs. While somewhat subtle, the revenue codes play an important role in providing the information necessary to generate the CCRs. The charges made by a hospital must be correlated to the costs on the cost report, and then everything must fit into proper categories of costs and associated charges.

> *Note:* There are different ways in which the charges can be correlated to the costs. The chargemaster will always be involved to some degree because this is the origin of the charges. However, a given hospital may correlate the costs and charges through the general ledger as opposed to using the revenue codes that are found on the chargemaster.

There are very different levels of specificity for CCRs. At the most general level, we can take the total (allowable) costs and divide by the total charges to obtain a ratio, perhaps 0.60000. This means that for each dollar charged, the costs are 0.60000 of the charges, or 60¢. Another breakdown might be between inpatient services and outpatient services. For instance, the Apex Medical Center might have the following CCRs:

- Inpatient—0.68000
- Outpatient—0.57500

The level of detail may be taken to any desired level. For instance, the costs and charges for blood, blood products, and transfusions may be segregated so that there is a specific CCR for this area.

When discussing APCs in Chapter 5, we note that some bundling of charges for services and items may occur at the chargemaster level through regulatory guidance.

Relative Weights

One of the more common approaches to determining payment for the groupings within the PPS is to determine the costs for services that have mapped into the given group. This is the general approach for the Medicare program. To use costs as the basis for determining payment, there must be a way to determine those costs. We have now discussed the two processes needed to determine and then use the costs, namely

1. Costs through the cost report
2. Charges through the chargemaster

By determining the cost-to-charge ratios (CCRs), the charges that appear on the claims can be converted into the costs or at least what the third-party payer thinks are the costs. In simplistic terms, the given charge is multiplied by the appropriate CCR to generate the costs. The process of determining accurate costs is absolutely dependent on correct charges and correct CCRs. If either or both of these numbers are skewed, the calculation of the costs will also be skewed.

CASE STUDY 3.14 PRICING DRUG-ELUTING STENTS

The service area personnel in the catheterization laboratory are setting the charges for the expensive drug-eluting stents that are used with coronary catheterization. Because these are expensive items, they are being marked up only 10% as per the tiered pricing formula for supply items and devices.

To illustrate this process, we consider Case Study 3.14. To understand the case study, here is the tiered pricing formula in use by the Apex Medical Center for supplies and devices:

Tier 1: Items less than $20.00, multiply by 3.50
Tier 2: Items between $21.00 and $75.00, multiply by 3.00
Tier 3: Items between $76.00 and $200.00, multiply by 2.50
Tier 4: Items between $201.00 and $1,000.00, multiply by 2.00
Tier 5: Items between $1,001.00 and $2,500.00, multiply by 1.50
Tier 6: Items between $2,501.00 and $5,000.00, multiply by 1.25
Tier 7: Items above $5,001.00, multiply by 1.10

This tiered approach is pervasive for supplies and pharmaceutical items. This is a popular approach because it makes logical sense relative to patient acceptance and understanding of the pricing structure. Also, the mark-up percentages do correlate to some extent to the associated overhead of these items.

When we calculate the overall CCR for supplies and devices, the different tiers will generate different CCRs. In the end there will be some sort of average CCR for all the supplies and devices. To actually calculate the CCR, we would need the volumes of items in each of the categories. For our purposes, assume the average is 0.6000. Note that for Tier 7 by itself, the CCR would be 1.00/1.10 = 0.91; the CCR for Tier 1 would be 1.0/3.50 = 0.29.

Now, the basic facts provided in Case Study 3.14 are quite common. So if there is a drug-eluting stent that costs (acquisition cost) $2,500.00, then the charge that is made is $2,500.00 × 1.10 = $2,750.00. However, we also need to know the overall CCR for these items, which we have assumed is 0.6000. Now when a claim is filed, the $2,750.00 charge for the drug-eluting stent will appear. For Medicare, the charge will be multiplied by the CCR, or 0.6000, to determine the cost. Then, $2,750.00 × 0.60000 = $1,650.00. So this $1,650.00 is what Medicare thinks is the stent cost, and payment will be calculated using this number, which is well below the true cost.[*]

Now we can move on to actually developing the relative weights. As we will discuss, calculating the relative weights for each of the categories in the given prospective payment system involves significant statistical calculations. While the idea is fairly simple, putting everything together is not so straightforward. In Chapters 4 and 5 we look at this statistical process in more detail. Actually, the statistical calculation is almost the same for the Medicare APCs (Ambulatory Payment Classifications) and MS-DRGs (Medicare Severity Diagnosis Related Groups).

Before discussing an extended example of the calculation, we need to review a statistical concept called the *geometric mean*. This is a concept that originally arose from geometry and relationships within the unit circle and associated triangles. Most of you are fully conversant with the **arithmetic mean,** or what many simply call the *average*.[†]

Let us assume that we have the following numbers or data points:

---

[*] This is a specific example of a more general issue called *charge compression*.
[†] In actuality, there are a number of different means provided in mathematics. The most common is the arithmetic mean or the simple average.

$$1, 2, 3, 4, 4, 6, 24$$

There are seven numbers, and the arithmetic mean is calculated by adding the numbers together and then dividing by the number of data points, which in this case is 7. Thus,

$$1 + 2 + 3 + 4 + 4 + 6 + 24 = 44,$$

and then 44 divided by 7 gives us 6.286.

To calculate the geometric mean, we really do the same thing but we elevate the order of arithmetic operations by one degree. Thus, instead of adding, we multiply; and instead of dividing by the number of data points, we take the root of the product, the degree of the root being the number of data points. Thus,

$$1 \times 2 \times 3 \times 4 \times 4 \times 6 \times 24 = 13{,}824$$

and then the 7th root of 13, 824 is 3.904.

If you think about our data set and you ask about an approximate average, you may well realize that the *true* average (whatever *true* means) should be something close to 4. This is what the geometric mean generated. The challenge with this data set is that the number "24" is an *outlier* and it skews the arithmetic mean upward.

Alright, so what does this have to do with our relative weights and prospective payment system categories? The data we use for calculating the relative weights turn out to have a lot of outlier data. The geometric mean is a much better indicator of the true average when there is outlier data present. Thus, we use the geometric mean as our main statistical tool in calculating central tendency for our data sets, which typically consist of cost data.

We now establish a very simple prospective payment system and the needed relative weights. Let us assume that we have the following information:

1. A set of 200 medical services
2. A classification system that groups five categories
3. 5,000 claims with charges for various services within the 200 medical services
4. Cost-to-charge ratios for each of charges on the claims

We designate our categories as A, B, C, D, and E. For each of the services on the claims, the grouping system will map each service to one of the five categories.

Now there are several calculations that must be made.

■ The charges on the claims must be converted to the costs for the services. We have the CCRs so that for each charge we can calculate the actual costs. The CCRs, as discussed above, come from the cost report (costs) and the chargemaster (charges).
■ For each of our five categories, we must calculate the geometric mean of the costs.
■ We also need the overall geometric mean of *all the costs for all categories*.

Here are some sample numbers for our calculation.

■ Geometric mean cost for each category:
   Category A: $ 150.00

Category B: $ 370.00
Category C: $ 600.00
Category D: $2,000.00
Category E: $4,200.00
- ▪ Overall geometric mean cost for all services is $500.00

Now we can easily calculate the relative weights by simply dividing each of our categories by the overall geometric mean costs. Thus,

Relative weight of Category A = $150.00/$500.00 = 0.30000
Relative weight of Category B = $370.00/$500.00 = 0.74000
Relative weight of Category C = $600.00/$500.00 = 1.20000
Relative weight of Category D = $2,000.00/$500.00 = 4.00000
Relative weight of Category E = $4,200.00/$500.00 = 8.40000

Now we have our relative weights for our five-category prospective payment system. The final element that we need is a way to calculate the actual payment that will be made for each of the categories. This is accomplished by establishing a dollar conversion factor (CF) that can be used for each of the categories.

Before establishing a conversion factor, we need to look at the different PPS categories to see what kind of cost data is present in a given category. We also need this information to establish the conversion factor. Let us look at PPS Category C. Here is the range of costs associated with services that map into PPS Category C.

$1,100.00 ← High Cost
$ 600.00 ← Mean Cost
$ 400.00 ← Low Cost

For those with a statistical background, what we really should do is for PPS Category C, take the data set of the costs, along with frequency of the given costs, and check to see what kind of distribution we have. This would include the standard deviation. What we are seeking is to check the *variation* in the costs for PPS Category C.

> ***Note:*** For the Medicare program, a favorite statistic for determining the mean cost is to use the *median*. The various averages and median are all measures of central tendency for a given data set, which for our purposes is cost data.

If you go back and look at Case Study 3.12, this involved a situation in which the hospital was performing most of the services within the given category with higher cost services. For instance, with PPS Category C, the hospital may be performing mainly services that cost $1,000.00 and the hospital's average costs are well above the mean cost of $600.00 in our example.

What we need is a way to check the variation of costs within the given category. A simple measure that is not statistically advanced is the so-called *2-times rule*. This rule checks to see if the highest costs with the given PPS category are more than twice the lowest costs. In our example, $1,100.00 is more than twice the lowest cost of $400.00. Thus, the variation is too high. Now we need to take some action to alleviate this situation because hospitals may be inappropriately underpaid or overpaid.

One approach is to adjust the mappings of the services into the groups. Perhaps there are high-cost services currently in PPS Category C that should instead map into PPS Category D, or low-cost services that should map into PPS Category B. Adjusting the mappings within the grouping process might reduce the variation.

Another approach is to take PPS Category C and break it into two categories: C1 and C2. We can then adjust the grouping process so that the lower-cost services go into Category C1 and the higher-cost services into Category C2. Such a splitting is not just a financial calculation; there would also be clinical issues because the services that map into any group need to have some clinical consistency and commonality. However, this is a fairly standard approach and shows why the number of categories or groups tend to increase over time within a given PPS.

Note that in the discussion of our simple PPS, the five groups or categories were already determined, as were the mappings of services into the five different categories. You may well ask, how were the categories determined? A very general answer to this is a two-stage process:

1. Determine groups that contain clinical associated services that require similar resource utilization.
2. Based on preliminary groupings, statistically check the cost data for such services from a database of claims and refine as necessary.

The refinement that is performed is similar to our example of dividing a category into two categories.

Conversion Factor

Setting the conversion factor can be quite arbitrary and sometimes controversial. In theory, the calculations that have been performed align the categories into groups with relative weights that were calculated using cost and charge data. Thus, the conversion factor should be set so that at least the costs are covered, again on an averaged basis. Assume for the purposes of our little example that the third-party payer wants to pay at 10% over the costs. So, for Category D, the reimbursement amount is set at $2,000.00 × 1.10 = $2,200.00. Dividing $2,200.00 by 4.0000 generates a CF = $2,200.00/4.00000 = $550.00.

> *Note:* The process for setting conversion factors is much more complicated than the discussion above. Also, the determination of the conversion factor may be secret, at least to some extent. Depending on the system, the conversion factor may be set to approximate a global payment for services from the given third-party payer over the period of a year.

Using our $550.00 conversion factor, we can now calculate the payments for each of our groups:

Category A: 0.30000 × 550.00 = $ 165.00
Category B: 0.74000 × 550.00 =   407.00
Category C: 1.20000 × 550.00 =   660.00
Category D: 4.00000 × 550.00 = 2,200.00
Category E: 8.40000 × 550.00 = 4,620.00

While the above calculation gives us the normalized payment, there may be a need to adjust the payment either slightly up or down. For instance, the healthcare facility may be in a metropolitan area where the cost of living is high. So, a geographic adjustment factor (GAF) should be applied. Perhaps a multiplying factor of 1.1000 should be applied. The conversion factor now becomes $605.00. This means that the payment rates are now as follows:

Category A: 0.30000 × 605.00 = $ 181.50
Category B: 0.74000 × 605.00 = 447.70
Category C: 1.20000 × 605.00 = 726.00
Category D: 4.00000 × 605.00 = 2,420.00
Category E: 8.40000 × 605.00 = 5,820.00

A third-party payer using this approach may want to increase payment by a fixed percentage for reporting certain quality indicators or perhaps an increased percentage for obtaining and implementing an electronic health record system. Whatever should be added in or taken away can easily be accomplished at the payment level using some sort of conversion factor or fixed payment rate.

You may need to read through this example several times to get the overall logical process in place. Note that this logic is but one approach. There are significant variations in cost, charges, relative weights, conversion factors, and the like. However, this discussion is a simplified example of how the Medicare program calculates the payment rates for both APCs (Ambulatory Payment Classifications) and MS-DRGs (Medicare Severity Diagnosis Related Groups), which we discuss in subsequent chapters.

Chapter Summary

There are a number of general characteristics for prospective payment systems. These systems have been developed as an alternative to cost-based payment systems that involve looking, retrospectively, back in time to determine costs by which reimbursement could be made. The first PPS was developed by Medicare in the mid-1980s to address hospital inpatient services. Since that time, other PPSs have been developed, mainly by the Medicare program, to address a number of other types of healthcare services.

Payment for services is fixed in advance, generally for a year. Each year the payment amounts are updated along with refinements to the payment system itself. PPSs have a classification process for reporting various services provided or items used in providing healthcare services. The classification systems can vary from highly detailed coding systems to more classification based upon extended patient assessments. Once the services are classified, then various services are grouped or amalgamated into a limited number of categories. These categories provide the basis for reimbursement and generally have relative weights developed to rank the resource utilization for each group. A conversion factor is a dollar amount that is paid for each relative value or relative weight unit. The conversion factor is multiplied times the relative weight to arrive at a payment amount for the case.

The payment calculation easily supports the addition or subtraction of payments based on other criteria. These additions or subtractions might involve geographic adjustments, incentives for quality reporting or implementation of electronic health records (EHRs), or possibly cost inliers and outliers.

The most distinguishing feature of prospective payment systems is that there is a great deal of bundling. Fee schedule payment systems tend to pay at a detailed level directly from the classification of services. PPSs take the classifications of services provided and/or items dispensed and group them together into a single payment or certainly payment for a limited number of groups. The way in which the groups within the PPS are developed and then the process for determining the payments for the group can be quite complicated.

While aggregation of services through clinical similarity is used, complicated statistical calculations based on costs are the norm in this area. Because charge and cost data for healthcare involve enormous variability with many outliers, instead of using the arithmetic mean (i.e., the average), the geometric mean is used. While the calculation for the geometric mean may seem almost esoteric, the geometric mean is a much better measure of the central tendency with healthcare data. Also, keep in mind that these calculations also involve index numbers. Index numbers are special in that they do not have any units; index numbers have meaning only on a relative basis when comparing a series of index numbers.

We will use the general discussions from this chapter to better understand the two most complex and detailed PPSs in use today: Medicare's inpatient prospective payment system (MS-DGRs) and Medicare's outpatient prospective payment system (APCs). In Chapter 6 we also briefly look at some of the more recent PPSs from Medicare that address service areas, such as skilled nursing, home health, and special types of hospitals. Keep the generalized process for PPSs in mind as we pursue these discussions. This involves the following sequence:

1. Service is provided/Items are dispensed.
2. Services are documented.
3. Services are classified.
4. Classified services are categorized or grouped.
5. Payment is calculated.

Chapter 4

Medicare Severity Diagnosis Related Groups (MS-DRGs)

Introduction

MS-DRGs represent Medicare's latest incarnation of DRGs, which were initially implemented for fiscal year 1984. This is a complex prospective payment system used to pay for hospital inpatient services referred to as an IPPS (inpatient prospective payment system). We discuss this topic at a conceptual level, addressing the salient features of MS-DRGs. A complete discussion of MS-DRGs or any other implementation of DRGs would involve thousands of details. Various forms of DRGs are pervasive in healthcare when reimbursing for inpatient services. In our discussions, please refer to Chapter 3, "Anatomy of a Prospective Payment System," for a general outline of common features of any PPS. We refer to some of the specific discussions in Chapter 3, including the cost report, cost-to-charge ratios (CCRs), the geometric mean, and associated topics. This chapter is filled with acronyms; be sure to check any acronym used with the acronym listing provided in Appendix B.

Terminology

DRG is an acronym for diagnosis related group (DRGs = diagnosis related groups). DRGs represent the standard hospital inpatient prospective payment system. There are many variations that have developed over the years. Thus, terminology becomes confusing. For our purposes, we use the following acronyms:

MS-DRGs—Medicare Severity DRGs: The current DRG system used by Medicare starting in FY2008.

M-DRGs—Medicare DRGs: Generally refers to the Medicare DRG system used from FY1984 to FY2007.

DRGs—Generic DRGs: Refers to various versions and refinements of the DRGs generally based on the Medicare program or M-DRGs.

Note also that references to the years are the federal fiscal year starting October 1 and ending September 30 each year. Other terminology and acronyms will be encountered as we discuss various features and characteristics of DRGs, both in general and then specifically for MS-DRGs.

Historical Background

Prior to DRGs, payment for hospital inpatient services was basically on a cost basis. Basing payments on costs involves retrospective payment, that is, looking back to determine costs. M-DRGs were the first prospective payment system developed and implemented for hospital inpatient services. Implementation occurred on October 1, 1983. Previously, payment for inpatient services was based on costs through the Medicare cost reporting process. In general, hospitals were not prepared for using M-DRGs, and there were several years of confusion and some very definite financial impacts. Over time, hospitals did adjust to the new system by understanding that the proper coding of diagnoses and procedures was critical. At that time, ICD-9 was used. Also, hospitals studied just how DRGs were constructed so that claims could be properly filed and appropriate reimbursement obtained.

In 1994, CMS did propose to implement a significant refinement to the Medicare DRG system by introducing a severity refinement. While this change was proposed, including the development of the modified DRG system, the proposal was never pursued by the Medicare program. We refer to this proposed system as SR-DRGs or severity refined DRGs.

SR-DRGs paved the way for the later refinement to MS-DRGs in FY2008. We will discuss how these severity refinements have been developed. Also, there have been significant refinements of the M-DRGs through the all patient DRGs (AP-DRGs) and all patient refined DRGs (APR-DRGs). Due to the design of DRGs in general, DRGs can be used as a payment system or, if properly refined, they can also be used as a method for determining severity of illness. There have been other offshoots of M-DRGs in the form of refined DRGs (R-DRGs) and all patient severity DRGs (APS-DRGs). We will see several other offshoots of the M-DRGs when we discuss the severity refinement implemented in FY2008. Also keep in mind that different third-party payers have also modified various DRG systems to meet their specific needs.

The bottom line is that if you are examining a specific DRG system, be certain to understand the context of the DRG system being discussed or used for inpatient services payment. We discuss the general characteristics of DRGs by first discussing the features of MS-DRGs that are a direct modification of M-DRGs, the original DRG system. As we discuss these features we will compare and contrast how features can be, and are sometimes are, altered for modifying DRGs.

MS-DRG Design Features

DRG payment systems, and MS-DRGs specifically, are complex payment systems that require careful study in order to properly use them for appropriate reimbursement. These systems are dynamic in that they change constantly with new services, new technologies, new drug regimens, and the like. Thus, learning DRGs and then maintaining a current knowledge base takes significant time and effort. Over the period of years, significant modifications and additions are made to these systems.

Coverage

DRGs have been developed to address hospital inpatient services. For MS-DRGs there are two levels of coverage. The first level is to determine which hospitals are covered by the IPPS (i.e., MS-DRGs) and which are not. The easier list to address is those hospitals not covered by MS-DRGs:

- Rehabilitation hospitals and rehabilitation units
- Long-term care hospitals (LTCHs)
- Psychiatric hospitals and psychiatric units
- Children's hospitals
- Cancer hospitals
- Critical access hospitals (CAHs)

Rehabilitation hospitals and rehabilitation units are referred to as inpatient rehabilitation facilities, or IRFs. These facilities have alternative payment mechanisms, including their own PPSs and some cost-based reimbursement. Generally, MS-DRGs apply to short-term acute care hospitals.

The second level of coverage relates to the services provided at the hospital. Most DRG systems are quite inclusive of all hospital inpatient services. Overall, MS-DRGs and most other DRG payment systems tend to cover virtually all the services provided and items dispensed during an inpatient stay—that is, admission through discharge. For MS-DRGs there are very few exceptions of services not included. One of the exceptions is for expensive hemophilia clotting factor pharmaceuticals.* There can also be subtle situations that arise. An example of this is when DME (durable medical equipment) is provided to an inpatient in anticipation of a discharge to home. The DME does not fall under MS-DRGs; payment is made through the DMEPOS fee schedule as billed by the DME supplier.

Unit of Service

The unit of service for virtually all DRG-type payment systems is a length-of-stay that involves an admission followed later by a discharge. Conceptually, this is simple. However, almost nothing is simple in these prospective payment systems. You may also encounter phrases such as *spell of illness* or *episode of care*. A hospital admission may be part of a larger set of services, that is, the episode of care that may start before the hospital admission and then even go beyond the discharge.

Another issue surrounding the unit of service is how days should be counted. For instance, a patient may be admitted late in the evening and then discharged early the next morning, or possibly transferred. Should this count as 2 days? Or because the actual stay was less than 24 hours, should it be counted as 1 day? For CMS and MS-DRGs, there are three different issues surrounding the counting of days:

1. Cost report
2. Utilization
3. MS-DRG pricer

---

* See CMS Publication 100-04, *Medicare Claims Processing Manual*, Chapter 3, §20.7.3.

CASE STUDY 4.1   PATIENT TRANSFERRED TO ANOTHER HOSPITAL

Stephen, an elderly resident of Anywhere, USA, has been at the Apex Medical Center since he was admitted on Tuesday. It is now Thursday and he is being transferred by ambulance to another hospital. He remains in the second hospital until Monday, when he is discharged.

We are interested in payment issues, more specifically MS-DRGs. Be sure that you understand how a given DRG payment system addresses this type of question. Let us consider some simple case studies that illustrate the challenges in this area.

For Case Study 4.1, the main question here is how to count or not count the day on which the transfer occurred. In this case, both hospitals will count the day of the transfer itself. So Apex will count 3 days (Tuesday through Thursday) and the second hospital will count 5 days (Thursday through Monday).

Normally, the day of admission and the day of discharge, even though only partial days, are counted in the day count.

In Case Study 4.2, quite logically, this will count as a single day although the Medicare program is quite sensitive to the concept of staying overnight. Consider the next case study.

In Case Study 4.3, the patient was actually in the hospital for only 32 hours, but the day count will be 3 days. Hospitals often use a census approach to count the number of patients in which the count occurs at midnight.

For MS-DRGs and most other DRG payment systems, the unit of service is also the unit that is paid. There are some situations in which an interim payment may be made for unusually long stays. For other types of PPSs, sometimes there is a distinction between these two concepts. See Chapter 6 for a discussion of PPSs for skilled nursing and home health.

Classification System

All PPSs must have some way of classifying the services provided. For MS-DRGs, and virtually all DRG payment systems, the classification mechanism is ICD-10 CM for diagnosis codes and ICD-10-PCS for procedure codes. Note that ICD-10 is relatively new and converting DRGs from ICD-9 may take years. While there will always be diagnosis codes, there may or may not be any

---

CASE STUDY 4.2   SAME DAY ADMIT AND DISCHARGE

Sarah presented to the Apex Medical Center's ED not feeling well. She was admitted as an inpatient at 7:30 a.m. Infusion therapy was provided and by 4:00 p.m. she was more than ready to go home. Her attending physician discharged her at 7:00 p.m.

CASE STUDY 4.3   ADMIT FOLLOWED SHORTLY BY DISCHARGE

A patient was admitted as an inpatient at 11:00 p.m. on Tuesday evening. First thing Thursday morning, the patient was discharged at 7:00 a.m.

procedures that are performed. You may encounter terms such as medical cases versus surgical cases, with surgical cases having codes for both diagnoses and procedures.

The diagnosis codes developed for a particular case or admission are particularly important. Diagnosis codes are separated into

- Principal diagnosis
- Secondary diagnosis or, more likely, diagnoses

The principal diagnosis is, by far, the most important code developed for any specific case under any DRG system. From the *ICD-10-CM Official Guidelines for Coding and Reporting* we have

> "The principal diagnosis is that condition established after study to be chiefly responsible for occasioning the admission of the patient to the hospital for care."

Diagnosis codes cover an enormous range of diseases, conditions, signs, symptoms, and associated types of information. Some diagnoses are appropriate as principal diagnoses (e.g., fractured hip, pneumonia, etc.) while other diagnoses cannot be used as a reason for admission (e.g., lives alone, cough, etc.). Thus, MS-DRGs separate out those diagnoses that can be used as principal diagnoses and then further group these diagnoses into more homogeneous, clinically related groups of diagnoses. These are the MDCs (or major diagnostic categories). The diagnoses in each MDC generally correspond to a single organ system or etiology and most often are associated with a particular medical specialty.

MS-DRGs use twenty-five MDCs and these have been relatively stable over the years. Almost all DRG systems use the same twenty-five MDCs. They are as follows:

MDC 1 Diseases and Disorders of the Nervous System.
MDC 2 Diseases and Disorders of the Eye.
MDC 3 Diseases and Disorders of the Ear, Nose, Mouth, and Throat.
MDC 4 Diseases and Disorders of the Respiratory System.
MDC 5 Diseases and Disorders of the Circulatory System.
MDC 6 Diseases and Disorders of the Digestive System.
MDC 7 Diseases and Disorders of the Hepatobiliary System and Pancreas.
MDC 8 Diseases and Disorders of the Musculoskeletal System and Connective Tissue.
MDC 9 Diseases and Disorders of the Skin, Subcutaneous Tissue and Breast.
MDC 10 Endocrine, Nutritional and Metabolic Diseases and Disorders.
MDC 11 Diseases and Disorders of the Kidney and Urinary Tract.
MDC 12 Diseases and Disorders of the Male Reproductive System.
MDC 13 Diseases and Disorders of the Female Reproductive System.
MDC 14 Pregnancy, Childbirth, and the Puerperium.
MDC 15 Newborns and Other Neonates with Conditions Originating in the Perinatal Period.
MDC 16 Diseases and Disorders of the Blood and Blood Forming Organs and Immunological Disorders.
MDC 17 Myeloproliferative Diseases and Disorders and Poorly Differentiated Neoplasms.
MDC 18 Infectious and Parasitic Diseases (Systemic or Unspecified Sites).
MDC 19 Mental Diseases and Disorders.
MDC 20 Alcohol/Drug Use and Alcohol/Drug Induced Organic Mental Disorders.
MDC 21 Injuries, Poisonings, and Toxic Effects of Drugs.

MDC 22 Burns.
MDC 23 Factors Influencing Health Status and Other Contacts with Health Services.
MDC 24 Multiple Significant Trauma.
MDC 25 Human Immunodeficiency Virus Infections.

As you read down the list, you will notice that toward the end of the list some of the MDCs become more general and may involve multiple body systems. For instance, MDC 22, Burns, can address multiple parts of the body or organ systems.

Typically, the principal diagnosis determines the MDC, and then the MS-DRG category within that MDC can be determined by the additional codes developed for the case. There are certain cases in which the principal diagnosis will map immediately to a DRG. These are called the pre-MDC categories. Most of these unusual mappings occur with various types of transplants and tracheostomies with mechanical ventilation. In other words, the pre-MDC categories involve fairly complicated services.

ICD-10 diagnosis codes and procedure codes drive the whole process of grouping a case to a single MS-DRG category. There are extensive coding guidelines for ICD-10 coding within the code set itself and also externally, such as the official coding guidelines referenced above. There is also a quarterly publication from the American Hospital Association called the *Coding Clinic* that continually updates guidelines on when to and when not to code in certain ways. Competent, well-trained, and experienced coding staff for MS-DRGs is essential to properly use this PPS. Note that extensive software programs, called *encoders*, have been developed to assist coding staff in developing appropriate ICD-10 codes.

MS-DRG Categories

The process of developing and then, over time, of refining the actual MS-DRG categories or groups is based on resource utilization, that is, the cost of providing services for different principal diagnoses within the MDC. One of the first concerns is to take into account whether or not there is a surgical procedure involved versus simply medical conditions. As appropriate, age, sex, and patient disposition are also taken into account. Through statistical processes, and with due regard for clinical similarity, the actual categories can be developed by statistically coalescing the principal diagnoses into groupings based on charge or cost analysis. Within these groupings there is a base category, or base MS-DRG, for the particular diagnoses or procedures as determined by identifying the MS-DRG categories. As appropriate, a base category, that is, the base MS-DRG, can be expanded to include severity refinements using secondary diagnoses and procedures if the statistical cost data support the refinements.

The statistical process employed to determine the MS-DRG categories within a given MDC is well beyond the scope of this text. As indicated above, the general idea is to take the principal diagnoses within the given MDC and then, using either charge data or cost data from hospital claims, to determine the relative ranking of the principal diagnoses within the MDC. The statistical measure used is generally the median. With the charge or cost data in hand, clinical characteristics within the different principal diagnoses can be considered in grouping principal diagnoses together into what will become the MS-DRG categories. Secondary diagnoses must also be included in the mix, particularly those that will generate a severity refinement. Thus, within a given MS-DRG category, if the charge or cost data shows significant variations, then certain principal diagnoses along with selected secondary diagnosis can then split the base MS-DRG into additional severity levels. MS-DRGs have two severity levels that we discuss below.

Note: Up until FY2008, CMS used charge data from the hospital inpatient claims for analysis. Starting with FY2008, the charge data analysis was phased over to cost data analysis. The charges were converted into costs using hospital-specific cost-to-charge ratios (CCRs). In Chapter 5 we will see that for APCs, the outpatient PPS, cost data have always been used in the statistical analyses.

As we discuss the selection of the principal diagnosis, which then drives to an MDC and then an MS-DRG category within the MDC, we are really starting to discuss the overall grouping logic within MS-DRGs. While an understatement, the full grouping logic for MS-DRGs is quite complex and requires extensive programming to develop what is called the MS-DRG grouper. The grouper takes the ICD-10 codes and eventually generates a single MS-DRG.

One of the first logic splits is whether or not there was an operating room procedure. Not all surgical procedures qualify as operating room procedures. The surgical MS-DRGs are based on a hierarchy that orders operating room procedures or groups of procedures by resource intensity as determined through cost analyses.

M-DRGs have one severity classification based on CCs (complications and comorbidities). MS-DRGs use two severity classifications:

1. CCs: Complications or comorbidities
2. MCCs: Major complications or comorbidities

CCs and MCCs are generated by secondary diagnoses in relationship to the base MS-DRG categories within an MDC. Some base MS-DRGs have both CC and MCC levels, while others may have CCs but not MCCs; and similarly, some have MCCs but not CCs. For each principal diagnosis, certain diagnoses are CCs or MCCs to the principal diagnosis. These specific diagnoses that generate CCs or MCCs for each principal diagnosis are listed in extensive tables* that are then programmed into the MS-DRG grouper.

To illustrate, let us take two examples from MDC 06, Diseases and Disorders of the Digestive System (see Table 4.1). The first three represent a triple of MS-DRGs that contains all three severity levels; that is, there is a base, another category with a CC, and a third category with an MCC. This triple involves surgical procedures as indicated from the description. The last two are medical MS-DRGs in which there are just two severity levels, the base plus an MCC level.

For MS-DRGs, there were 745 MS-DRG categories at the time this text was prepared. Over time there is a tendency for the number of DRGs to slowly increase as needed refinements are

Table 4.1 Sample MS-DRG Categories

MS-DRG	Type	MS-DRG Title
326	Surgical	Stomach, Esophageal & Duodenal Proc w MCC
327	Surgical	Stomach, Esophageal & Duodenal Proc w CC
328	Surgical	Stomach, Esophageal & Duodenal Proc w/o CC/MCC
391	Medical	Esophagitis, Gatroent & Misc Digest Disorders w MCC
392	Medical	Esophagitis, Gatroent & Misc Digest Disorders w/o MCC

---

* See supplemental materials from the CMSIPPS web site.

identified. In 1994 when CMS proposed the SR-DRGs, the number was 652. For other DRG payment systems, the number may run into the thousands.

The MS-DRG categories are carefully studied to ascertain whether additional splits should be inserted. This may mean taking a base MS-DRG and splitting it into two base MS-DRGs, or it may mean taking an MS-DRG that has only one severity refinement and making it into two severity refinements, that is, have a full triple. These kinds of decisions are made based on the costs within each MS-DRG category. If there is too much variability in the costs for a given MS-DRG, as reported by hospitals through their charges, then that MS-DRG is a candidate for further refinement. Such proposed and finalized changes are discussed at some length in the annual *Federal Registers* addressing IPPS.

MS-DRG Grouping

The grouping process (Figure 4.1) of taking the principal diagnosis, secondary diagnoses, the principal procedure, and any secondary procedures that are then mapped into a single MS-DRG category is quite complex. While we have given you a conceptual snapshot of how the principal diagnoses are used to generate MDCs and then the actual MS-DRG categories using secondary diagnoses and procedures, the actual statistical calculations to align resource utilization based on costs is well beyond the scope of this text.

The process of developing and programming the MS-DRG grouper requires significant programming and the inclusion of a number of factors that we have not discussed. One of the general factors is the Medicare code editor (MCE). The important point is that the diagnoses and procedures are input to the grouper and then one, and only one, MS-DRG is generated.

One of the first concerns is exactly how many diagnoses and procedures are actually allowed for inclusion in the grouping process. For the UB-04 claim form and the equivalent 837-I data format, there is room for up to twenty-five diagnosis codes (one principal diagnosis and twenty-four secondary diagnoses) and twenty-five procedure codes (one principal procedures and twenty-four secondary procedures). For any DRG payment system, be certain to check how many of these codes are actually accepted for the grouping process for that DRG system. Care should be taken to include the more significant secondary diagnoses and procedures on the claim form in the earlier positions to make certain they are included in the grouping process.

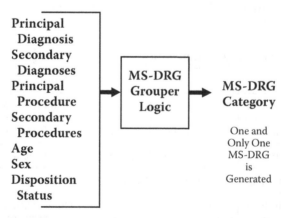

Figure 4.1   General MS-DRG grouping process.

Note that you may also see the grouper referenced in connection with the MS-DRG pricer. Often, these two pieces of software are integrated. As the title implies, the pricer takes the single MS-DRG that is generated and determines the actual payment amount for a specific hospital. Again, the logic used by the pricer is also quite complicated and requires extensive programming.

MS-DRG Relative Weights

To calculate payment, relative weights must be developed for each of the MS-DRG categories. This process is very much like the general example discussed in Chapter 3, "The Anatomy of a Prospective Payment System." MS-DRGs, and DRGs in general, have a significant advantage for the statistical calculations used, namely the MS-DRG grouper generates one, and only one, MS-DRG category for any given case. Thus, virtually all inpatient cases for which a claim is filed can be used in the statistical calculations.

The base data used in this process come from the claims filed by hospitals to the Medicare program for inpatient services. Up to FY2008, the CMS used the charges made as the base data that was used to generate the relative weights. Starting in FY2008, the CMS started to use charge data converted to cost data. This process involves converting the charges on the line-items on the claim into the costs for the various line-items. This is performed on a hospital-specific basis using the hospital's cost-to-charge ratios (CCRs) as generated from the hospital's cost report.

In addition to converting charges on the claims to the hospital's costs, each claim must be grouped to a given MS-DRG category. Remember that with MS-DRGs, and virtually all other DRG systems, the grouping process results in one and only one MS-DRG being generated. The result of this is that for each MS-DRG category we have a significant data set of costs for the MS-DRG.

> *Note:* There are some low-volume MS-DRGs that may not really have enough cost data for proper statistical analysis. These exceptional situations must be handled differently. The exact processes utilized will vary depending upon the amount of cost data available.

While there are some statistical refinements that are used, the basic conceptual steps are as follows:

1. For each MS-DRG category, calculate the geometric mean cost for the *given group*.
2. For all MS-DRG categories, calculate the geometric mean cost for *all groups*.
3. For each MS-DRG category, divide the geometric mean cost by the overall geometric mean cost for all MS-DRGs.

This then generates the relative weights for each of the MS-DRGs. If we expand Table 4.1 and fill in some more information, we obtain Table 4.2.

The numbers in Table 4.2 have been simplified so that it is easier to study the numbers and their relationships. If you study the sequence MS-DRG 328 through MS-DRG 326, you will note that each step up in severity[*] is almost a doubling of the relative weight. The same is generally true with both the GMLOS and AMLOS numbers.

We have not yet discussed the GMLOS and AMLOS. CMS also calculates these statistics based on the length-of-stay (LOS) for each of the MS-DRGs. The arithmetic mean and geometric mean were discussed in Chapter 3. For MS-DRGs, only the GMLOS is actually used. Later

---

[*] Strangely the actual sequence of the MS-DRGs is the opposite of increasing severity.

Table 4.2 Sample MS-DRG Weights along with AMLOS and GMLOS

MS-DRG	Weight	Geometric Mean Length-of-Stay (GMLOS)	Arithmetic Mean Length-of-Stay (AMLOS)
326	5.9000	13.0	17.0
327	2.8000	7.0	9.0
328	1.4000	3.0	4.0
391	1.2000	4.0	5.5
392	0.7000	2.8	3.5

in this chapter, we will see this when discussing transfer cases relative to the payment process. Historically, the AMLOS is utilized for calculating what are called day outliers. Generally, the AMLOS is no longer used by the CMS. Other payers may use it, and the CMS has continued to make this statistic available. The acronym ALOS (or average length-of-stay) may be used; be certain to determine whether this refers to the AMLOS or the GMLOS.

> *Note:* The geometric mean is always less than or equal to the arithmetic mean. There are other means that are defined mathematically, such as the harmonic mean. Be careful when reading CMS documents; sometimes there are nebulous references to the *average* that are really referencing the geometric mean. Also, in some circumstances, CMS likes the median as a measure of central tendency.

The information in Tables 4.1 and 4.2 is readily available from the *Federal Register*, which indicates the final changes for the coming fiscal year. These *Federal Registers* generally appear on or about August 1st of each year with implementation on October 1st of each year. In these IPPS update *Federal Registers*, it is usually Table 5 that lists this information and even more, as we will discuss in calculating the payment for a particular MS-DRG.

Case-Mix Index (CMI)

The relative weights assigned to each MS-DRG and the fact that for any inpatient case there is one, and only one, MS-DRG assigned give us the ability to develop a simple statistic that simultaneously represents the severity of inpatient cases at a given hospital and also provides the key to the level of reimbursement. This is the case mix index (CMI). Financial personnel often monitor the CMI with great care. If the CMI is going up, then reimbursement is most likely going up also.

The formula for calculating the CMI is to take all the discharges over a period of time, array them by MS-DRG, multiply the frequency of each MS-DRG times the weight for the MS-DRG, accumulate the sum total of all the weights, and then divide by the overall frequency of the MS-DRGs. Table 4.3 provides a very simplified example that illustrates this process.

So, we take the cumulative total of the weights (3,960) and divide by the total frequency (1,700) to obtain a CMI of 2.3941. As with other index numbers, this particular CMI has little meaning by itself. However, when we start tracking the CMI on a monthly basis, then there is some meaning. Consider the sequence of monthly CMIs in Table 4.4.

Table 4.3 Simplified CMI Data

DRG	Weight	Frequency	Cumulative Weights
DRG A	1.2000	500	600.0000
DRG B	0.7000	450	315.0000
DRG C	4.1500	300	1,245.0000
DRG D	3.0000	400	1,200.0000
DRG E	12.0000	50	600.0000
Totals		1,700	3,960.0000

Table 4.4 Sequence of CMIs

Month 1	Month 2	Month 3	Month 4	Month 5
2.3941	2.4001	2.3850	2.3502	2.3010

As with any statistics, you should ask questions as to how these calculations were actually made. These could literally be the CMIs for each month or they could be the CMIs calculated each month based on the preceding 12 months, that is, a moving average of sorts. Whatever the case, the overall trend is downward in this example. Could this create some consternation on the part of financial personnel?

While the situation described in Case Study 4.4 is not uncommon, even a moment's reflection should indicate that there may be other factors at work. For instance, there may be some problems with the completeness or timeliness of the documentation. The biggest factor may be that there are more or less severe cases being addressed by the hospital. In other words, hospitals cannot necessarily control the types and severity of cases for inpatient admissions.

After discussing the payment process, we return to the case mix index and show how it correlates directly with the overall payment to a hospital under MS-DRGs and/or other DRG payment systems.

ICD-10 Coding: The Key for Optimizing MS-DRG Reimbursement

Although we have not discussed the relatively complex payment calculations by which payments for MS-DRGs are determined, we now have enough conceptual information to discuss how to

---

CASE STUDY 4.4   DECLINING CASE MIX INDEX

The CFO at the Apex Medical Center has been tracking the CMI on a weekly basis and has noted that it is slowly decreasing and has been doing so over the past several years. An outside consulting firm has also been tracking this decline and has informed the CFO that the coding staff at Apex is incorrectly undercoding cases and their incompetence is causing the decline.

gain proper reimbursement under MS-DRGs. The key is developing the *best codes*, relative to MS-DRGs, that are properly supported by the documentation. The phrase *best codes* simply means the principal diagnosis, secondary diagnoses, and/or procedure codes that generate the highest weighted MS-DRG. The process for gaining proper reimbursement consists of two basic steps that apply to virtually all DRG systems:

1. Develop the best principal diagnosis
2. Find a secondary diagnosis code that generates a CC or, better yet, an MCC for the principal diagnosis

This two-step process does not explicitly include the procedure coding, but developing the best procedure code(s) is assumed.

As previously mentioned, there are extensive coding guidelines due to the multitude of situations that can occur. We will go through a simple conceptual example and then look at two of the many coding situations that can arise.

Case Study 4.5 involves the triple of MS-DRGs shown in Table 4.5.

While we do not go into the intricacies of coding and the MS-DRG grouping process, you should be able to understand that this case will probably group to the lowest level of the triple of MS-DRGs listed in Table 4.5, that is, MS-DRG 195 with a weight of 0.7000. Now what if there were better documentation and more tests? Say, the pneumonia is bacterial in nature and the organism is identified. Dehydration is documented. Worsening cough is documented. Shortness of breath is documented. This list can go on, but you should realize that what we are doing is improving the principal diagnosis (pneumonia with specified etiology) and we now have the possibility of several secondary diagnoses, one of which might be a CC to the principal diagnosis. This could easily move this case to MS-DRG 194 with a weight of 1.5000. With some luck we might even find a secondary diagnosis that generates an MCC.

Table 4.5   Simple Pneumonia MS-DRGs

MS-DRG	Title	Weight
193	Simple Pneumonia and Pleurisy with MCC	1.5000
194	Simple Pneumonia and Pleurisy with CC	1.0000
195	Simple Pneumonia and Pleurisy without CC/MCC	0.7000

CASE STUDY 4.5   ELDERLY PATIENT WITH PNEUMONIA

Sally has been admitted to the hospital with cough, congestion, slight fever, and she is not feeling well. The physician documents a diagnosis of pneumonia and proceeds to provide intravenous antibiotics. Oxygen is provided because the oxygen saturation is low. While there are other services provided, there are no other real diagnoses documented. Sylvia, an inpatient coder, is reviewing the case. For some reason the physician did not have tests to identify the organism causing the pneumonia. Also, according to the documentation, Sally appeared dehydrated but there is no diagnosis.

The question in Case Study 4.6 is which diagnosis to use as the principal diagnosis. In the discussions above, we want the best principal diagnosis, that is, the one that will generate the higher weighted, and thus higher paying MS-DRG. However, is it appropriate to choose based on payment? From Section II-C of the *ICD-10-CM Official Guidelines for Coding and Reporting:*

> "In the unusual instance when two or more diagnoses equally meet the criteria for principal diagnosis as determined by the circumstances of admission, diagnostic workup and/or therapy provided, and the Alphabetic Index, Tabular List, or another coding guidelines does not provide sequencing direction, any one of the diagnoses may be sequenced first."

Alright, this seems to indicate that you can choose either of two equally qualified diagnoses as the principal diagnosis. Do you suppose that an auditor might question whatever decision is made?

The issue in Case Study 4.7 concerns the propriety of coding the acute respiratory distress even though no supporting documentation is present. In situations of this type, coding staff will normally check with the physician to verify that the diagnosis as stated is correct. If the diagnosis is correct, then the physician may be queried for additional information so that the diagnosis can be coded with confidence. Generally, if a physician documents a condition, then due consideration should be given to coding the condition. The physician may make judgments based on observations and data that might not be specifically listed in the documentation. While this type of situation should be avoided—that is, conditions should be documented—this type of situation will occur from time to time.

The two case studies discussed above are simply two of hundreds of coding situations that can be encountered for which decisions must be made by coding staff based on interpreting the documentation from the record. This is why there are extensive coding guidelines and why this is an area where compliance is a significant issue.

Conversion of M-DRGs to MS-DRGs

Our next logical discussion point is the payment calculation for MS-DRGs. Before tackling the payment process, it is instructive to briefly discuss how the venerable M-DRGs were expanded into the current MS-DRGs. As previously discussed, MS-DRGs have, potentially, two levels of severity of illness above the given base MS-DRG category, namely those generated by a CC or an MCC.

In considering a severity refinement to M-DRGs, the first step was to examine other severity refined DRG payment systems. The CMS contracted with RAND to evaluate and assess current DRG systems. The study examined the following systems:

- CMS-DRGs (What we are calling M-DRGs)
- CMS + AP-DRGs
- HSC-DRGs
- Sol-DRGs
- MM-APC-DRGs
- CS-DRGs

This list is a further indication of how prolific DRG payment systems have become. While each of these systems has rather interesting characteristics, the CMS did decide simply to refine its own DRG system, that is, what we are calling M-DRGs. Figure 4.2* provides a summary of the characteristics of these DRG systems.

The CMS used a specific process to develop the final 745 MS-DRGs:

	CMS-DRG	CMS+AP-DRG	HSC-DRG	Sol-DRG	MM-APS-DRG	Con-APR-DRG
#MDCs	25	25	25	25	25	25
#Base DRGs	379	379	391	393	328	270
Total # DRGs	538	602	1,293	1,261	915	863
# Severity CCs	2	3	3-Med 4-Surg	3-Med 4-Surg	3	4
CC Subclass	w CC w/o CC	c/o CC w CC w MCC	No CC Class C CC Class B CC Class A CC	Min/No CC Major CC Major CC Catastrophic CC	w/o CC w CC w MCC	Minor Moderate Major Severe

Figure 4.2   Comparative DRG payment systems.

---

* Based on Table A, August 22, 2007 (72 FR 47143).

Step 1: Consolidate the M-DRGs to just the base DRGs. Basically, the purpose of consolidating was to remove the severity refinement by consolidating the M-DRG categories with CCs into the associated base category. Conceptually, this appears fairly straightforward, but significant decisions were necessary with burn DRGs and pediatric DRGs, among others. This process resulted in 335 base DRGs.

Step 2: Categorize diagnoses into three levels. The three levels were the non-CC, CC, and MCC. The numbers of diagnoses in each category are

Levels	Number of Codes
MCC	1,096
CC	4,221
Non-CC	8,232
Total	13,549

Step 3: Develop additional CC exclusions. This step involves looking for redundant secondary diagnosis codes.

Step 4: Analysis of secondary diagnosis. In this step, the CMS subdivided the secondary diagnosis per base MS-DRG into the three levels: non-CC, CC, and MCC. Part of this analysis involved looking for monotonically increasing average charges.*

Step 5: Divide proposed MS-DRGs by CCs and MCCs. Some rather complex statistical methods were used to determine whether there should be a three-level split or a two level split, or just the base MS-DRG by itself. Among other considerations, this involved analysis of the charge data.

All this work finally resulted in what we have today, namely 745 MS-DRGs with 335 base MS-DRGs and a two-level severity refinement based on CCs and MCCs. Anticipate that the MS-DRGs will be further refined over time. Now back to the payment process for MS-DRGs.†

Payment Process

The payment process for MS-DRGs is conceptually straightforward. The software that calculates the payment is called the MS-DRG pricer. After the inpatient stay (i.e., admission followed by discharge), the case is coded using ICD-10 diagnosis and procedure codes. These codes, along with charges for all the services provided and items used, are placed on the claim form and the case can then be grouped using the MS-DRG grouper. Some additional information such as age, sex, and disposition status will also be needed.

The grouping process as discussed above will result in exactly one, and only one, MS-DRG category. The given MS-DRG category has an associated weight. To calculate the payment, all you need is some sort of conversion factor that is generally called the base rate for MS-DRGs. The

---

* The CMS used an analysis of charges instead of charges converted to costs prior to FY2008.
† Further details are available in the *Federal Register*, August 22, 2007, starting on page 47138. (72 FR 47138).

payment rate or rates are updated annually, often using a percentage increase based on a standard index, such as the hospital market basket price index. The adjustment of the payment rates is called rebasing. Technically, rebasing involves more than just a cost-of-living percentage increase. Rebasing implies going back through the cost determination processes using updated cost and resource utilization data, which involves special studies.

The determination of the base rate for a particular hospital in a particular location is not at all straightforward. There are many influencing factors that must be considered when calculating the final payment for the specific MS-DRG for a specific hospital. Let us take a simple example to start our discussions and then discuss some of the additional provisions for refining the actual payment amount. Keep in mind that you need not perform these calculations manually. The MS-DRG pricer will actually perform this for you after you establish the necessary parameters (e.g., location, special designations, etc.). Continuing with our example,

1. Assume that the MS-DRG weight is 1.8750.
2. The operating payment rate or conversion factor is $6,000.00.
3. Therefore, the operating payment is simply 1.8750 × $6,000.00 = $11,250.00.

As you might guess, the payment rate is adjusted geographically relative to the wage index for the particular geographical location. Generally, the split between labor-related and non-labor-related is 60% versus 40%. This means that 60% of the payment rate is adjusted, up or down, based on the wage index while the other 40% is not adjusted. Over time, this 60%–40% split has become skewed to a ratio that is closer to a 70%–30% split. You can find the current split in the annual *Federal Register* that is issued on or about August 1st of each year. Look for Table 1. You will probably find that there are slightly different splits based on whether the wage index is above or below 1.0000.

This calculation is for operating costs. MS-DRGs also pay for capital costs so that there is a portion of the overall payment that addresses capital costs. This payment rate can also be found in Table 1 of the annual *Federal Register* for MS-DRGs. To pay for capital costs we also need a geographic adjustment factor for the location of the hospital. Here is a simple example continuing the example above:

1. Assume that the MS-DRG weight is 1.8750.
2. The capital payment rate is $400.00.
3. The GAF is 0.9150.
4. Therefore, the capital payment is simply 1.8750 × 0.9150 × $400.00 = $686.25.

The final payment is then the sum of the operating and capital payments: that is, $11,250.00 + $686.25 = $11,936.25.

There are a number of mechanisms for additional payments and/or reductions in payments.

Now that we have the basic payment calculation, we can return to two previous case studies for further analysis. First is Case Study 4.4, which involved calculating the CMI (case-mix index). The CMI is directly related to overall reimbursement under MS-DRGs, or any other DRG system for that matter. A sequence of CMIs was provided in Table 4.4. We consider Month 1 at 2.3941 and Month 5 at 2.3010. We want to calculate the overall reimbursement and a fixed number of cases will be used, say 500 discharges.

- For Month 1, the total reimbursement is 500 × 2.3941 × $6,000.00 = $7,182,300.00.
- For Month 2, the total reimbursement is 500 × 2.3010 × $6,000.00 = $6,903,000.00.

Clearly, with the declining CMI, reimbursement is dropping and financial personnel will be concerned.

Case Study 4.5 had to do with elevating the MS-DRG severity level through better coding and documentation. The objective is to find a CC or MCC for a higher level and associated relative value.

Moving from MS-DRG 195 to MS-DRG 194 means an increase of 1.0000 − 0.7000 = 0.3000. and
Moving from MS-DRG 195 to MS-DRG 193 means an increase of 1.5000 − 0.7000 = 0.8000.

An increase of 0.3000 means a payment increase of 0.3000 ′ $6,000.00 = $1,800.00. Moving to the MCC severity level means an increase of 0.8000 ′ $6,000.00 = $4,800.00. Now, this is for a single case, so proper coding and documentation can reap huge benefits under MS-DRGs. This increase in payment is also the reason why there are significant compliance concerns about upcoding.

Transfers

MS-DRGs, and DRGs in general, make payment when a patient is discharged from the hospital. All the diagnosis and procedure codes drive the grouping process and a payment is calculated. What happens if a patient is admitted to one hospital and is then transferred to another hospital for the completion of care? This is basically a transfer but there can be complications. MS-DRGs represent an inpatient prospective payment system. What if the patient is transferred to a special hospital that is not paid under MS-DRGs but under some sort of cost-based system? Here are some of the variations that can occur in this area:

- Transfer is from one PPS hospital to another PPS hospital.
- Transfer is from a PPS hospital to a non-PPS hospital.
- Patient is admitted, leaves against medical advice, and is later admitted to a PPS hospital.

There is also a special rule under MS-DRGs called the post-acute care transfer (PACT) rule; this special rule is discussed later in this chapter.

To discuss the typical transfer and the way that MS-DRGs treat these transfers, consider Case Study 4.8.

The receiving hospital will be paid the normal MS-DRG payment, presuming that Sam is discharged home. If he is transferred to skilled nursing or home health and/or if within 3 days comes under the care of such a provider, then there could be a decrease in payment. The main concern is how MS-DRGs will treat the transferring hospital because the patient was only there for 2 days so

---

CASE STUDY 4.8   TRANSFER TO HIGHER LEVEL OF CARE

Sam has been in the hospital for 2 days with an unusual respiratory condition. His condition has been diagnosed as needing a higher level of care. He is taken by ambulance to a larger hospital where he completes his recovery over the course of 6 days.

that full payment is probably not appropriate. We need some additional information in order to actually calculate the payment reduction:

■ The GMLOS of the MS-DRG that the case groups to is 5.0.
■ The full MS-DRG payment for the case is $20,000.00.

The first calculation is to determine the per-diem payment rate for this MS-DRG. This is simply $20,000.00 divided by 5.0; that is, $4,000.00 per day. The transferring hospital will then receive payment for 2 days; but because the costs for the hospital are loaded at the front end, the hospital will receive a double per diem for the first day. Thus, the transferring hospital will receive three per diems, or $12,000.00.

Casey Study 4.9 illustrates a different type of situation.

In this case study, there really has not been a transfer, but for MS-DRGs this will be treated as if it were a transfer. Thus Apex, as the transferring hospital, will receive payment on a per-diem basis. Obviously there are many different types of situations that can arise. Another example would be a patient being transferred to a critical access hospital (CAH) that is reimbursed on a cost basis. In this case, the transferring hospital would receive the full MS-DRG payment and the receiving hospital (CAH) would be paid as usual.

Typically, in Case Study 4.10 this would simply be a discharge from the hospital followed, later in the day, by an admission to the skilled nursing facility. The concept of a transfer is from a hospital to another hospital of some sort. However, as we discuss below, MS-DRGs have a special payment policy called the post-acute care transfer. As you might infer from the title of this payment policy, under certain circumstances, the movement of a patient from the hospital to a sub-acute provider (e.g., skilled nursing or home health) is construed or deemed as a transfer, not a discharge followed by an admission.

There are other circumstances that can create concerns relative to MS-DRGs and associated payment policies. Let us consider two more case studies to illustrate possible challenges:

For Case Study 4.11 certainly this is not any sort of transfer. However, is it a discharge and then a new admission? Or is it a continuation of the initial stay? Based on the apparent facts in Case Study 4.11, the readmission is a continuation of the initial stay. Of course, the return to the hospital could be for a reason that is unrelated to the initial admission. For instance, the patient

---

CASE STUDY 4.9   INPATIENT LEAVES AGAINST MEDICAL ADVICE

Stephen has been admitted to the Apex Medical Center for care. He is rather disgruntled and after lunch on the second day, he leaves. Unfortunately, later the same day, he is taken by family members to another hospital about 60 miles down the road where he is admitted and stays for 5 days.

CASE STUDY 4.10   DISCHARGE TO SKILLED NURSING

Sam has been at the Apex Medical Center recovering from an illness. He has been in the hospital for 5 days and the physician determines that he can be discharged and placed in a skilled nursing home to complete his recovery.

CASE STUDY 4.11 PATIENT RETURNS JUST AFTER BEING DISCHARGED

Steve has been in the hospital for 4 days and he is ready to go home. Family members pick him up after he has been discharged from the hospital. However, in driving some 40 miles back to his home, he has a significant relapse. He is driven back to the hospital, proceeds through the emergency department, and his attending physician decides to readmit him.

CASE STUDY 4.12 PATIENT DISCHARGED AND ADMITTED TO DIFFERENT HOSPITAL

Sydney has been at the Apex Medical Center for the past 5 days. He is cleared for discharge and family members have picked him up to go home. The trip takes an hour and a half and about 70 miles down the road Sydney is obviously not doing well. His family members decide to take him to a nearby hospital. He is assessed and then admitted to the hospital.

---

may have fallen or been involved in an accident. In this latter case, the admission later in the day would be considered a new episode of care.

In Case Study 4.12 there is the distinct potential for a transfer as opposed to a new admission. If the reason for the second admission is simply a continuation of the first episode of care, then should this be considered a transfer? Certainly if there is some new and separate reason (e.g., accident of some sort) occasioning the second admission, then this would be a discharge from the first hospital and an admission to the second hospital.

Case Study 4.13 illustrates a situation that is not a transfer.

There is no transfer in this case. MS-DRGs and other DRG payment systems will pay for this service through the normal grouping process; there is no extra payment for the ambulance services. There are certainly extra costs involved. The MRI services will also be paid through the MS-DRG payment. So how does the hospital performing the MRI services get paid? Generally, payment will be made by Apex to the other hospital on a contractual basis.

The whole concept of transfers seems conceptually simple, but the payment process and associated policies in MS-DRGs and other DRG type payment systems must address many different variations that can occur in practice.

Cost Outliers

Years ago, M-DRGs had both day outliers and cost outliers. Day outliers have been phased out. A day outlier payment is a process that occurs when a patient stays in the hospital longer than

---

CASE STUDY 4.13 MRI AT ANOTHER HOSPITAL

Sam has been admitted to the Apex Medical Center. His physicians have determined that he needs immediate MRI (magnetic resonance imaging) service. Unfortunately, Apex's MRI equipment is temporarily down. Sam is put in an ambulance and driven 60 miles to another hospital. The test is performed and Sam is brought back by ambulance.

the AMLOS (arithmetic mean length-of-stay). In theory, if a length-of-stay goes beyond a certain threshold, then there are significantly increased costs and thus there should be increased payment. For instance, a day outlier threshold might be set at two times the AMLOS. If this threshold is exceeded, then extra payment is made. Today, MS-DRGs do not use day outliers, but other implementations of various types of DRGs may still use this concept.

Cost outliers represent the same sort of logic. If an inpatient case becomes extremely costly to the hospital, then an extra payment, the cost outlier payment, can be made. For MS-DRGs, both operating costs and capital costs must be considered in the calculation. Note also that we will need to convert the hospital's charges to costs using appropriate hospital cost-to-charge ratios (CCRs). If this seems complicated, it is because it is complicated!

Even in a simplified example, here are the basic factors that we need to consider:

- The case groups to an MS-DRG, which for this hospital pays $25,000.00.
- The cost outlier threshold (fixed loss outlier threshold) is $30,000.00.
- The covered charges are $100,000.00.
- The marginal payment rate is 80%; that is, the extra payment made will be 80% of the difference between the costs and the threshold.
- The hospital's CCR is 0.4000.

Now we can start calculating the actual cost outlier.

The costs to the hospital are found by multiplying the covered charges ($100,000.00) by the CCR. In this case, 0.4000 × $100,000.00 = $40,000.00.
Now we check to see if the costs are above the cost threshold; that is, is $40,000.00 greater than $30,000.00, which it certainly is. The difference is $10,000.00.
The actual cost outlier payment will be 80% of the difference or 0.80 × $10,000.00 = $8,000.00.
The MS-DRG payment of $25,000.00 will be added to the cost outlier payment of $8,000.00 to arrive at the final payment of $33,000.00.

Note that this is a simplified example intended only to illustrate the conceptual process. The actual calculation will involve operating costs, capital cost, CCRs for both operating and capital costs, any additional payments (e.g., indirect medical education or disproportionate share), geographic adjustments, and the like. The good news is that the MS-DRG pricer software will actually perform the calculation. Of course, hospitals receiving a cost outlier should check to make certain that the calculation is correctly performed so that there is no overpayment or underpayment.

Cost outliers are fairly common for different types of PPSs. In the next chapter we will discuss Medicare's APCs (Ambulatory Payment Classifications), which also have a complicated cost outlier calculation.

The MS-DRG payment can be enhanced either directly or indirectly for certain special classifications of hospitals, which is our next topic.

Special Types and Designations of Hospitals

For payment purposes, particularly with the Medicare program, there are a number of special types of hospitals or hospitals with special designations. As noted earlier in this chapter relative to coverage for MS-DRGs or the IPPS, some special hospitals are paid through different mechanisms, including modified MS-DRGs. In Chapter 6 we review some other relatively new PPSs for certain types of hospitals. Here is a brief listing of some of these special situations:

- Children's Hospitals (cost-based reimbursement)
- Cancer Hospitals (cost-based reimbursement)
- Disproportionate Share Hospitals (DSHs)
- Medicare Dependent Hospitals (MDHs)
- Sole Community Hospitals (SCHs)
- Rural Referral Centers (RRCs)
- Long-Term Care Hospitals (LTCHs) (modified MS-DRG system)
- Inpatient Rehabilitation Facilities (IRFs) (modified MS-DRG system)
- Psychiatric Hospitals or Inpatient Psychiatric Facilities (IPFs) (modified MS-DRG system)
- Critical Access Hospitals (CAHs) (cost-based reimbursement)

Each of these designations involves meeting certain requirements. Generally, these designations accrue from Medicare although some other private payers may recognize selected designations as well and may even adjust their payments. These special designations have been designed to better reimburse or to provide payment incentives under certain circumstances. This is particularly true in rural areas. If there were no special incentives, quite likely there would be fewer rural hospitals.

The CAH designation applies to small, generally rural hospitals that are located some distance from any other hospital. The usual distance is 35 miles, but there are exceptions. There are also bed limitations and a host of other criteria to meet. CAHs are cost-based reimbursed and thus they do not use MS-DRGs. Well, they do not use MS-DRGs for Medicare but they may well use other DRG systems from non-Medicare payers. Because they are not under MS-DRGs, there are certain rules that do not apply, such as the post-acute care transfer rule and the 3-day pre-admission window. Also, for Medicare, CAHs are not required to use the present-on-admission (POA) indicator, but other payers may require the use of this indicator.

We discuss LTCHs, IRFs and IPFs in Chapter 6. These types of hospitals use modified forms of DRGs that are more tailored to their needs. Children's hospitals and cancer hospitals are cost-based reimbursed. These facilities are relatively few in number and are dispersed across the country.

Of greater interest for our discussion are DSHs, MDHs, SCHs, and RRCs. Disproportionate share hospitals, as the name implies, treat a high percentage of low-income patients. DSHs receive a percentage add-on payment applied to the MS-DRG-adjusted base payment rate. This add-on, known as the DSH adjustment, provides for a percentage increase in Medicare payment for hospitals that qualify. DSHs are often found in rural areas. Similarly, MDHs have a preponderance of Medicare patients so that special payment incentives are put into place.

Another type of rural area hospital is the sole community hospital (SCH). As the name implies, these hospitals are the only hospital within a given area. No other hospitals should be within 35 miles of the SCH, although for mountainous areas or where transportation is a problem, there are other geographic proximity tests. Payment under MS-DRGs is somewhat increased based on a hospital-specific basis. Also, SCHs are not subject to the special transfer rule so that there is no reduction in payment for transfers to subacute settings.

RRCs (rural regional centers) are larger hospitals located in or close to rural areas. The hospital must have at least 275 beds, certain percentages of patients must be referred, and there are extensive rules in order to qualify. The main benefit is that inpatient operating costs for RRCs are reimbursed at a higher urban rate rather than the lower rural rate.

These special designations are well worth the effort to attain. Typically, a hospital that has a special designation, such as a sole community hospital, will see significantly increased reimbursement under MS-DRGs through special payments and/or payment adjustments.

Note that the enhanced reimbursement for these special types of hospitals can accrue directly through MS-DRG payments or can accrue through the cost report settlement process.

Documentation Features

MS-DRGs use an extremely complex coding system for classification of services. The ability to properly code one diagnosis versus a slightly different diagnosis may make the difference between a CC versus a MCC secondary diagnosis, which then results in a payment difference that can range into the thousands of dollars. Likewise, the choice of the principal diagnosis is critical for proper grouping and ultimately appropriate payment.

Professional coding staff will quickly indicate that the ability to properly code and to code in a manner that optimizes reimbursement under MS-DRGs requires documentation that is clear, concise, and complete. Not only is complete documentation essential, the actual process of diagnosing and then the course of treatment can affect the coding that, in turn, affects the MS-DRG assignment. For instance, a long-standing issue in pneumonia cases is identifying the causative organism. If the precise cause is determined, the coding can be affected. Physicians may not be overly interested in the causative organism because the course of treatment may not be affected by this information.

Situations also arise in which a physician prescribes a course of treatment involving certain combinations of drugs but there is no documentation as to a diagnosis or disease process that would typically use such a drug protocol. This is simply one example of the challenges faced by hospitals using MS-DRGs and/or other DRG payment systems. While the documentation may be in place, often there are gaps, either obvious or invisible, that can affect the coding process.

The documentation and associated coding become a process or flow issue. Historically, with inpatient services, hospitals have waited until the patient is discharged before the coding takes place. After the patient is discharged, all the documentation is assembled, that is, the laboratory reports, radiology reports, admission history and physical, discharge summary, progress notes, orders, and the like. The coding takes place after the fact of the care itself. This can create some problems because there may be gaps in the documentation and there also may be delays, sometimes significant delays, before any questions are raised.

An alternative approach is called *concurrent coding,* of which there are variations. However, the basic idea is that the documentation is reviewed and preliminary coding is performed at the time that care is being provided. Nursing staff with clinical expertise and the ability to communicate with physicians and practitioners can monitor the care and documentation being developed. Questions can be raised in real-time relative to any missing documentation or possible missed diagnoses. In some cases, nursing staff will actually work on the inpatient floors of the hospital while in other cases, the review is performed outside the actual care setting. The important point is that such reviews are performed concurrently with the patient's time in the hospital.

Because of the sensitivity, small code variations can create significant payment differences within MS-DRGs; techniques such as some form of concurrent coding can generate significant increases in overall reimbursement.

Documentation for hospital inpatient services tends to involve a fairly standard set of documents. These include items such as

CASE STUDY 4.14   CODING WITHOUT THE DISCHARGE SUMMARY

Several physicians at the Apex Medical Center are notorious for not completing the discharge summary documentation in a timely manner. These summaries can become lengthy because they review the overall case and then list all the diagnoses and any procedures that were performed. Due to the need for developing the claims on a timely basis, coding staff go ahead and code the case without the discharge summary.

**CASE STUDY 4.15   SEQUENCING CODES
FROM THE DISCHARGE SUMMARY**

During a recent inpatient audit at the Apex Medical Center, the auditor noted that for two of the coding staff, the sequencing of the diagnosis and procedure codes was always the same as the physician listed in the discharge summary. The first diagnosis automatically became the principal diagnosis and then the other codes were reported in the same order as the physician listed the diagnoses and procedures.

- Pre-admission history and physical
- Progress Notes and Physician Orders
- Diagnostic test results – laboratory, radiology, and cardiology
- Specialty physician consultations
- Operative reports
- Drug administration
- Discharge summary

Obviously there may be other documentation and for long-term cases there may be hundreds of pages of documentation. One of the tasks for coding staff, whether the coding is performed retrospectively or concurrently, is to read through and organize the documentation in order to more effectively code the case. Case Studies 4.14 and 4.15 are from the perspective of an auditor who is validating the codes that were developed.

Even if you do not code, you will probably realize that this is not a good practice. Sometimes the physician will include vital information at the very end of the case in the discharge summary. Also, the physician may include answers to queries about the case in the discharge summary.

Based on all of our discussions about correct coding and being careful to choose the very best principal diagnosis, the findings in Case Study 4.15 are disturbing and should be thoroughly investigated. While everything may be as it should be, there is the suspicion that the coders in this case are not going through the entire record to develop the best codes based on the documentation.

Additional Features for MS-DRGs

Three-Day Preadmission Window

Payment systems that include paying for surgical services often have some form of global surgical package (GSP). The Medicare physician fee schedule (MPFS) has an extensive and well-defined

GSP for surgeons. As we discuss in Chapter 5, APCs (Ambulatory Payment Classifications) have a very weak GSP that is essentially delimited to the date of service on which the surgery is performed. DRGs in general, and more specifically Medicare's MS-DRGs, do not have a GSP as such. However, DRGs do typically have some bundling and/or reduction in payment relative to pre-admission services and possibly post-admission services. We discuss MS-DRGs and then also make some comments relative to other policy decisions that can be made by third-party payers using some form of DRG. The first of these is the 3-day pre-admission rule, which is sometimes called the *3-day payment window.* Note that this window applies to any hospital admission, whether services are purely medical and/or surgical.

First, the 3-day window applies to PPS hospitals; that is, hospitals are paid by Medicare through MS-DRGs. There is an equivalent 1-day window for psychiatric hospitals, rehabilitation hospitals, long-term care hospitals, children's hospitals, and cancer hospitals (i.e., non-IPPS hospitals). Neither version of this window applies to critical access hospitals (CAHs).

Second, this window is a bit complicated because it is divided into two distinct time periods:

1. On the date of admission, the time period before the time of the actual admission
2. Three dates of service prior to the date of admission

Third, we must distinguish between diagnostic and therapeutic services. The basic idea of this window is that all outpatient diagnostic services must be included in the inpatient billing whether or they meet any relatedness criteria. Certain therapeutic services are included in the billing if they are *related* to the inpatient admission but only for the three dates of service preceding the admission. All diagnostic and therapeutic services prior to the time of admission on the date of admission must be included in the inpatient billing.

The most difficult aspect of the 3-day window is: Exactly what outpatient services are included in the inpatient billing? The trigger for applying this rule is a bit unusual; it includes all facilities that are wholly owned or wholly operated by the admitting hospital. In Chapter 5 we discuss to some extent the provider-based rule (PBR). Provider-based clinics are those clinics that are owned by, operated by, and fully integrated into the hospital by virtue of meeting the requirements delineated in the PBR. Provider-based clinics are certainly subject to the trigger for applying the 3-day pre-admission window. However, the trigger also applies to any freestanding physician clinics that are owned or operated by the hospital. The application of this rule to such freestanding clinics can become quite complicated.

> ***Note:*** At the time this text was prepared, a major change to the 3-day window was rippling through the regulatory process. The change began on June 25, 2010, with the signing of the Preservation of Access to Care for Medicare Beneficiaries and Pension Relief Act of 2010. Section 102 modified the Social Security Act (SSA) so that related diagnostic services are bundled into the inpatient billing. Be certain to check for specific changes and new rules and regulations in this area.

For the purposes of Case Study 4.16, both the provider-based clinics and the freestanding clinics will trigger the application of the 3-day pre-admission window. Keep in mind that the trigger is wholly owned or operated; this would also apply to the freestanding physician clinics.

In Case Study 4.17, neither of the hospitals owns any of these clinics; thus the 3-day pre-admission window does not apply when patients are admitted to the either of the hospitals. The

CASE STUDY 4.16   FREESTANDING CLINIC NETWORK

The Apex Medical Center has four provider-based clinics and five freestanding physician clinics. The freestanding clinics are 25 to 50 miles from the hospital, while the provider-based clinics are right in Anywhere, USA. Some of the outlying freestanding clinics have stand-alone laboratories and basic radiology services.

CASE STUDY 4.17   HOSPITAL SYSTEM

The Pinnacle Health System owns two separate hospitals located about 30 miles apart. The system also owns twenty-five clinics in the general catchment area of the two hospitals. These clinics are all freestanding. There is a separate clinic organization owned by the system that operates these clinics.

organizational structuring of hospitals, clinics, and other associate healthcare providers becomes important when analyzing the application of the 3-day pre-admission window.

All diagnostic services and related therapeutic services must be included in the inpatient billing. The major question then becomes: Just what are *related services*? Prior to June 25, 2010, there was a very precise test for determining related services. Namely, the principal diagnosis for the inpatient admission had to match exactly the primary diagnosis for the outpatient services. With the change in the SSA language, everything reverted back to bundling related services without a precise definition. Hospitals are to judge whether the therapeutic services are related or unrelated.

Case Study 4.18 seems rather innocuous, but there are some very significant concerns relative to the 3-day pre-admission window. The visit to the clinic is certainly in the window. The laboratory tests and x-rays are diagnostic and will be included in the inpatient billing. What about therapeutic services? Any therapeutic services were provided by the NP under the supervision of a physician. So is there anything to bundle? The general answer is yes, although specific guidelines are needed from the CMS to address this type of situation. The services of the NP were incident-to those of the physician; remember that the physician billed for the services on an incident-to billing basis (i.e., the physician billed for what the services provided by the NP). For the application of the 3-day pre-admission window, these NP services are actually paid to the hospital; that is, all

CASE STUDY 4.18   RELATED THERAPEUTIC SERVICES

On Monday afternoon, Sam goes to one of the Apex Medical Center's freestanding clinics complaining of fever, cough, and some congestion. He is examined by a nurse practitioner (NP) who makes an assessment, runs laboratory tests, and takes chest x-rays. The nurse practitioner briefly confers with a physician and then provides Sam with a prescription for a course of antibiotics and sends him home to rest. The claim for these services will be under the supervising physician's name. On Wednesday, a neighbor brings Sam to the hospital and he is admitted with pneumonia.

CASE STUDY 4.19   PRE-ADMISSION AND POST-ADMISSION WINDOW

Sandra, the director of patient financial services at Apex, is grappling with a difficult situation. One of their major insurance companies is using a modified form of DRGs and has now implemented 10-day pre-admission and 10-day post-discharge windows. While it is difficult to even determine what should be bundled, now they have wait about 2 weeks after discharge before the claim can be developed and filed.

---

services provided in a facility setting incident-to those of a physician are paid to the hospital. Thus, all the billing for the NP services should be bundled into the inpatient billing.

Even assuming that the physician personally performed the services in the above case study, there should be a payment reduction to the physician for providing the services in a facility setting (i.e., the freestanding clinic is considered a facility when applying the 3-day pre-admission window). This is the Medicare site-of-service differential that would be applied on the 1500 claim form. See Chapter 5 for a discussion of this payment reduction.

In summary, the 3-day pre-admission window or 3-day payment window is a complicated feature of MS-DRGs and quite likely this type of bundling can be used with other DRG implementations. Note that there can be variations on this same theme. For the Medicare program, the OIG (Office of the Inspector General) has recommended extending the window to 14 days.[*] This same concept can also be used to establish a post-discharge window. For instance, any services provided by a hospital facility, however the term facility is defined, would be bundled into the inpatient billing if performed within 3 days of discharge—or perhaps 14 days of discharge might be chosen.

What is illustrated in Case Study 4.19 is basically some sort of global package that includes any related, or sometimes unrelated, service provided before the admission and then after the admission. From a billing standpoint, this type of feature for any DRG system significantly complicates the claims filing process.

Post-Acute Care Transfer

While we have discussed the typical transfer issues for DRGs, the Medicare program has provisions to make a reduced MS-DRG payment for certain MS-DRGs if the patient is discharged from the hospital to subacute facilities, such as skilled nursing or home health.[†] The reduction in payment is invoked only if the MS-DRG involved is on the post-acute listing.[‡]

As with other transfer cases, the GMLOS is used to determine payment; however, the formula is different. For instance, if the GMLOS for a given MS-DRG is 5.0 and the patient was in the hospital for only 3 days and then discharged to skilled nursing, this discharge is considered a transfer. The payment to the transferring hospital will be 50% of the MS-DRG payment plus 50% of the normal transfer payment. Of critical importance is the discharge status reported by the hospital at the time of discharge. It is the discharge status that will drive the reduction in payment. Here is a simplified example:

---

[*] See OIG report A-01-02-00503 issued on August 20, 2003.

[†] This rule also applies for certain special hospitals such as cancer or children's hospitals, inpatient rehabilitation facilities, long-term care hospitals, and psychiatric hospitals.

[‡] At the time this text was prepared, only select MS-DRGs were on the list; be sure to check for the current listing.

CASE STUDY 4.20   DELAYED TRANSFER TO SKILLED NURSING

Sandra, the director of patient financial services, is reviewing a claim. Sam was in the hospital for several days and then discharged home. The claim was filed with home as the discharge status. However, Sandra has become aware that Sam went to a skilled nursing home 2 days after he was discharged.

The GMLOS for the given MS-DRG is 5.0.
The length-of-stay is 3 days.
The normal MS-DRG payment is $20,000.00.
The per-diem amount is thus $20,000.00 / 5.0 = $4,000.00.
The payment is then $(0.50 \times \$20,000.00) + (0.50 \times 4 \times \$4,000.00) = \$18,000.00$.

Remember that the transfer payment is two per-diems the first day, so for 3 days the multiplying factor times the per-diem is 4.

While this is the general process, there are some rather convoluted issues that can arise from the MS-DRG post-acute transfer rule. Consider Case Study 4.20.

For Medicare, application of the post-acute transfer rule starts with admission to skilled nursing or to a home health plan of care that occurs within 3 days of the discharge. In case study 4.20, Apex correctly coded the case. At the time of discharge, Sam was discharged home. However, if this case were reviewed, an overpayment would be claimed. In this case, Sandra did become aware of the transfer within three dates-of-service so that the claim can be refiled correcting the error so that the reduced payment will occur.

The exact opposite can also occur. For instance, a patient may be discharged from the hospital with the intention of going under a home health plan of care. However, the patient may not end up using home health services. If the patient's stay is less than the GMLOS for the given MS-DRG, then there will be a reduction in payment based on the discharge status to home health. However, under this circumstance, the hospital is entitled to the full MS-DRG payment.

Present on Admission (POA)

The POA indicator is a single character attached to the diagnosis codes that appear on the inpatient claim. The five options are

- Y – Yes
- N – No
- U – Unknown
- W – Clinically undetermined
- 1 – Uninterpreted, not used

The basic idea is that under MS-DRGs there should be no payment for conditions that developed during the inpatient stay. For instance, a patient might contract a hospital-acquired infection that must then be treated. Such an infection would be most common with surgical procedures. If the POA indicator is that the infection was not present on admission, then that diagnosis will be removed from the set of diagnoses that actually go into the MS-DRG grouping process. Thus there is the potential of a lower-level category assigned by the MS-DRG grouper and thus payment is reduced.

CASE STUDY 4.21   PRESSURE ULCERS ON ADMISSION

Stephen is a long-term resident of a nursing facility. He has been transported by ambulance to the Apex Medical Center's ED. He is suffering from what appears to be pneumonia and his condition is deteriorating. He is rushed through the ED to an inpatient bed. Unfortunately, he has several pressure ulcers that are developing and this is not noted during the admission. He is in the hospital for 12 days and significant efforts are involved in not only taking care of the pneumonia, but also addressing the pressure ulcers.

Based on our previous discussions, if certain diagnosis codes are removed from the grouping process, then there is the real possibility that payment will be reduced through the use of a lower-level MS-DRG group. Thus, when a patient is admitted to the hospital, it is very important to report all conditions that are evident and present at admission.

Consider Casey Study 4.21 in which the patient had signs of pressure ulcers at the time of admission. To actually determine if there is any reduction in payment in this case, the specific codes would be needed and processed through the MS-DRG grouper/pricer. However, there is a good chance that the payment would have been higher if the pressure ulcers were identified at the time of admission and then the POA could be used correctly to ensure full payment.

Updating Process for MS-DRGs

Throughout this chapter, reference has been made to the annual *Federal Register* entry that occurs on or about August 1st of each year. This *Federal Register* provides the final rule with all the changes to MS-DRGs for the next fiscal year, starting October 1st. In theory, there is a 60-day time period for hospitals, and vendors supporting the MS-DRG grouper/pricer software, to update everything in preparation for October 1st of the given fiscal year. The base classification system— that is, ICD-10 diagnosis and procedure coding systems—is also updated on October 1st. If there are significant changes to ICD-10, then coding staff will need to take appropriate workshops and/ or otherwise update themselves.

The actual process that the CMS uses to update a payment system is more complicated than just the final *Federal Register* and is referred to as the national public rulemaking (NPRM) process. To start the process there must be a *Federal Register* entry that proposes all of the changes anticipated for MS-DRGs in the coming fiscal year. While the date for the final *Federal Register* entry is generally well fixed (i.e., close to August 1st), the date for the proposed changes is much more variable. For everything to work properly, the proposed *Federal Register* should be out no later than April. Let us take a hypothetical schedule. Keep in mind that there is a 60-day comment period relative to the proposed changes.

> April 15: Proposed *Federal Register* issued
> June 15: End of the 60-day comment period
> August 1: Final *Federal Register* issued
> October 1: Final rules go into effect

Note that in our hypothetical sequence, the time period from June 15 to August 1 provides the CMS with the time to take all the comments, sort them, read them, and then develop responses to the comments, along with possibly altering the proposed changes. What happens if the proposed *Federal Register* does not appear until, say, May 15th? Then either the comment period will be shortened or the time that that CMS has to respond will be shortened, or possibly both. Of course, the final *Federal Register* could also be delayed beyond August 1st. This would then shorten the time that hospitals have to prepare for the changes to MS-DRGs.

The *Federal Register* entries for MS-DRGs and hospital payments are typically quite long, running from about 300 pages on up to 500 pages. Note that inpatient hospital payment is generally addressed and goes beyond MS-DRGs for short-term, acute-care hospitals and includes updates for long-term care hospitals, inpatient rehabilitation facilities, and even critical access hospitals.

> *Note:* Be extremely careful to check the exact contents of these MS-DRG update *Federal Registers*. Other issues may find their way into these *Federal Register* entries, including discussion of topics such as the provider-based rule.[*]

After the changes have been implemented on October 1st, MS-DRGs will not ordinarily be changed during the year. There is always the possibility of correcting errors of some sort, but substantive changes are quite uncommon.

In Chapter 5 we discuss this same process for updating APCs, the hospital outpatient prospective payment system. The dates will be shifted because the changes for APCs go into effect on January 1st of each year.

Variations of DRGs

There are numerous variations on the M-DRGs, the original Medicare DRGs, and also the newer MS-DRGs. Based on the discussions above, you should realize that a detailed discussion of any one specific variant can become quite lengthy. In Chapter 6 we look at extensions of the MS-DRG system to certain types of hospitals that are generally specialized. There is one specific payment system that does use MS-DRGs with just a few changes. This is the TRICARE DRG-based payment system.

TRICARE previously was CHAMPUS, the Civilian Health and Medical Program of the Uniformed Services.[†] Both M-DRGs and MS-DRGs have been developed and refined over the years to primarily address a population of elderly Medicare beneficiaries. Medicare's DRG system is also used for neonatal, pediatric, and young adult populations, but the vast majority of Medicare beneficiaries are the elderly. Because of these demographic considerations, over the years most of the problems and associated adjustments to MS-DRGs have been made for the elderly population.

Recognizing this weakness and other possible weaknesses in MS-DRGs, TRICARE has made some adjustments in the actual MS-DRGs. Some of the DRGs are changed, there are some TRICARE-specific DRGs, and all these changes must be programmed in the grouper software

---

[*] The provider-based rule applies to hospital inpatient activities as well as outpatient activities so that, technically, updates can be included in the MS-DRG update *Federal Registers*.

[†] There is also a closely aligned acronym, CHAMPVA, Civilian Health and Medical Program of the Veterans Administration.

Table 4.6 TRICARE DRG Age Refinement Example

MS-DRG	Description	TRICARE DRG	Description
193	Simple pneumonia & pleurisy w MCC	193	Simple pneumonia & pleurisy age >17 w MCC
194	Simple pneumonia & pleurisy w CC	194	Simple pneumonia & pleurisy age >17 w CC
195	Simple pneumonia & pleurisy w/o CC/MCC	195	Simple pneumonia & pleurisy age >17 w/o CC/MCC
		140	Simple pneumonia & pleurisy age 0–17

that groups under the TRICARE version of MS-DRGs.* For example, TRICARE is much more concerned about age-related refinements within their payment system. Thus, there is greater emphasis on DRG categories for patients in the age range 0 to 17 years. Refining this even more is the age category of less than 29 days. An example of this is with pneumonia. The MS-DRGs have significant refinements in this whole area, including CCs and MCCs. Consider the frequently used triple depicted Table 4.6.

Table 4.6 illustrates the process of taking a standard triple of MS-DRGs with no age differentiation and then introducing an age break by adding in a new TRICARE DRG 140 for the age group 0–17 and adjusting the other categories to a description with age greater than 17. This kind of refinement allows greater specificity in properly paying for pediatric cases within this disease category.

Now the addition, elimination, and/or refinement of the actual DRG categories is a major concern when assessing a modified MS-DRG payment system or a refinement of any of the standard DRG systems. There are other concerns because of specific features in MS-DRGs. Here are some typical questions:

1. Does the modified system pay for both operating and capital costs? The TRICARE DRG payment system pays for operating costs through their DRGs. Capital costs are reimbursed through a different mechanism, namely, on a pass-through basis.
2. How are indices, such as the wage index, labor-related portion, and geographic adjustments, handled?
3. What about cost outliers and the formula for the threshold?
4. Is indirect medical education paid separately through the modified DRGs?
5. What about the post-acute care transfer reduction in payments?
6. How are the various hospital cost-to-charge ratios handled? For TRICARE, a national CCR is used.
7. How are the payment rates and DRG weight adjusted?
8. Are other special features of MS-DRGs used, such as the present-on-admission indicator or the 3-day pre-admission window?

Even with these relatively basic questions, developing a modified form of MS-DRGs or a modification of any other DRG system takes a great deal of care, and many decisions must be

---

* See http://www.tricare.mil/drgrates for additional information.

made. Often, hospitals must deal with several different DRG systems along with MS-DRGs as the primary inpatient prospective payment system.

Compliance Considerations

DRG payment systems in general and MS-DRGs specifically are prime targets for allegations of overpayment. As we have discussed the concepts of grouping and payment processes, even relatively small changes in the diagnosis or procedure coding can significantly affect final payment. Thus, governmental audit programs, including the recent recovery audit contractor (RAC) program, tend to focus on MS-DRG validation (correct coding based on documentation), medical necessity (correctly coded but not needed), proper application of the transfer rule, proper application of the pre-admission window, and proper coding of the present on admission (POA) indicator. This list can certainly be extended.[*]

One of the areas of concern is short-stay admissions. While a short stay can result because of a transfer, in many cases the patient is admitted and then they either recover quickly or their condition did not really justify an inpatient admission. In some cases, the short-stay admission should really have been an observation, outpatient encounter. For the Medicare program this is a major issue, that is, inpatient admission versus observation for short stays. Also, the Medicare program has a number of rather technical issues addressing the process for changing an inpatient admission, paid by MS-DRGs, to an outpatient encounter, ostensibly observation, that is paid under APCs. Consider Case Study 4.22.

In this case study, the actual claim filed will be for the outpatient services, including the ER visit. Because observation can only be billed from the time that it is ordered, there is only 1 hour of observation. Thus, under APCs, there will be no payment for observation because observation must be provided for at least 8 hours in order for payment to occur.

> *Note:* The situation described in Case Study 4. 22, along with numerous variations on the same theme, represent a major compliance issue. The Recovery Audit Contractors (RACs) routinely find cases that they determine should not have been inpatient admissions. Generally, overpayment for the entire MS-DRG is claimed and the hospital may end up receiving little if any reimbursement for these cases unless an appeal can be successfully pursued.

CASE STUDY 4.22   SHORT-STAY ADMISSION CHANGED TO OBSERVATION

Early in the week, an elderly patient was started on a diuretic and instructed to take extra potassium supplements. On Friday morning, the individual was brought to the ED suffering from a life-threatening potassium deficiency. The patient was started on intravenous potassium and admitted to the hospital. By mid-afternoon the patient was feeling quite well and laboratory tests indicated that the electrolytic imbalance was corrected. Utilization review intervened just as the physician was discharging the patient. The physician agreed that this should have been an observation case and the physician wrote an order for observation, which, in this case, lasted for 1 hour.

---

[*] See any one of the four regional RACs for a current listing of approved issues that are being addressed by the given RAC.

CASE STUDY 4.23   KNEE REPLACEMENTS AND 3-DAY STAYS

Sydney, the Chief Compliance Officer at the Apex Medical Center, has requested a computer run of Medicare beneficiaries over the past 6 months who have had a unilateral knee replacement and who then went on to skilled nursing for recovery. Sydney is amazed to find that there were 408 such cases and that 371 of the cases involved exactly a 3-day stay, nine cases involved just a 2-day stay, and the other twenty-eight cases involved more than a 3-day stay.

Case Study 4.23 illustrates a slightly different issue. Skilled nursing services are under a special prospective payment system that is briefly reviewed in Chapter 6. One of the coverage issues for SNF services is that there must be a 3-day inpatient qualifying stay in order for SNF services to attain coverage and thus payment by the Medicare program. Is it possible that a patient might be kept in the hospital for exactly 3 days in order for them to qualify for SNF coverage?

If you were the chief compliance officer (CCO) at Apex, how would you react to this report? The point in question is whether or not the 3-day stays were really medically necessary or whether they were 3 days in order to qualify for the SNF coverage. As a result of this report, the CCO did decide to have an audit conducted to judge whether medical necessity was being achieved in a sampling of cases.

Case Study 4.24 combines the concepts discussed in the previous two case studies:

The 2 days in observation do not count toward the required 3-day stay. However, the sequencing in Case Study 4.24 represents the fundamental idea that observation involves holding the patient to see if an inpatient admission is really necessary. However, from the patient's perspective, not qualifying for payment for skilled nursing will be highly disconcerting.

We have briefly examined some compliance issues involving MS-DRGs. There are many more. The long-term compliance issue with all DRG payment systems is over-coding in order to gain increased reimbursement. This may involve questionable coding, or it may involve soliciting documentation from physicians for diagnostic statements that may not be fully supported. Additionally, with all the intricacies found in MS-DRGs, the possibility of both over-payments and under-payments is significant.

**CASE STUDY 4.24   OBSERVATION FOLLOWED BY INPATIENT
ADMISSION FOLLOWED BY SKILLED NURSING**

The medical staff at the Apex Medical Center has become sensitive to admitting patients for possible short stays. Instead, observation is being ordered and then, if necessary, an inpatient admission can be made after the observation. One of the physicians is concerned because a patient was in observation for 2 days and is now in the hospital as an inpatient for 2 days. The patient is now ready to go to skilled nursing to complete his or her recovery. However, the necessary 3-day stay has not been met, so the skilled nursing services are not covered. The physician is very concerned about this situation.

Quality Initiatives and Electronic Health Records

Healthcare payment systems tend to make payment for healthcare services that are covered, ordered by a physician, medically necessary, and properly documented. The realm of whether the services were of an appropriate quality has been left to medical/legal liability issues in case there are mistakes or some form of malpractice. In recent years, payment systems including MS-DRGs have been drawn into the whole issue of quality and associated reporting of quality of care. Today, if a Medicare-participating hospital does not appropriately participate in quality reporting, then there is a payment penalty. The penalties are in the range of several percentage points, which can make a significant difference in the hospital's MS-DRG payments.

Using payment systems as a mechanism for ensuring quality of care is a process that will probably grow in the coming years. Hospitals and other types of healthcare providers should be prepared to develop reporting processes as they are developed in order to maintain optimized reimbursement levels.

Electronic health records (EHRs) are rapidly coming into common usage by healthcare providers, particularly hospitals and clinics. For MS-DRGs and other DRG systems, coding is preeminent, but the coding can be no better than the underlying documentation. Thus, if EHRs can provide a more efficient platform for developing documentation and/or if such systems will encourage better, more complete documentation, then EHR systems should be pursued aggressively. In some cases, there may be extra payment made for implementing such systems and meeting meaningful use criteria.

Summary and Conclusion

MS-DRGs are complex. DRG payment systems have been designed to pay for hospital inpatient services. The Medicare DRG system, which we have referred to as M-DRGs, was first implemented in FY1984 even though hospitals were woefully unprepared at that time. This is truly a prospective payment system in that once a payment category is determined (i.e., the MS-DRG category), full payment will be made regardless of the charges. This is distinctly different from fee schedule payment systems in which the payment is the lesser of charges or the fee schedule payment amount.

MS-DRGs cover almost everything that is involved with an inpatient stay. Thus, MS-DRGs probably represent the most inclusive bundling payment system that exists.

The coding system that is used to classify inpatient services is ICD-10. ICD-10 includes diagnosis coding (ICD-10-CM) and procedure coding (ICD-10-PCS). While the exact number of MS-DRGs will probably grow over time, there were about 745 at the time this text was prepared. There are two general classes of MS-DRGs: medical and surgical. The grouping process involves complicated logic. The basic idea is that the all-important principal diagnosis, along with carefully selected secondary diagnoses, and, if appropriate, procedure codes, are input to the grouper and one, and only one, MS-DRG is generated. In some cases the age, sex, and discharge status of the patient may enter the grouping process. Using this single MS-DRG and the relative weight for the given MS-DRG, the pricer software can then take into account other variables such as the base rate, geographic location, special hospital designations, transfer cases, length-of-stay, cost outliers, and indirect medical education to generate the actual payment for the case.

The payment rates for MS-DRGs are updated each year using a percentage increase. Every few years the payment rates are revisited and adjusted through statistical processes. The process is termed *rebasing*.

The full calculation of an MS-DRG is quite involved and such calculations are typically performed through the pricer software so that hospital personnel do not have to constantly recalculate the payments. While hospitals do not have to actually perform the grouping and pricing—CMS will do that when the claim is adjudicated—the hospital will have no idea whether a correct payment has been made unless the case is sent through the grouper/pricer software.

The relative weights for the MS-DRG categories are calculated each year (i.e., recalibrated) through a rather sophisticated statistical process using the geometric mean. The base data used in the statistical calculations are the costs incurred for each claim that has grouped to a single MS-DRG. Given the fact that the data CMS uses is from the claims that contain the charges, not the costs, then how are the costs calculated? The answer is that the charges must be converted into costs using cost-to-charge ratios (CCRs) that are calculated on a hospital-specific basis through the Medicare cost reporting process. These CCRs can be troublesome if the hospital's charges are not correctly aligned with the hospital's costs as reported through the cost report.

Because MS-DRGs have relative weights and the fact that a single MS-DRG is generated through the grouping process, an interesting statistic can be calculated, namely the case-mix index, or CMI. The CMI is, in some sense, an indication of the average weight for all cases provided by the hospital. Thus, there is a direct correlation between the CMI and payment to the hospital. Financial personnel often track the CMI with great care in hopes that this index is increasing over time, indicating that greater payments are being received.

Compliance with particular attention to up-coding has been a long-term concern with M-DRGs and continues with MS-DRGs. A great deal of auditing is performed on inpatient cases paid under MS-DRGs. The latest, highly pervasive audit program is with the recovery audit contractors, or RACs.

In Chapter 5 we look at a newer and even more complicated prospective payment system, namely APCs that are used for hospital outpatient services.

Chapter 5

Ambulatory Payment Classifications (APCs)

Introduction

Hospital outpatient services are highly diverse, represent a wide range services, and are provided in a variety of settings. Designing and implementing a prospective payment system for hospital outpatient services is a distinct challenge. In Chapter 4 we discussed prospective payment for hospital inpatient services using MS-DRGs as the prime example. By any standard, MS-DRGs are complex, as are the other specific implementations of DRGs. While subjective, hospital outpatient prospective payment systems (HOPPS) are even more complex. The same fundamental principles are in place, as discussed in Chapter 3, and there are significant intricacies and many design decisions that must be considered.

We address APCs or ambulatory payment classifications as the prime example of a HOPPS. This is the Medicare approach for outpatient services. As with DRGs, there are alternative implementations of APCs themselves, as well as various versions of ambulatory patient groups (APGs), a precursor system to APCs. Thus, in the outpatient setting there may be a dozen or more versions of APCs or APGs that will be used to provide reimbursement. As with our discussion of DRGs, we discuss alternative decisions that can be made in developing the implementation parameters for a given APC implementation.

Historical Background

After the successful implementation of DRGs by the Medicare program, there was a significant movement from Congress to develop a similar prospective payment system for hospital outpatient services. The impetus for this new system was to cut Medicare costs. Various approaches for outpatient prospective payment processes were studied and researched during the 1980s. One such system, the Ambulatory Visit Groups (AVGs), analyzed the possible groupings of different types of ambulatory services. A much more detailed system, namely Ambulatory Patient Groups (APGs), was developed by 3M/HIS* with funding from Medicare. The first implementation of APGs was made with the Iowa Medicaid program in 1994.

While the healthcare community anticipated that APGs would be implemented by Medicare in the mid-1990s, there were significant delays and Medicare finally implemented a related, but different, system called Ambulatory Payment Classifications (APCs). This new system was implemented starting August 1, 2000.

> *Note:* As with all Medicare payment systems, the various rules and regulations are published in lengthy *Federal Register* entries. For anyone who wishes to fully understand APCs, the April 7, 2000, *Federal Register* is a classic, must-read document. This *Federal Register* basically set all the decisions that were made relative to implementing the new system. Although significant changes have been made over more than a decade, this document is still quite instructional. Note also that in this same *Federal Register* entry, CMS formalized what is called the Provider-Based Rule (PBR).† Provider-based clinics (i.e., generally hospital-based clinics) are paid for their services through both APCs and the Medicare Physician Fee Schedule (MPFS).

Since the mid-1990s, various forms of APGs have been implemented and with Medicare's entry into this area with APCs, there have also been numerous variations of APCs implemented. Keep in mind that these are all dynamic systems that change and evolve over time. While the basic thrust of both APGs and APCs is essentially the same, there are variations; sometimes the differences are startling and other cases almost trivial.

During the past two decades, during which APCs were developed, there has been a significant movement in the organizational structuring of healthcare providers. Not too far in the past, hospitals provided hospital services, that is, inpatient services and outpatient surgeries. Physicians provided services in their clinics and then also did rounds at the hospital. Skilled nursing services were provided in SNFs that were independent of other healthcare providers. Today there is a great deal more integration and a much greater concentration on hospital-based services that may encompass a broad array of outpatient services. Because of this organization structuring, payment systems such as APCs must be designed and implemented to accommodate these newer, integrated organizations.

In our discussions we will concentrate on the implementation parameters for the general concept of a hospital outpatient prospective payment system (HOPPS) using more specific rules and logic for APGs and then even more details for Medicare's implementation of APCs. In these discussions we will further specify the concepts discussed in Chapter 3, that is, the anatomy of a prospective payment system. As appropriate, we also reference common features with MS-DRGs discussed in Chapter 4.

Challenges for Hospital Outpatient Prospective Payment

One of the challenges on the hospital outpatient side is to define exactly what services are included for payment in a given implementation of an outpatient PPS. Hospital inpatient services are those

---

* HIS is the Health Information System division within 3M.
† See *Code of Federal Regulations* (CFR) at §413.65.

that are provided after a patient has been admitted to the hospital. A simplistic definition of outpatient services would, quite literally, be all the services that hospitals can provide that are not inpatient services. Thus, a truly comprehensive outpatient PPS would need to address all hospital services other than those that must be provided on an inpatient basis. This would include an enormous range of services, including medical visits, surgeries, diagnostic services, therapy service of different types, hearing services, vision services, pharmacy services, laboratory services, and the list becomes quite lengthy.

Add to this general list the fact that there are many different types of nonhospital providers that offer some of these services and thus there is a need for any hospital outpatient PPS to interface to the payment systems used by these other providers. For example, hospitals typically provide physical therapy (PT) and occupational therapy (OT) services to patients of the hospital. These patients can be inpatients or outpatients. At the same time there are independent or freestanding physical therapy and occupational therapy clinics that provide many of the same services that hospitals provide to outpatients. Thus when designing a HOPPS, the way that PT/OT services are paid must be considered in the context of other payment systems, most likely fee schedule payment systems in the case of PT/OT services.

Today, many hospitals have developed integrated delivery systems (IDSs), sometimes on a small scale and in other cases on a very large scale. For instance, even small rural hospitals often offer medical clinical services through specialty clinics. Specialists, often from nearby metropolitan areas, may come to the small hospital periodically and see patients and perform procedures as necessary. While there are different ways to organize business arrangements between the specialty physicians and the hospital, one way involves hospital-based clinics in which there is both a professional charge and a technical component (i.e., hospital) charge. Thus, any HOPPS would have to at least consider how to pay for the hospital component of clinic visits.

For large hospitals, hospital systems, and academic medical centers, there may be dozens of clinics that are part of the integrated delivery system centered on the hospital itself. These clinics may simply be owned and organized as freestanding clinics, or they may be organized as hospital-based clinics as discussed above with the specialty clinics. Additionally, there may be an array of diagnostic services that are provided at special centers located some distance from the hospital. There may also be special centers in which outpatient or ambulatory surgeries are performed. When an outpatient PPS is designed, all these different types of providers and associated business arrangements must also be considered.

For instance, physical therapy and occupational therapy services can be included in an outpatient prospective payment system, or payment can be made through a separate fee schedule payment system. As we will discuss, the Medicare program has decided that PT and OT services should be paid through the Medicare Physician Fee Schedule (MPFS) and not through APCs. While this division is fairly clean, there can be services provided by physical therapists that can come under either the fee schedule or the prospective payment system, depending on specific service location and need for the service.

The question in Case Study 5.1 is how this should be coded and billed. Embedded within this question is determining whether this service should be paid under APCs or paid through the physician schedule for physicians, that is, MPFS. With the facts represented in Case Study 5.1, this service would fall under APCs. There are special modifiers for physical therapy and occupational therapy to indicate when the services should be paid through MPFS. If we include speech language pathology in our discussion, here is the triple of Level II HCPCS modifiers:

CASE STUDY 5.1   SPLINTING IN THE EMERGENCY DEPARTMENT

The ED at the Apex Medical Center is quite busy today. One of the ER physicians has requested that a PT come to the ED to fabricate and apply a splint for a dislocated elbow. The PT provides the services and then returns to the Therapies Department at AMC.

- "-GP": Physical therapy under a plan of care
- "-GO": Occupational therapy under a plan of care
- "-GN": Speech therapy under a plan of care

If these modifiers are used on a hospital outpatient claim (i.e., UB-04), then payment will be calculated using the MPFS. If these modifiers are not used, then payment will be calculated using APCs if the service is covered under APCs. In this particular case study, ostensibly, there is no physical therapy plan of care and thus the GP modifier would *not* be used.

There is a key difference in the grouping process for both APCs and APGs. The difference is important enough to discuss before any lengthy discussions take place on related topics. In MS-DRGs, the result of grouping the ICD-10 diagnosis and procedure codes was one, and only one, MS-DRG category or group. There is also a grouping process for APCs and APGs. The coding classification system used CPT and HCPCS code sets. However, the result of the grouping is that there can be more than one category generated; in many cases there are multiple groups generated. Each of these groups must then be considered for the payment calculation. This is conceptually indicated in Figure 5.1.

Later in this chapter, this distinction will become important in understanding a significant challenge that is encountered in using a statistical methodology to determine the relative weights for the different APCs or APGs.

Ambulatory Patient Groups (APGs)

Late in the 1980s and then on into the early 1990s, significant research was conducted on developing a hospital outpatient prospective payment system (HOPPS). The main impetus for this work came from the Medicare program, which, at that time, was the HCFA (Health Care Finance Administration). Early work included concepts found in Ambulatory Visit Groups (AVGs) and the

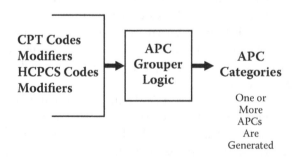

Figure 5.1   Conceptual APG grouping.

Medicare Outpatient Groupings (MOGs). 3M/HIS with financing from the Medicare program did develop a rather extensive HOPPS called APGs, which is an acronym for Ambulatory Patient Groups.

> *Note:* The use of acronyms such as APGs or APCs really represents a generic form of the given payment system. There are hundreds of implementation parameters for either of these generic approaches. Also, either APCs or APGs can be considered a variation of the other. Thus, when there are two different third-party payers who are both using APGs, there are probably two different implementations. When specifying APCs or APGs, be certain to identify the specific system, that is, the particular implementation and the third-party payer using the given system. Even with a given implementation, these systems tend to change over time, which creates even more variation.

In order to better understand APCs, the Medicare HOPPS, we now discuss a few of the salient features of the general form of APGs.

Three-Day Window of Service

An encounter is fundamental to virtually all hospital outpatient prospective payments as the unit of service for which payment is made. However, defining exactly what constitutes an encounter can be difficult. One approach is to use a sliding 3-day window-of-service. When an outpatient claim is adjudicated and processed through the grouper, the dates of service are considered within the grouping logic. Of course, the grouper must have all the services listed with the appropriate dates of service. To use a sliding window there may be claims filing requirements in which the hospital is required to accumulate services in the 3-day window and/or the claim adjudication software would need to have the ability to check on any services provided in the window itself.

If you start analyzing different scenarios, the use of a 3-day sliding window-of-service can become complex.

With the basic facts from Case Study 5.2, the 3-day moving window will consider the Monday visit to the hospital-based clinic as part of the presentation for the colonoscopy. Typically, there will be no separate payment to the hospital for the visit with the physician on Monday. The E/M (Evaluation and Management) service on Monday will be bundled into the payment to the hospital for the colonoscopy on Wednesday because the two services are in the same encounter (i.e., 3-day window) and the services are related.

> *Note:* In the case above, it is assumed that two claims will be filed, one by (or for) the physician and one for the hospital. The physician claim will address the professional component, and the hospital claim will address the technical component. Most likely, the physician will be paid through a fee schedule payment system with the E/M on Monday and the colonoscopy on Wednesday will be paid separately. Separate payment

---

CASE STUDY 5.2   3-DAY WINDOW OF SERVICE — SURGERY

On Monday, Sarah went to one of Apex Medical Center's hospital-based clinics. In this case she saw a gastroenterologist concerning a colonoscopy. On Wednesday, she went to Apex to have a colonoscopy performed.

CASE STUDY 5.3   MULTIPLE VISITS WITHIN 3-DAY WINDOW

Sally has not been feeling well. On Tuesday evening she goes to the Apex Medical Center's ED where several diagnostic tests are performed but no definitive diagnosis can be made. She is given a mild analgesic for pain. On Thursday she goes to one of Apex's clinics and is examined by a family practice physician. Further tests are ordered. On Saturday evening, Sally presents to the ED in significant distress. She is taken to an operating room where an appendectomy is performed on an urgent basis.

will be made unless the specific fee schedule payment system has a preoperative window of some sort.

For Case Study 5.3, the question is which 3-day window will be used? Typically, the adjudication process will take Tuesday through Thursday as a window and then Saturday as a separate window. However, if Thursday through Saturday were used as the window, then the reimbursement amount could be significantly affected.

Because the concept of an *encounter* is so fundamental to a hospital outpatient prospective payment system, be certain to understand exactly what definition is being used by the specific system in use. Be prepared for possible inconsistencies between the stated definition and the way in which the computer software comprising the grouper is actually programmed.

> *Note:* Be careful to distinguish the above discussion of a 3-day window, which could easily be 2 days or 4 days, from the DRG 3-Day Preadmission or 3-Day Payment window. This concept is discussed in Chapter 4 and involves bundling certain outpatient services provided at a wholly owned or wholly operated facility of the admitting hospital.

Significant Procedure Consolidation

The hallmark of any prospective payment system is the bundling of services. As discussed in Chapter 4, DRG payment systems provide the ultimate in bundling. For APGs, one of the mechanisms for bundling services, particularly surgical services, is called *significant procedure consolidation*. The basic idea is that if several, related surgeries are performed, then there will be payment only for the most extensive surgery. The bundling through consolidation requires that extensive tables of related surgeries be developed and included in the grouper.

While Case Study 5.4 could be a coding exercise for lacerations, under APGs using significant procedure consolidation, all of these lacerations would be paid through the payment for the one deep laceration on the left forearm. Because these surgeries are related, the grouper

CASE STUDY 5.4   MULTIPLE LACERATIONS

While visiting a friend, Sally inadvertently crashed through a plate glass doorway. She was not seriously injured, but she did sustain several lacerations. There was a deep laceration on the left forearm, several minor lacerations on the other arm, and five lacerations on the legs.

will group together all the lacerations into a single category for the deep laceration repair. Obviously, using this approach requires very careful definitions of what services are or are not related.

E/M Service Bundling

Evaluation and management (E/M) services involve services provided by physicians and practitioners relative to the assessment of patients for any sort of medical complaints and conditions. These are the clinic visits, ED visits, consultations, hospital visits, and the like. Most physicians routinely provide E/M services along with other outpatient services. For the architects of a hospital outpatient prospective payment system, the question is whether or not to pay separately for E/M services that are provided within a given encounter. Depending on how the encounter is defined, this bundling decision may involve a given date of service or it may involve several dates of service within a window-of-service.

Alternative approaches can be taken. One approach involves simply bundling any E/M service that is provided with some other service (e.g., outpatient surgery) within the encounter or window-of-service. Even with a 3-day window-of-service, another approach is to bundle payment for the E/M service only if it is on the same date of service and otherwise pay for the E/M separately.

Yet another approach is to only pay separately for the E/M service if it is *unrelated* to the other service provided during the encounter. If the E/M service is related, then there is no separate payment. If the E/M service is unrelated, then separate payment will be made. Obviously we must now define exactly when an E/M service is related to the associated service(s). Current Procedural Terminology (CPT) does provide a coding mechanism to address the billing issue, namely the "-25" modifier. This modifier is used only on E/M CPT codes and indicates that the E/M service is a significantly, separately identifiable service from any other services provided on the same date of service. Note that CPT presumes a date-of-service encounter window that is generally applicable to physicians for professional billing. On the hospital outpatient side, this modifier may be used differently. As usual, be certain to fully understand how E/M services are treated by the given grouper for the specific APG implementation.

In summary, we have discussed three of the key implementation parameters that were generally developed as part of APGs. These three parameters, among many others, must be considered for any outpatient PPS that uses an approach similar to APGs, which then includes APCs. As you study APCs, check to see how these three issues are addressed; that is, were these three parameters applied to APCs as they were for APGs?

APC Design and Implementation Parameters

For any hospital outpatient PPS, there are literally hundreds of decisions that must be made in designing the system and putting all the pieces together. In the following discussion we use APCs as the vehicle of discussion and then also look at alternative ways in which the parameters can be developed and implemented. Most hospitals will be paid under APCs for Medicare, and then the hospitals will also be subject to a dozen or more other outpatient payment systems that involve modified forms of APCs, including APGs. Keeping everything straight in order to properly code, bill, and be reimbursed is a significant challenge. Using a payment system like APCs requires that hospitals develop personnel resources that study and monitor the various details of APCs in order to ensure correct coding, billing, and reimbursement. Many aspects of APCs are also subject to various governmental auditing entities, including the RACs (Recovery Audit Contractors). Fully understanding and keeping up-to-date with APCs requires dedicated effort.

We now discuss a number of APC features. Our discussions of various implementation parameters include those that can be established by different third-party payers. For Medicare's APCs, the implementing organization is the CMS.

Medicare APC Coverage

For any payment system, the first question to answer is to identify just what services are included, that is, covered by the payment system. Given the extreme diversity of hospital outpatient services, fully answering this question on the outpatient side is not trivial. Generally, APCs cover outpatient surgical services and medical services provided by or at hospitals. Always keep in mind that we are addressing the so-called *technical* component or hospital component services that are billed and claims filed on the UB-04 or the electronic equivalent. Physicians and other qualified practitioners file *professional* claims on the 1500 claim form or the electronic equivalent.

What APCs *do not* cover is a little easier to approach, but there are always exceptions. Here is a brief listing:

■ Physical Therapy/Occupational Therapy: APCs do not generally cover these services. Payment is made through the Medicare physician fee schedule (MPFS).
■ Laboratory: These services are generally paid through the clinical laboratory fee schedule (CLFS). However, pathology in some cases is paid through APCs.
■ Durable Medical Equipment (DME): DME is generally paid through a separate fee schedule, namely the DMEPOS fee schedule.
■ Ambulance Services: APCs do not cover ambulance services as such. These services are generally paid through the ambulance fee schedule (AFS).

Also keep in mind that the services listed above are covered under the general Medicare program with payment made through various payment systems. There are some services that are not covered under Medicare at all without regard to the specific payment system. For example, self-administrable drugs in the outpatient setting are not covered at all. Such drugs are a Medicare beneficiary liability.[*]

> *Note:* Self-administrable drugs can create significant public relations challenges with Medicare beneficiaries. When a Medicare patient presents to the ED and is given several analgesic tablets, receiving a bill for the tablets can come as a surprise and the amount billed will generally be significantly more than obtaining a prescription of the same drug at the local pharmacy.

A little later in this chapter we discuss the status indicators (SIs) that are part of APCs. For all the CPT and HCPCS codes, the coding systems used by APCs, there is an SI assigned. We will see that status indicator "A" indicates services paid through other payment mechanisms, and status indicator "B" indicates codes not acceptable for the APC grouping process. While this list does not change dramatically from year-to-year, be certain to check the status indicator listing that is

---

[*] A discussion of drug coverage, particularly with the Medicare Part D program, is beyond the scope of this book. Be certain to check for current rules and regulations concerning drug coverage.

provided with the annual APC update *Federal Register*. These status indicators delineate what is and what is not a part of APCs.

Encounter Driven

The unit of service, as discussed in Chapter 2, for almost all outpatient ambulatory services is an *encounter*. As discussed above with APGs, the concept of an encounter can be defined as a window-of-service that can include several dates of service. Or an encounter can be limited to a single date of service. Specifically defining the *encounter* is fundamental to any given APC or APG type payment system. For any system that you are using, be certain to explicitly understand the definition in use.

In normal parlance, an encounter seems simple. An individual, presumably a patient, goes to a healthcare provider (e.g., physician, clinic, diagnostic testing center), services are provided, and the individual then leaves. The time period for an encounter is thus generally brief, being measured in minutes or possibly an hour or more depending on the services. When we start to look at specific examples, particularly for hospital outpatient services, significant challenges arise with this simplistic definition. Consider the flowing case studies.

All five of these case studies are typical. However, a hospital outpatient payment system like APCs must provide precise guidance as to what constitutes an encounter and thus the unit of service by which the grouping and eventual payment will be made. Case Study 5.5 is straightforward and fits the general concept of an encounter. That is, patient presents, services are provided, and patient leaves all within a fairly tractable time period.

In Case Study 5.6, the time period over which the encounter occurs is now measured in hours. In some cases, such surgeries may also cross dates of service. In Case Study 5.7 the two separate blood transfusions now start to really strain our conceptual definition of an encounter. Many would say that these two separate transfusions constitute two separate encounters. That is, the

---

CASE STUDY 5.5   ER VISIT

On Saturday mornings, Sam washes his car. Unfortunately, on this Saturday morning he cuts his hand on the windshield wiper blade. A neighbor takes Sam to the Apex Medical Center's ED where Sam is examined and his laceration is repaired using two sutures and some wound adhesive. Sam's neighbor returns him home.

CASE STUDY 5.6   OUTPATIENT SURGERY

Sarah has presented to the Apex Medical Center at 8:00 a.m. for an elective outpatient surgery. She is taken to the pre-operative room where she changes clothes and receives some preliminary medications. She is taken to surgery, anesthesia is induced, and the operation is performed. Recovery only takes 3 hours and she then returns to the post-operative room, which is the same as the pre-operative room. She relaxes for several hours and then returns home.

CASE STUDY 5.7   BLOOD TRANSFUSIONS

Sally has been having some very real difficulties with anemia. Her family practice physician sees her at 9:00 a.m. and orders the transfusion of a unit of blood over at the hospital. By late afternoon, Sarah is still not feeling quite right and she again goes to see her physician, who then orders that a second transfusion be performed over at the hospital. The second unit is transferred and Sally is feeling much better and goes on home.

CASE STUDY 5.8   ER FOLLOWED WITH OBSERVATION

On Thursday evening, Sam has been having some chest pains. His daughter-in-law takes him to the ED at the Apex Medical Center. A thorough workup is performed, including a battery of laboratory and radiology tests. A definitive diagnosis cannot be made. A cardiologist is called in and a decision is made to place Sam in observation. Sam stays in observation until Saturday afternoon, at which time he is discharged home.

CASE STUDY 5.9   SECOND ER VISIT

It is now Saturday afternoon and Sam, from Case Study 5.5, is relaxing at home after his laceration repair. Now he is beginning to have some abdominal pains and he finally decides to go to the Apex Medical Center's ED for the second time in a day. Luckily, after a fairly complete workup including diagnostic radiology and ultrasound, Sam apparently has a mild case of gastroenteritis. He is given a prescription and sent home.

---

patient came, received a service, and then left, only to return a second time. If two units of blood had been transfused one immediately following the other, then it would be one encounter.

> *Note:* While there is some confusion in the Medicare guidance for this particular case, CMS seems to allow the use of CPT code 36430, blood transfusion, only once per date-of-service even if it appears that two separate encounters took place.*

In Case Studies 5.8 and 5.9, the ER visit followed by observation occurs over three different dates of service although all of these services are considered part of the same encounter. Thus we have an outpatient encounter that spans three dates of service. Later in this chapter we discuss the APC composites for observation services. Observation, as such, is not separately paid. In this case study, payment will be paid for an extended ER visit that includes observation.

In Case Study 5.9, we have a second ER visit on the same date of service. As indicated in the case study, the first and second visits are for completely different reasons. This would be established through the associated diagnosis coding. For APCs, these are considered separate encounters. Even if the two encounters were related, that is, for the same or related reasons, APCs still

---

* Of course, be certain to check for current guidance.

CASE STUDY 5.10   ER VISIT REQUIRING A CAT SCAN

Sandy has been brought to the Apex Medical Center's ED. She suffered a fall and has several minor injuries. During the workup by the ER physician, the ER physician determines that a CAT scan should be performed. Unfortunately, Apex's CAT scanner is down for repairs. Sandy is carefully bundled into an ambulance, which then transports her to another hospital about 45 miles away. A CAT scan is performed and Sandy is brought back and placed in observation for 2 days before being discharged home.

consider them separate for payment purposes. Is it possible that other third-party payers implementing some form of APCs would also adopt this policy? Or would related encounters on the same day be considered part of the same encounter?

Consider Case Study 5.10.

At first glance, it would appear that the hospital down the road should code and bill for the CAT scan, but the ambulance trip and services at the other hospital are all part of a single encounter. Thus, everything must be coded and billed by Apex. Note that the ambulance services are not billable in this case, and the hospital will need to pay for the ambulance services.

If you are coding, billing, and being paid under some sort of APC payment system, then you must be extremely sensitive to unanticipated situations that will strain the definition and concept of an encounter. The bottom-line for APCs, as well as for any APC type payment system, is that the way the concept of an *encounter* is defined is critical.

APC Classification Systems: CPT and HCPCS

For MS-DRGs, the system used to classify services was ICD-10. For APCs, two different, but related, code sets are used to classify services and sometimes report items provided. These two code sets are

1. CPT: Current Procedural Terminology
2. HCPCS: Healthcare Common Procedure Coding System

These are standard code sets under the HIPAA transaction standard/standard code set rule.

CPT Codes and Modifiers

CPT® was developed by the American Medical Association (AMA), and this code set is updated annually with the new codes going into effect on January 1st each year. HCPCS was developed and is maintained by CMS. The major update for HCPCS occurs on January 1st, but there are also minor quarterly updates throughout the year.

These two code sets are also used as the classification process for the Medicare physician fee schedule (MPFS). Physicians use mainly the CPT code set with some use of the HCPCS. Hospitals tend to use HCPCS more frequently. Note that the *coding process* used by physicians and hospitals is based on different fundamental principles. Here are the two different approaches:

1. Physicians code for the services they provide.
2. Hospitals code for resource utilization, regardless of who provides the services.

> *Note:* A major area of concern for APCs is the availability of official coding guidelines for both CPT and HCPCS on the hospital side. The American Hospital Association (AHA) does have the *Coding Clinic for HCPCS*. This is similar to the *Coding Clinic for ICD-10* although the code set addressed is different.

This difference in the basis for coding may appear trivial; however, there can be some very significant shifts in the way we think about coding for the professional side versus the technical side. Now for surgical coding, the surgeon and the hospital will, or should, have the same surgical codes. Consider Case Study 5.11.

In this case study, some sort of remedial action should definitely be taken. While there can be some variation in surgical coding, the 20 cases out of 100 cases appears suspicious.

While the surgery codes should be the same, the one area where there can be significant variation between physicians and hospitals is with the E/M or evaluation and management codes. These are the office visit codes, emergency department codes, and other assorted codes that include services such as critical care. The E/M codes generally come in series or levels. Three of the most frequently used series of E/M codes are given in Table 5.1.

For physicians, on the professional billing side, there are extensive coding and documentation guidelines. The CPT manual itself has rather detailed guidelines based on factors such a level of history, level of examination, and medical decision making, among others. CMS has issued additional guidelines; one set in 1995 and another update set in 1997, the latter of which has been withdrawn but may still be used by physicians.

For hospitals under APCs, on the technical component side, there are no guidelines at all! In the April 7, 2000, *Federal Register,* the CMS instructed hospitals to develop their own mappings of resources utilized into the various levels of E/M codes.[*] Ostensibly the plan was that the CMS would develop national guidelines in a year or two so that hospitals could start using standard guidelines. However, this has never happened and, at the time this text was prepared, it does not appear that it will happen. Hospitals have done what the CMS directed back in 2000, namely, they have developed mappings of resource utilization into the various levels. Of course, all these mappings are potentially different and may be developed based on very different approaches.

CASE STUDY 5.11   SURGICAL CODE CORRELATION AUDIT

The Chief Compliance Officer at the Apex Medical Center has become aware that because they now have a new regional MAC (Medicare Administrative Contractor), the MAC can easily compare the codes on the physician's 1500 claim form and the hospital's UB-04 claim form. With the cooperation of several surgeons, 100 cases have been selected to see if the physicians' surgical codes are the same as the hospital's surgical codes. Surprisingly, the audit shows that there were 20 cases in which the codes were different.

---

[*] See the April 7, 2000, *Federal Register,* 65 FR 18451.

Table 5.1 Some Frequently Used Series of E/M Codes

New Patient Clinic		Established Patient Clinic		Emergency Department	
99201	New Level 1 Clinic	99211	Est Level 1 Clinic	99281	Level 1 ED
99202	New Level 2 Clinic	99212	Est Level 2 Clinic	99282	Level 2 ED
99203	New Level 3 Clinic	99213	Est Level 3 Clinic	99283	Level 3 ED
99204	New Level 4 Clinic	99214	Est Level 4 Clinic	99284	Level 4 ED
99205	New Level 5 Clinic	99215	Est Level 5 Clinic	99285	Level 5 ED

Under APCs, these series of E/M codes are simply placeholders to indicate relative resource utilization. Consider the E/M code 99211. On the physician side, this code is very special. Physicians do not use this code; CPT 99211 is reserved for nursing services. Thus, for established patients, physicians start with 99212 and work up. For APCs, CPT 99211 is simply a Level 1 placeholder and has no special meaning outside that given to it by the resource mapping.

Another small issue with the clinic visit E/M codes is the meaning of *new* versus *established*. For physicians, there is a 3-year rule in that if the patient has not been seen by the physician, or specialty group, then the patient is new. On the hospital side, CMS has adopted a similar approach after considerable discussion. Currently, the rule is that if the patient has not been registered for a service at the hospital within the past 3 years, the patient is new. Early in the APC implementation, the directive was that if the patient had a medical record number, then they were considered established.

> ***Note:*** Great care must be taken to guard against physician coding conventions migrating over to the hospital side without anyone really noticing. For instance, under MPFS, physicians have a global surgical package and coding staff tends to think in terms of pre-operative and post-operative coding directives. However, on the hospital side under APCs, the only pre-operative and post-operative services are those provided on the date of service of the surgical procedure. This potential carryover is particularly true with the CMS National Correct Coding Initiative (NCCI) edits and policies.

Proper CPT coding is paramount for receiving appropriate reimbursement under APCs. Thus, professional coding staff must be utilized in any of the CPT areas in which coding can become complicated. Good examples of complex coding areas are cardiovascular interventional radiology and various endoscopy services. In some areas, the CPT coding is fairly direct, such as in diagnostic radiology. In the areas of hospitals where coding is straightforward, hospitals will often place the CPT codes in their chargemasters and allow service area personnel to perform the coding through charge entry.

Regardless of how the coding process is addressed, constant attention is required to ensure accurate coding. As with MS-DRGs and for physicians using MPFS, correct coding is the key factor. Most of the compliance issues surrounding inappropriate payments—both overpayments and underpayments—tend to revolve around coding issues.

CPT also has a robust set of modifiers that can be attached to the CPT codes to provide additional information. Several of these modifiers will arise in our discussions of APCs and various implementation parameters. You can find the listing of CPT modifiers that apply to hospital

---

CASE STUDY 5.12   LACERATION ON THE ARM

Sam has presented to the Apex Medical Center's Urgent Care Clinic that is located about a mile from the main hospital. Sam was gardening when he suffered a laceration on the left forearm about 3.0 cm in length. The wound is not deep but needs attention. The nurse does a general assessment, thoroughly cleanses the wound, and obtains a suture tray. One of the physicians comes in, examines the wound, sutures the wound, and also uses a skin adhesive. The nurse applies a dressing and instructs Sam to return immediately if there are any problems. Otherwise he is to return in a week to have the sutures examined for removal.

---

outpatient services and ambulatory surgical centers delineated in the CPT manual. There are two critical CPT modifiers for APCs:

1. "-25" modifier: Significant, separately identifiable E/M service
2. "-59" modifier: Distinct procedural service

The "-25" modifier is used only on E/M codes and indicates that there was an E/M service provided on the same date as another service. Under APCs, if the "-25" modifier is not used on the E/M code, then payment for the E/M service will be bundled into the other service provided on the same date.

For our purposes, although not stated in Case Study 5.12, we assume that the urgent care clinic is provider based. Thus, two claim forms will be filed: (1) a professional claim form for the physician and (2) a technical claim form for the nursing services, supplies, and any other resources consumed. We also assume that Sam is an established patient. This is not really a coding exercise as such. The laceration repair will probably be CPT code 12002. Both the physician and the hospital will code and bill for the laceration repair using CPT 12002.

The real question here concerns any possible E/M levels and then the use or non-use of the "-25" modifier. On the physician's part, there really was not much of an evaluation and what evaluation was performed appears to relate to the laceration itself. Thus, the physician will not code an E/M level because the E/M services are part of the surgical procedure. On the hospital side, the situation is different. The nurse did provide a general assessment along with assessing the laceration. Thus, on the hospital side, there would be an E/M level that will be determined by the hospital-developed mapping of resources utilized. Let us assume that this is a Level 2 or CPT 99212. For both the 99212 and 12002 to gain payment, we will have to append the "-25" modifier to the 99212.

We discuss the "-59" modifier at greater length when discussing the Medicare National Correct Coding Initiative (NCCI) edits and associated coding policies (later in this chapter).

HCPCS Codes and Modifiers

CMS initially developed the HCPCS code set to address identifying supply items. Over the years this code set has grown significantly and not only are supplies addressed, but a host of other services are also addressed. There are more than a hundred modifiers. This code set and the associated modifiers are used by both physicians and hospitals. While this code set has been developed by CMS, other private payers also sometimes use these codes.

Generally, CPT codes consist of five numeric digits. The AMA has started to use a single alphabetic character in certain special CPT codes. The HCPCS uses a five-place format with the first position being alphabetic and the second through fifth positions being numeric. Thus, we can refer to HCPCS by the letter in the first position. For instance, A-codes are generally supply items, D-codes are dental codes, E-codes are durable medical equipment, and J-codes refer to pharmaceuticals. G-codes are temporary procedure or professional services codes.[*] For example, the sequence G0380–G0384 refers to the five levels of services provided in a type B emergency department. "Type B" indicates an emergency department is not open 24/7/365.

HCPCS modifiers are frequently used even on CPT codes. Among the more common modifiers are the anatomical modifiers "-LT" and "-RT," referring to left and right. Also, fingers and toes have series of modifiers: "-F1"–"-FA" and "-T1"–"-TA," respectively. Another common modifier is the "-TC" modifier for "technical component;" the CPT modifier "-26" is for "professional component."[†] Generally, HCPCS modifiers are two alphabetic characters although some of them have a numeric value in the second position.

> ***Note:*** You will see references to Level I HCPCS and Level II HCPCS. Level I HCPCS equates to CPT while the Level II or national codes come from the CMS. Historically there were also Level III HCPCS or local codes; these are no longer used.

There are a number of special modifiers that are used specifically for APCs. One of them is the "-CA" modifier, which has the following description:

> "Procedure payable only in the inpatient setting when performed emergently on an outpatient who expires prior to admission."

In the next section we discuss status indicators for APCs and illustrate the way in which the "-CA" modifier is used.

National Correct Coding Initiative (NCCI) Edits

The NCCI edits were developed starting in the 1990s for physician coding. These edits involve both CPT and HCPCS. The basic idea behind the edits is that certain code combinations should not be used together. In some cases, the two codes would never be used together under any circumstances, while in other cases the codes would not ordinarily be used together but there could be extenuating circumstances. Thus we have *absolute* edits and *relative* edits. For the relative edits, if there is a good reason for using both codes together, then we must append a modifier to separate them. The usual modifier is "-59," which indicates a distinct procedural service.

While Case Study 5.13 does not give us enough detail to actually code the case, the very fact that a stent placement was performed on the right leg and then an angioplasty was performed on the left leg will cause an NCCI edit to occur. This is due to the way the coding structure in CPT has been established. Because both legs were addressed, it is appropriate to get around this edit. In theory, using the "-LT" (left) and "-RT" (right) modifiers should get us around the edit and get

---

[*] The word "temporary" is used in the Medicare context, which can be measured in years and sometimes decades.
[†] Be careful not to confuse the "-PC" modifier with the concept of the professional component.

CASE STUDY 5.13   VASCULAR CATHETERIZATION ON OF BOTH LEGS

A lower extremity revascularization procedure is being performed on Sam. Conscious sedation is used, the surgeon using a femoral puncture of the left leg. Both legs are addressed. In the right leg, a stent is placed. In the left leg, a balloon angioplasty is able to open an artery. A vascular plug is placed and Sam goes to recovery.

---

both services paid. However, the "-59" modifier will probably be used and it will get us around the edit.

It is amazing that these edits have now grown to approximately 300,000 in number. The only real way to keep track of them is through computer programs that check for any possible violations. Another factor that is sometimes overlooked is that there is a rather extensive *NCCI Coding Policy Manual*. These coding policies are sometimes quite significant and coding staff must be fully aware of the policies because there are some of the policies that cannot be implemented through code pair edits.

Now you may ask, what does this have to do with APCs? When APCs were implemented on August 1, 2000, the CMS also brought all the edits, and ostensibly the coding policies, over to APCs. Thus, hospital coding staff using CPT and HCPCS were now also subject to the edits and associated policies that were developed for physicians. Unfortunately, not all the edits and coding policies apply to hospitals. For instance, physicians have a global surgical package while hospitals do not. This can cause significant confusion. In the next case study, 5.14, we illustrate several of these situations.

Coding is needed for both the professional and technical components. The CPT codes for the laceration repairs are 12002 for the simple repair and 12032 for the intermediate repair. Based on the information in the case study, there was a general E/M level performed by the physician. This general assessment is required by law, namely EMTALA (Emergency Medical Treatment And Labor Act), and is called the medical screening examination (MSE). This MSE must be performed by a qualified medical person, that is, typically a physician or practitioners.

This means that we will have an E/M code for both the physician and the hospital. Let us assume that the physician meets the criteria (history, examination, medical decision making) for a level 3 ER visit, 99283. On the hospital side, assume that the resource mapping generates a 99282, that is, a level 2. Note that the E/M levels can be different because they are coded based on different criteria. Table 5.2 shows the coding.

CASE STUDY 5.14   LACERATION REPAIRS IN THE ED

Susan was out riding her bicycle when there was a slight mishap. She is not seriously injured; she has a laceration (3.0 cm) on the left arm and another deeper laceration (3.2 cm) on her right arm. Upon presentation to the ED, she is triaged and then seen by an ER physician who performs a general examination. After the general examination, the two lacerations are examined. The left arm requires a simple laceration repair while the right arm requires an intermediate closure. The nurse applies dressings and gives Susan the discharge instructions to return to the ED in a week to have the sutures removed or to come back immediately if there are any problems.

Table 5.2 **Physician versus Hospital Coding**

Physician Coding	Hospital Coding
99283-25	99282-25
12002-59	12002-59
12032	12032

Except for the E/M levels, the coding is essentially the same. The "-25" modifier has been included for both the physician and the hospital to separate the E/M level from the operative procedures so that the E/M level will be paid separately. Now why is the "-59" modifier included on the 12002? The reason is that the code pair 12002 and 12032 may violate an NCCI edit. You would have to check the current set of edits because they change from time to time. The logic behind 12002 and 12032 being on the edit list is that someone may incorrectly code the 12032 for the layered closure and then also code the simple closure.

The coding and use of the "-59" modifier would seem to address Case Study 5.14, but there is a complicating factor. The complication arises from NCCI coding policies. From the *NCCI Coding Policy Manual*, Version 15.3, Page III-2, we have:

> "If a procedure has a global period of 000 or 010 days, it is defined as a minor surgical procedure. The decision to perform a minor surgical procedure is included in the payment for the minor surgical procedure and should not be reported separately as an E&M service. However, a significant and separately identifiable E&M service unrelated to the decision to perform the minor surgical procedure is separately reportable with modifier 25."

The general idea in this policy statement is that the E/M level is generally included in the payment for the minor surgery. If the documentation shows that there is a separately identifiable E/M service that goes beyond that normally provided with the laceration repair, then it can be coded separately and the "-25" modifier applied. A subjective judgment is necessary to determine if the MSE provided by the ER physician meets this requirement.

Interestingly enough, there is another glitch in this NCCI coding guidance, although it is somewhat difficult to recognize. The problem is with the phrase *minor surgical procedure*. On the physician side, this phrase is well-defined using the 0-day or 10-day post-operative period as the criterion. However, on the technical component side, that is, APCs, there is no definition of a minor surgical procedure and thus the application of this coding guideline is called into question.

If we return to Case Study 5.12 in which Sam had a laceration at an urgent care center, the way the case reads, the physician did not really perform a general assessment. Therefore, with the above NCCI coding guideline, will the physician code and bill an E/M level? The answer is probably not, but does that mean that the hospital cannot code and bill an E/M level? Noting that the nurse did perform a general assessment along with other services, there should be a technical component E/M level based on the resource mapping in use by the urgent care clinic. Let us look at another aspect of this same topic in Case Study 5.15.

Because there is a post-operative period on the physician side, the ER physician will not code and bill for this service. The ER physician has already been paid. However, for the hospital, this is a new encounter because there is no post-operative period under APCs other than any activities on the date of the surgical procedure itself.

CASE STUDY 5.15   RETURN TO ED FOR SUTURE REMOVAL

Susan, from Case Study 5.14, is now returning to the Apex Medical Center's ED to have her sutures removed. It has been 6 days and the lacerations are pretty well healed. The nurse encounters Susan and determines that the medical condition with which Susan is presenting is not an emergency. The nurse obtains a tray. One of the ER physicians briefly examines the wounds and orders the nurse to remove the sutures. The nurse completes the work and sends Susan on her way.

CASE STUDY 5.16   UNCOMPLICATED FRACTURED RIB

Sam is presenting to the ED after he fell off his horse. Other than some bruises and a contusion, he is complaining of some upper chest pain. Laboratory tests are run and x-rays taken. He is diagnosed with a simple fracture of one rib that is uncomplicated. He is provided with an analgesic, educated on how to delimit activities until the rib can heal, and then he is discharged home.

While the discussion of using the code sets CPT and HCPCS has been brief, the intent is to show that proper coding can sometimes be quite difficult. There are many modifiers to master, and the CMS has applied the NCCI edits and NCCI coding policies on the hospital side as well. However, regardless of the challenges, gaining proper reimbursement under APCs is totally dependent on the codes. The APC mantra is truly, *no code, no payment.* If a service is not coded, then the service will never be paid under APCs because APCs represent a prospective payment system.

With Case Study 5.16 we provide one more case study to illustrate challenges with coding. There is a perfectly good code for the closed treatment of a rib fracture, namely CPT 21800. The coding question is whether or not closed treatment was actually provided. That is, was hands-on service provided to address the fracture? Some coding staff will code this out along with an ED E/M level. Other coding staff will not code the 21800 but will elevate the E/M code to account for resource utilization for the fracture.

APC Status Indicators (SIs)

The next two concepts for our discussion of APCs are packaging and discounting. To provide examples in this area we need to understand a technical aspect within APCs. These are the *status indicators.* While we certainly have status indicators, or we will use the acronym SI, formally defining them is not straightforward. SIs are applied within APCs at two different levels:

1. At the individual APC level for application of the grouping logic
2. At the individual CPT/HCPCS level, which also involves grouping but before the APC categories are developed

Here is a simplified listing of the SIs that are current at the time this text was developed:

- SI = A: Services furnished to a hospital outpatient that are paid under a fee schedule or payment system other than OPPS:
  - Ambulance services
  - Clinical diagnostic laboratory services
  - Nonimplantable prosthetic and orthotic devices œ EPO for ESRD patients
  - Physical, occupational, and speech therapy
  - Routine dialysis services for ESRD patients provided in a certified dialysis unit of a hospital
  - Diagnostic mammography
  - Screening mammography
- SI = B: Codes that are not recognized by OPPS when submitted on an outpatient hospital Part B bill type (12x and 13x)*
- SI = C: Inpatient procedures
- SI = D: Discontinued codes
- SI = E: Items, codes, and services:
  - That are not covered by any Medicare outpatient benefit based on statutory exclusion
  - That are not covered by any Medicare outpatient benefit for reasons other than statutory exclusion
  - That are not recognized by Medicare for outpatient claims but for which an alternate code for the same item or service may be available
  - For which separate payment is not provided on outpatient claims
- SI = F: Corneal Tissue Acquisition; Certain CRNA Services and Hepatitis B Vaccines
- SI = G: Pass-through drugs and biologicals
- SI = H: Pass-through device categories
- SI = K: Nonpass-through drugs and nonimplantable biologicals, including therapeutic radiopharmaceuticals
- SI = L: Influenza vaccine; pneumococcal pneumonia vaccine
- SI = M: Items and services not billable to the fiscal intermediary/MAC
- SI = N: Items and services packaged into APC rates
- SI = P: Partial hospitalization
- SI = Q1: STVX-packaged codes
- SI = Q2: T-packaged codes
- SI = Q3: Codes that may be paid through a composite APC
- SI = R: Blood and blood products
- SI = S: Significant procedure, not discounted when multiple
- SI = T: Significant procedure, multiple reduction applies
- SI = U: Brachytherapy sources
- SI = V: Clinic or emergency department visit
- SI = X: Ancillary services
- SI = Y: Non-implantable durable medical equipment

As you read through and study the status indicators, you will realize that

1. There are quite a few different status indicators.
2. There are significantly different reasons for having certain status indicators.

---

* Type of Bill (TOB) 12x and 13x are for hospital Part B as inpatient or outpatient.

CASE STUDY 5.17 EXTENDED OUTPATIENT SURGICAL PROCEDURE

Sam has presented to the outpatient surgery unit of the Apex Medical Center. An outpatient hernia repair is scheduled. However, as the procedure progresses, a much more extensive procedure must be performed. Sam goes to recovery and after 7 hours is placed in observation. He is discharged after 2 days of observation. Coding staff at Apex are now coding the case and realize that the actual procedure performed is on the CMS inpatient-only list.

All these status indicators go into the overall APC grouping logic. We discuss several of the status indicators in this section and then we also encounter of number of them in discussing other features of APCs.

Consider SI = C; this status indicator is entitled *Inpatient Procedures*. A more accurate descriptor is *Inpatient Only Procedures*. The CMS has developed a listing of surgical procedures that will be paid only if they are performed on an inpatient basis. Interestingly enough, this listing transcends APCs and also applies to Critical Access Hospitals that are paid on a cost basis. Note that there are some procedures on the list that can be, and are, performed appropriately on an outpatient basis. The issue is that the Medicare program will not pay for these services if performed on an outpatient basis. This listing is updated each year and even the concept of an inpatient-only listing is questioned by commenters through the *Federal Register* process.

In Case Study 5.17 because the procedure performed was on the inpatient-only list, the CMS will not pay for the surgery if performed on an outpatient basis. The patient then becomes liable for payment, but as a practical measure Apex will probably not charge anyone for the services. We will see a variation on this concept when we discuss the "-CA" modifier.

SI = G and SI = H involve the concept of a pass-through payment. Generally, these are new drugs, biologicals, and/or devices that are paid at cost until their costs can be properly integrated into associated APC categories. For pass-through items, the hospital must be very careful to charge correctly for the given item. In the overall adjudication process, the charge for the item is converted into the presumed cost by multiplying the charge times a cost-to-charge ratio (CCR) from the hospital's cost report. Clearly, if the hospital does not charge correctly, then improper payment will be received. Pass-through items have a life of only a few years before their payment is integrated.

Brachytherapy sources are classified to SI = U. Given the fact that APCs generally bundle any drugs, biologicals, and/or other items with the service that uses the given item, having a separate status indicator shows that the brachytherapy sources are paid separately from the associated procedures. While brachytherapy sources are expensive, there is also great variability in the costs and amount used; this is an area where permanent pass-through payment would be appropriate. Instead, the CMS has decided to develop a separate payment process that uses the fundamental logic of APCs. In other words, the CMS has developed a mini-APC system to pay for just the brachytherapy sources.

We will encounter more status indicators as we discuss additional features of APCs. Keep in mind that all these processes must be programmed into the APC grouper/pricer software.

Packaging

Significant bundling is a hallmark of any prospective payment system. For APCs, one form of bundling is called *packaging*. Under APCs, the whole process of bundling is multifaceted and occurs at different levels. The most visible level is at the CPT and HCPCS coding level. Certain codes are classified as status indicator N. Informally, the N is interpreted as *no payment*. Technically, we should say "no separate payment" because payment is made on a packaged basis. We now look briefly at two of the many codes that have status indicator N, namely

- 99292: Subsequent half-hour of critical care
- 99143: Moderate conscious sedation

Now, the CPT code 99292 is one of a pair of codes. The 99291 code addressees the first hour of critical care and then the 99292 code addresses additional half-hour increments. APCs have been established to pay for the 99291, but any additional 99292 services are packaged into the payment for the 99291. This creates significant challenges for hospitals, particularly for proper charging and appropriate coding. If a hospital chooses to include 99292 in its chargemaster, then there must be an appropriate charge based on costs, that is, resources utilized. On the other hand, if a hospital decides not to include a line-item for 99292 in its chargemaster, then the charge made for 99291 must contain, on average, costs that are incurred for cases that involve critical care that goes beyond the first hour.

> *Note:* While we are addressing only the concept of packaging of payment of 99292 into payment for 99291, there are additional coding and billing issues with these codes. Critical care is a timed service and the amount of time devoted to critical care must be carefully documented. Also, embedded in CPT is the inclusion of certain associated services such as interpretation of chest x-rays. This phraseology applies to physicians, that is, the interpretation, but according to CPT, facilities may separately report the technical component of providing the chest x-ray. (See Q3 status indicator discussed below.)

Conscious sedation, CPT code 99143, is also part of a sequence but we will address only 99143. Conscious sedation is status indicator N so that this service is packaged into the associated procedure. Conceptually, this is fairly straightforward; however, in practice, this area becomes complicated. CPT has an additional annotation for certain procedures in which the conscious sedation is an inherent part. These are mainly procedures in the gastroenterology area (e.g., colonoscopies, esophagoscopy) and catheterization laboratory procedures (e.g., heart catheterizations, vascular catheterizations). The annotation is the "bull's-eye" or "⊙". The guidance from CPT is that conscious sedation is not to be reported separately.

From a coding and billing perspective under APCs, what does this mean? While the guidance from the CMS is less than explicit, reporting separately or billing separately seems to imply that a CPT or HCPCS code is on the claim. If there is no code on the claim, there can still be a separate charge for the conscious sedation, but no code. The fact that 99143 is status indicator N seems to make this whole discussion moot because there will be no separate payment anyway!

For conscious sedation, hospitals must make some difficult policy decisions about charging for this service at all. If charges are made, then the inclusion or exclusion of the CPT code must also be considered. Keep in mind that when a hospital sets up its chargemaster and associated coding through the chargemaster, payers other than Medicare must also be considered. Conscious sedation may be separately payable by some private payers.

Note: Conscious sedation has also become a compliance issue. While CPT indicates that conscious sedation is an inherent part of a number of procedures, physicians performing these procedures sometimes request that the moderate sedation services be provided by an MD Anesthesiologist (MDA) or CRNA (Certified Registered Nurse Anesthetist). If these requests become routine, the question of medical necessity for such services becomes a concern. If a nurse provides the conscious sedation under the supervision of the physician performing the associated service, there is no additional payment made by Medicare. However, if an MDA or CRNA performs the service, then there is an additional, separate professional payment above and beyond the packaged payment for the conscious sedation inherent to the given procedure.

While status indicator N is common, there is a series of status indicators Q1, Q2, and Q3 that involve what can be called *conditional packaging*. If certain conditions are met, the given code and associated service will not be paid separately; payment is packaged. A simple example of this is with the chest x-ray mentioned in our critical care discussion above. While there are several chest x-ray codes, let us use CPT 71010, chest x-ray, single view, frontal. This code has status indicator Q3 for APCs. Generally, chest x-rays are paid separately and would ordinarily be status indicator S. Because APCs do not pay separately for chest x-rays in connection with critical care, status indicator Q3 is used to establish the programming for the APC grouper to bundle the chest x-ray into the payment for critical care.

Note: Status indicator Q3 is generally used for composite APCs, which are discussed later in this chapter. The bundling of chest x-rays and certain other services into critical care is unusual.

Another simple example of packaging is with fluoroscopy. Currently, CPT has two codes:

■ 76000: Fluoroscopy up to 1 hour
■ 76001: Fluoroscopy more than 1 hour

For APCs, CPT 76001 is status indicator N so that it is always packaged. However, CPT 76000 is status indicator Q1 so that it is packaged only if performed with some other service that is categorized by status indicator S, T, V, or X. For practical purposes, this means that APCs will pay for fluoroscopy only if it is performed all by itself. As you can probably envisage, generally fluoroscopy is used in conjunction with some other procedure. Can you think of a situation in which fluoroscopy would be used all by itself?

As discussed above, packaging can be quite explicit, to the point of being able to program the bundling into the APC grouper logic. Some packaging occurs at the coding level. There is an extensive set of coding edits, namely the Medicare National Correct Coding Initiative (NCCI) edits, as discussed above for the CPT/HCPCS code set.

Along with the NCCI edits themselves, there are some rather extensive coding policies that have been developed. Some of these coding policies form the basis for developing the NCCI edits themselves, while other policies go beyond the edits and give directions for certain inclusions and exclusions. Case Study 5.18 is an example of a coding policy that involves bundling by not allowing separate coding. This is an example of packaging through a coding and billing policy.

According to NCCI coding policy directives, all injections and infusions provided surrounding the provision of a surgical procedure are not separately reportable. In other words, these

---

CASE STUDY 5.18 INJECTIONS DURING SURGERY

The billing personnel at the Apex Medical Center are concerned about proper billing for injections before surgery. For some patients, the surgeon will order a pre-surgery antibiotic injection. These injections are performed only when medically necessary and are not a routine part of the surgery itself.

---

injections and infusions should not be coded separately.* See also the separate discussion of the global surgical package (GSP) concept elsewhere in this chapter.

There are even more primitive packaging processes that take place at the chargemaster level. While there are numerous examples, we consider here only one involving supply items. The whole issue of supply categorization, particularly for APCs and to a lesser degree for DRGs, has become a very difficult area for hospital chargemaster personnel. While the CMS discusses various aspects of this issue at some length, ensuring compliance from a charging perspective for hospital is difficult.

Basically, the CMS has indicated that supply items fall into two categories:

1. Routine or non-ancillary
2. Non-routine or ancillary

The routine supply items are not charged separately. This means that these supply items do not even appear in hospital chargemasters and thus the charges, let alone payments, are bundled. Non-routine supply items can be charged separately and thus will appear in the hospital's chargemaster and also on the itemized statement. In almost all instances, there is no separate payment. Thus, the payment is packaged although there can be separate charges.

Routine supply items are very common items that are used whenever needed and in whatever quantity is needed. For instance, cotton balls, tongue depressors, steri-strips, gauze, etc. fall into this category. Non-routine or ancillary supply items are ordered by a physician and are specific to the patient and generally include specific quantity identification. While many of these ancillary supply items do not have CPT or HCPCS codes, for some of the more expensive items, HCPCS codes may be required. For example, expensive vascular catheters or coronary stents must be reported with certain Level II HCPCS C-Codes. These items are status indicator N so that there is no separate payment; that is, the payment is packaged. However, under APCs, a hospital must appropriately charge for the expensive items so that CMS gathers appropriate charge data that can be correctly converted into cost data.

Consider Case Study 5.19. The reason for the perceived low payment on the part of Apex is that Apex may not be appropriately charging for the more expensive drug-eluting stents. In this case, payment for the stent placement includes the stent or stents; but if there is not an appropriate charge associated with the C-Code for the stents, then payment for the entire APC category may be depressed. This occurs when hospitals across the country are not charging appropriately for drug-eluting stents and the CMS is converting the low charges into low costs for the stents.

Other items generally packaged (i.e., status indicator N) are inexpensive pharmaceuticals or drugs. While the threshold for packaging can vary, a threshold of $60.00 to $80.00 is typical. Thus, drugs whose cost is below the threshold are packaged. Drugs above the threshold can be considered

---

* See Page III-12 of Version 15.3 of the NCCI policy manual for explicit OPPS guidance.

CASE STUDY 5.19   DRUG-ELUTING STENTS

The Apex Medical Center is performing more and more coronary catheterization services using the more expensive drug-eluting stents. The financial analysts at the hospital cannot understand why the payments for the drug-eluting stent placements do not pay for the full difference between regular stenting and drug-eluting stenting.

---

for separate payment. Typically, drugs on APC claims are reported with Level II J-codes although there are some convoluted billing instructions for drugs that are considered an integral part of a procedure.

For APCs, as well as variations such as APGs, there is a great deal of bundling of payments through packaging and through coding and billing limitations. While APCs have significant bundling features, DRGs still represent the ultimate PPS for overall bundling.

Composite APCs

Status indicators Q1 and Q2 directly address packaging. Status indicator Q3 involves a slightly different feature of APCs, namely composite APCs. These are special APC categories that involve two or more services that are grouped for a single payment when they are provided together. Otherwise, the individual services may qualify for separate payment when not performed together. There are composite APCs for families of radiological services (e.g., ultrasound, CTs and MRIs), cardiac electrophysiological studies, and prostate brachytherapy.

As an example, we will take two related composite APCs:

1. 8002: Level I Extended Assessment & Management Composite
2. 8003: Level II Extended Assessment & Management Composite

Although there is nothing in the descriptions, these two composite APCs provide payment for observation services under certain circumstances. Over the years, the Medicare program has refused to pay separately for observation services because of concerns about hospitals inappropriately charging for such services. These two composites do pay for observation service, but only when there are associated E/M services. The Level I composite pays if there is an evaluation and management service in connection with a direct observation admission. This involves the HCPCS code G0379. Also, if there is a Level 5 clinic visit, established or new patient (CPT 99215 or 99205, respectively), then the observation composite can be paid. While not immediately obvious, the clinic visit would have to occur with a provider-based (i.e., hospital-based) clinic. If the clinic visit were to occur in a freestanding clinic, the physician would order the observation admission, a so-called direct admission to observation, and there would be a nursing assessment and thus HCPCS code G0379.

In Case Study 5.20, Sam is assessed by a nurse at the hospital and this assessment generates a G0379, which along with observation charges drives the payment for observation. Case Study 5.21 is a little different in that Sarah, by virtue of being at the clinic, is actually on hospital property and it is the physician's assessment that drives the observation payment. When Sarah is placed in the observation bed, a nurse will probably perform an assessment, but the main assessment from the physician is already in the hospital record.

CASE STUDY 5.20   DIRECT OBSERVATION ADMISSION

Sam has not been feeling well. His daughter-in-law takes him to the doctor's office. After a thorough examination, the physician decides that Sam should go into observation over at the hospital. The physician writes an order and Sam is taken to the hospital where he is placed in an observation bed after a nursing assessment.

CASE STUDY 5.21   OBSERVATION ADMISSION FROM A PROVIDER-BASED CLINIC

Sarah has made it to one of the Apex Medical Center's provider-based clinics. The clinic is located in a medical office building right next to the hospital. After a thorough workup, the physician decides that Sarah should be taken over to the hospital and placed in an observation bed. Hospital personnel, via a wheelchair, move Sarah to the hospital along with the clinical record showing the physician's assessment and order for observation.

The higher-level composite, APC 8004, is quite similar except it is a Level 4 or Level 5 ED visit that drives the payment for the composite. Critical care, CPT 99291, also drives payment, as does HCPCS code G0384, which is a Level 5 visit at a type B ED. If observation services are billed with any other service that is status indicator T, then the observation is bundled into the payment for the status indicator T service that is most likely a surgical procedure. This way, the APC grouper is programmed so that post outpatient surgery observation is never separately paid. However, this particular logic generates some interesting idiosyncrasies. Consider Case Study 5.22.

All the requirements for the higher-level observation composite are met. Certainly a higher-level ED visit will be coded (i.e., level 4 or 5) and thus observation should be paid. However, there was the laceration repair, which will generate a CPT code that is status indicator T and thus the observation payment will be bundled into the payment for the laceration repair. Thus, instead of an observation payment of about $700.00, there will be a payment for the laceration repair of about $100.00.

> *Note:* Observation services under APCs is a major area of controversy concerning both payment and utilization issues. The development of these two composites is a welcome step; however, the Medicare program has been slow to respond with appropriate payment for observation services under APCs.

CASE STUDY 5.22   CHEST PAINS WITH A MINOR LACERATION

Sam has been having some chest pains and his son takes him to the ED at the Apex Medical Center. Upon exiting the car, Sam does sustain a minor laceration on his hand. In the ED, a fairly complete workup is performed and he is placed under the chest pain protocol. The laceration on his hand is repaired and he is in observation for 2 days and then released home.

CASE STUDY 5.23   MULTIPLE SURGERIES – ED

Steve, a Medicare beneficiary, has been driven to the ED at Apex. He was in an accident and hurt his right leg and suffered a laceration on the left forearm. In the ED, Steve is assessed, x-rays are taken, and laboratory services are provided. There is a nondisplaced fracture of the right leg and the laceration on the forearm is sutured. A cast is applied to the leg to address the fracture.

Discounting

Discounting is a payment issue but we discuss this process at this point because it fits in quite nicely with the concept of bundling services. Discounting involves multiple services for which full payment is made for the first, generally highest-paying, service and then the remaining services are paid at a reduced percentage, typically 50% for APCs. This type of process is also used in other types of payment systems, including fee schedule payment systems such as MPFS.

For APCs, the main indicator for discounting is through the status indicator T. Status indicator T services are typically surgical procedures. Status indicator S indicates that discounting is not applied and this status indicator often involves radiological procedures. There can be variations with the application of discounting, so be prepared to encounter unanticipated results from the APC grouper. While we can deal with processes such as discounting at a conceptual level, the real test is to see how the grouper is programmed.

In Case Study 5.23 the complete claim will have a number of different items, our interest is with the two surgical procedures. There will be a CPT code for the fracture care and another CPT code for the laceration repair. When the APC grouper processes these two codes, there will be full payment for the fracture care but only a 50% payment for the laceration repair. This assumes that the fracture care is the higher-paying service.

The logic behind discounting is that the additional surgeries can be performed with less cost and thus the payment should be reduced. Case Study 5.23 does not really support this logic because the laceration repair is unrelated to the fracture care, and resource utilization on the part of the hospital is most likely not reduced.

When Case Study 5.24 is coded, there will be two different CPT codes for the colonoscopy, namely one for the polyp removal using the snare technique and then one for the small polyps removed using the cold biopsy forceps. Most likely, these two codes will group to the same APC and then full payment will be made for one and a 50% payment for the other. Certainly in this case, there is a reduction in cost and effort for providing the services.

Question: If you were designing a HOPPS, would you include discounting? If so, would you discount only if the two procedures in question were related?

CASE STUDY 5.24   MULTIPLE SURGERIES   COLONOSCOPY

Sarah is presenting to the Apex Medical Center to have a routine colonoscopy. This is her fifth colonoscopy. Under conscious sedation, the colonoscopy proceeds fairly smoothly. There are two polyps removed by the snare technique. There are also four small polyps removed using the cold biopsy forceps. Samples of the polyps are forwarded to pathology. She is awakened and recovers within 2 hours, at which point she is taken home by her daughter.

Global Surgical Package (GSP)

Healthcare payment systems that involve any sort of payment for surgical procedures tend to have a global surgical package of some sort. The basic idea is that payment for the surgical services includes certain defined services prior to the surgery and then possibly some services post-surgery. In the Medicare Physician Fee Schedule (MPFS), there is a well-defined GSP that actually centers more on the surgeon rather than on the surgery itself. So, what about APCs and other similar OPPSs?

Rather surprisingly, for APCs, the approach taken involves the definition of an encounter or a window-of-service. For APCs, the surgical encounter is generally envisaged to involve a single date of service. Thus, services that are related to the surgery on the given date of service, either before the surgery or after the surgery, are included in the grouping process and this generates a GSP at least for that date of service. For some variants on APCs, there may be a 3-day window-of-service that tends to capture services related to the surgery within the window. Thus, there are no complex definitions and associated implementation of a GSP for APCs. This approach does, however, create some interesting situations. Consider Case Studies 5.15 and 5.16.

While the surgery itself was provided on a single date of service, with the post-operative observation we now have spanned two dates of service although this is all considered a single encounter for APC grouping purposes. For APCs, post-operative observation is always bundled into the payment for the surgery. This bundling is enforced using status indicator T as a test. If there is a surgical service with status indicator T provided in connection with observation, then there is no separate observation payment. This logic basically establishes a special case for post-operative bundling and is a weak form of a GSP.

Case Study 5.26 involves a pre-surgery visit. Strangely, pre-surgery clinics are controversial under APCs. These clinics are generally provider based and billing is performed on the UB-04 with an E/M level for the nursing resources utilized, along with the appropriate radiology and laboratory tests performed. While hospital resources are utilized by the anesthesiologist, payment on the anesthesiology side is bundled into the professional payment for the anesthesiologist for

---

CASE STUDY 5.25   POST OUTPATIENT SURGERY OBSERVATION

An elderly patient has presented to the hospital for an outpatient surgical procedure. The surgery proceeds according to plan and the patient is taken to recovery. The patient recovers very slowly with nausea and discomfort. After 6 hours, the surgeon orders the patient taken to observation where the patient spends the night and discharge occurs mid-morning.

CASE STUDY 5.26   PRE-SURGERY CLINIC

To better care for surgery patients, the Apex Medical Center has established a pre-surgery clinic. Surgeons send patients to this clinic several days before the scheduled surgery. A nurse performs a thorough assessment, radiology and laboratory services are provided, and the anesthesiologist examines the patient and completes the anesthesia questionnaire. The patient is also given detailed instructions on where and when to report, along with what should be expected.

CASE STUDY 5.27   PRE-SURGERY HISTORY AND PHYSICAL EXAMINATION

The Apex Medical Center performs a high volume with a wide variety of outpatient surgical procedures. A problem has been encountered that patients sometimes present for surgery without a pre-surgery history and physical (H&P) or an H&P that is not current. The hospital has hired a Nurse Practitioner (NP) who is in the operative areas in the mornings to perform or update an H&Ps so that surgery can take place.

---

services provided during the surgical procedure. The "-25" modifier is usually attached to the E/M level because there are radiology services provided, and, under APCs, if the "-25" were not present, the payment for the E/M level would be bundled into the payment for the radiology service. Although there is no pre-operative period for APCs, other than services on the date of the operation, billing for pre-surgery clinics as described in Case Study 5.26 has been questioned relative to the proper use of the "-25" modifier.

> *Note:* If the anesthesiologist, generally an MD anesthesiologist or CRNA, performs the assessment and documents the anesthesia questionnaire and the surgery does not take place, then the anesthesiologist can file a professional claim using an E/M level.[*]

In Case Study 5.27, the work of the NP occurs on the same date of service as the surgical procedure. Is the H&P performed by the NP distinct and separately identifiable? Is this H&P service above and beyond that which is normally provided for surgeries on the date of the surgery? If the answer to these questions is "yes," then the "-25" modifier can be used on the technical component E/M level that will appear on the UB-04 from the hospital. If the NP has billing privileges with Medicare, then a professional claim can also be filed for professional payment. As you might guess, billing for this type of service does raise compliance issues relative to using the "-25" modifier because the only services provided by the NP is the H&P.

The rules and regulations for the physician global surgical package were discussed at some length in the companion volume entitled *Fee Schedule Payment Systems*. For physicians under the Medicare physician fee schedule (MPFS), there are post-operative periods of 0 days, 10 days, and 90 days. Medicare has struggled with attempting to define *normal complications* that would be paid as part of the surgical payment. In other words, the payment would be part of the physician GSP. The exception to this concept occurs if the patient must be returned to the operating room during the post-operative period. There are two CPT modifiers that address this type of situation, namely the "-76" and "-77" modifiers. Both of these modifiers are available for hospitals, but their interpretation is quite different because APCs have no post-operative period other than the date of service on which the surgery was provided.

See Case Study 5.28, where the GSP for physicians is well-defined. The physician will file a claim for the first day with the operative procedure. The physician will file a second claim for the second day and use the "-76" modifier and be appropriately paid. What about the hospital under APCs? In theory, there is no post-operative period for the hospital. Thus, the second day would be coded and billed as a second encounter and the "-76" modifier would not be used. In other words, the hospital will only use the "-76" (or "-77") modifier if the return to operating room is on

---

[*] See the National Correct Coding Initiative (NCCI) policy manual for further details.

> **CASE STUDY 5.28 RETURN TO OPERATING ROOM**
>
> An elderly patient presented to the Apex Medical Center for an outpatient surgical proce-
> dure. The procedure took longer than usual and the patient had difficulty in recovery. The
> patient was placed in observation. The next day the patient was examined and the surgeon
> determined that the operation must be performed again. The patient was returned to the
> operating room and the surgery was successfully performed. The patient remained in obser-
> vation for 2 days and was discharged.

the same date of service. However, the observation services are certainly a complicating factor in
proper coding, billing, and reimbursement.

Payment under APCs

The determination of payment for each of the APC categories involves a rather convoluted process.
There are a number of concepts and processes that must be mastered in order to understand how
payments are determined. In Chapter 3, "Anatomy of a Prospective Payment System," we began
the discussion of topics such as

- The cost report
- Cost-to-Charge Ratios (CCRs)
- Geometric and arithmetic means
- Weights and relative values
- Conversion factor
- Index numbers

We even set up a highly simplified example of calculating the weights or relative values for prospective payment. In Chapter 4, "Medicare Severity Diagnosis Related Groups (MS-DRGs)," we
discussed this process as applied to an inpatient prospective payment system. The basic process
discussed in Chapter 3 was also extended to include concepts such as geographic adjustments of
payments to reflect the relative cost of living in geographic areas.

Now we discuss this process for APCs. While not evident at the time we discussed
MS-DRGs, there is a significant advantage on the inpatient side for calculating the payments.
The advantage is that for any inpatient case when grouping is performed through the MS-DRG
grouper, one and only one MS-DRG category is generated. This means that all the charges on
the given claim can be easily associated with the given MS-DRG category that results from
the grouping. The charges on the claim can be converted to costs at the hospital level by using
the specific CCRs from the hospital's cost report. The costs from all hospitals for the specific
MS-DRG can then be statistically analyzed to generate the MS-DRG relative weight and thus
payment levels.

For APCs, this process is much more difficult. While APCs and APGs were designed to mimic
this MS-DRG process, when APC grouping takes place, there can be—and often will be—more
than one APC category generated. To properly associate the costs with a given APC category, only
claims that group to a single APC category can be used. These are called *singleton claims* because
they group to a single APC category. While there are some methods that can be used to use certain

CASE STUDY 5.29   E/M VISIT WITH LABORATORY AND X-RAY

Sarah has awakened with a stuffy nose and sore throat. She calls the Acme Medical Clinic only to find that her primary care physician is out of town and the clinic personnel direct her to go to the ED at Apex. She presents, is screened, and then sees a physician. A chest x-ray and laboratory tests are run, as well as a brief examination. She is sent home with several prescriptions.

claims that group to more than one APC, fundamentally, many claims will never be used in the statistical process to determine the payment levels for APCs.

This situation arises partially because APCs involve a great deal of bundling, mainly through packaging. A given claim may have dozens of line-items involving supplies, pharmacy items below the packaging threshold, and claim level line-items that are packaged and the like. This claim may then group to two or possibly three or more APC categories, and there is no way to properly associate the line-item costs to the multiple APCs.

In Case Study 5.29, because EDs are provider based under the Medicare program, both a professional claim for the ER physician and a technical component claim for the hospital will be filed. For APCs we are interested in the technical component claim that is filed on the UB-04 claim form or the equivalent electronic version. For APCs, the E/M visit and x-ray will group to separate APCs. The laboratory services are paid separately through the clinical laboratory fee schedule (CLFS). Thus we have a claim that does not fit into the necessary singleton category for use in determining APC payments. Presuming that there were no separately charged supplies (i.e., only routine or non-ancillary supplies) and no pharmacy items were used, this may be a two line-item claim, and each line-item will group or map to an APC. If this type of simple claim could be identified, could it be used for the process of determining payments? The general answer is yes. This is an overly simple example of what is called a *pseudo-singleton claim*. This claim could be considered two separate claims because we can easily associate the charges with the proper service.

Proper coding and billing for the services provided in Case Study 5.30 is a definite challenge. There will be multiple codes, and numerous supplies coded and billed for the catheters and the drug-eluting stent. The placement of the vascular plug along with a charge for the vascular plug itself can be considered, but for APCs these devices and the associated services are packaged. Also, the nonselective angiography at the renal level (commonly called a "drive-by shooting") will be coded but payment will be packaged.*

CASE STUDY 5.30   CORONARY CATHETERIZATION LABORATORY

Sam has presented to the Apex Medical Center's Catheterization Laboratory. He has been having some chest pains and associated problems. Using conscious sedation, through a left femoral puncture, the catheter is advanced to the heart, diagnostic tests are performed, and a drug-eluting stent is placed using an angioplasty balloon. Additionally, an atherectomy is performed on a different coronary artery. Upon withdrawing the catheter down through the aorta, the physician performs nonselective angiography at the renal level and then also performs bilateral lower extremity angiography with the catheter located at the aortic bifurcation. A vascular plug is deployed for closure.

Because of the complexity of a claim like the one in this case study, and the fact that multiple APCs will be generated, this type of claim is not a good candidate for use in the statistical process for determining APC payments. If proper payment is to be developed for placement of a drug-eluting stent, what kind of claims would be needed to go into the statistical mix? The basic answer is that we would need claims that involve only the APC for placement of the drug eluting stent.

In summary, for APC payment determination, we can use only singleton claims or pseudo-singleton claims. This delimitation in using claims is a major challenge with APCs. Let us consider one more case study to illustrate this challenge. Case Study 5.31 involves what is called "autologous blood salvage." During a surgical procedure (outpatient because we are discussing APCs), the blood that is lost can be collected and processed through a device that reconditions the blood so that it can be infused back into the patient.

From a coding and billing perspective, we will have a charge and associated CPT code for the operation, and there will also be a charge and separate CPT for the autologous blood salvage. Considering just these two services, there will be two separate APCs generated, one for the surgery and one for the autologous blood salvage. Thus, this claim will not be a candidate for inclusion in those claims that can be used in determining payment for the APCs. The question then becomes: Under what circumstances would there be a singleton claim for autologous blood salvage? The answer is that there would never be such a circumstance because autologous blood salvage can only be provided in connection with a surgical procedure. So are hospitals appropriately paid, under APCs, for autologous blood salvage? Most likely payment does not cover costs.

We are now ready to go through the process of determining the weights or relative values for the APC categories. We use a conversion factor in the final step to determine the actual payment. Here is the general process:

1. All of the singleton and pseudo-singleton claims that hospitals across the country filed for outpatient services are amalgamated into a database.
2. The charges for services covered under APCs are converted into costs at the hospital-specific level using claims from the given hospital and the CCRs from the cost report of the given hospital.
3. For each APC category, all the costs are amalgamated.
4. The geometric mean cost *for each* APC category is calculated.
5. The geometric mean cost *for all* APC categories is calculated.
6. For each APC category, the geometric mean cost for that category is divided by the overall geometric mean cost for all categories.

CASE STUDY 5.31   AUTOLOGOUS BLOOD SALVAGE*

Sally is having an operative procedure performed. The operation itself takes about an hour and during the operation, any blood that is lost is being collected, processed, and infused back into Sally. The operation goes smoothly; Sally is taken to recovery and is sent home 6 hours later.

---

* See CPT code 89861.

Clearly this is the conceptual form of a much more intricate process. For instance, the database of claims will typically be a year or two in the past. For CY2015, the claims data base would probably come from CY2013 because the calculation for CY2015 is actually made in CY2014 and, with luck, the CY2013 claims database is available. Also, there are additional statistical processes that may be employed, such as trimming the data to exclude outliers that are much too high or much too low for the given APC category.

Now the result of all this work is a set of relative values for each APC category. We discussed the same process in Chapter 4 for MS-DRGs. We need two other pieces in order to put everything together. These are the

1. Conversion factor (CF)
2. Geographic adjustment process

As with the Medicare physician fee schedule, the conversion factor can become politically sensitive. The APC CF was originally set when APCs commenced back on August 1, 2000. While the statistical processes used are beyond the scope of this text, the CF was set to approximate cost reimbursement to some extent. Since that time, the CF has been updated annually, taking into consideration a number of different factors. For readers interested in this process, refer to the annual update *Federal Register* entries for APCs; some of the discussions can become somewhat detailed and convoluted.

Now that we have the relative values and the conversion factor, at least conceptually, we can now move on to the last stage, the geographic adjustment. A relatively simple approach is taken using a 60%–40% split. The 60% part of the split is adjusted according to the wage index. The 40% is not adjusted. This split is basically borrowed from the DRG methodology, which at one point in time was also a 60%–40% split.

As an example, let us take the autologous blood salvage discussed in Case Study 5.31. The CPT code for this service is 86891. This code maps or groups to APC 0345, which is Level I Transfusion Laboratory Procedures. While the specific weight will vary somewhat from year to year, let us use 0.2190 as the weight. A typical conversion factor is $70.000. This means that the payment, without geographic adjustment, would be $0.2190 \times \$70.000 = \$15.33$.

> *Note:* As an exercise for the reader, do you think that this payment would cover the cost of the equipment, supplies, and personnel time for performing the blood salvage?

The final step is to apply the geographic adjustment. Assume that Apex is in an area where the wage index is 0.9980. This is an area that is slightly below the average for the country. Now we can apply our 60%–40% split:

$$(0.60 \times 0.9889 \times \$70.00) + (0.40 \times \$70.00) = \$41.50 + \$28.00 = \$69.50$$

Thus, for Apex, the payment for the blood salvage is $0.2190 \times \$69.50 = \$15.22$.

This type of calculation must be made for all the APC categories and specific geographic locations. While this can be accomplished using a spreadsheet, the normal process is to use APC grouper/pricer software just as we did for MS-DRGs.

Special Payment Considerations

There is basically only one mechanism in APCs to accommodate any unusual costs that might be incurred by a hospital for outpatient services covered under APCs. This is the *cost outlier* that is also found, in a different form, in MS-DRGs. Because the weights and ultimate payment for an APC category is based on averaging costs within the APC category, it is possible that a hospital might have an unusually high cost for services within the APC category that are not even close to being covered. Thus, a formula is instituted that makes extra payment if the costs, as determined by converting charges to costs using the appropriate CCRs, exceed a given threshold. Actually, there is a double threshold formula. The costs for the given APC must exceed both (1) 1.75 times the APC payment *and* (2) $2,175.00.

The fixed cost threshold tends to change each year, while the 1.75 times criterion has been fairly stable over the past several years. The Medicare program generally limits the outlier payments to a small percentage of overall APC payments.

Consider Case Study 5.32. We have all the information that is needed to determine if this unusually expensive case qualifies for a cost outlier payment and, if so, how much the payment would be.

1. The cost of the procedure is 0.50 × $6,000.00 = $3,000.00.
2. 1.75 × $550.00 = $962.50. The $3,000.00 is greater than $962.50, that is, the first threshold.
3. $3,000.00 is greater than $2,175.00, the second fixed cost threshold.
4. Now the cost outlier payment will be 50% (the marginal rate) of the difference between the cost and 1.75 times the APC payment. In this case: 0.50 × ($3,000.00 − $962.50) = 0.50 × $2,037.50 = $1,018.75.

For this case study, the numbers have been simplified to a certain extent; however, the important point is to understand the overall formula for calculating APC cost outliers. The actual numbers in this formula can change each year. The CMS monitors very carefully the overall cost-outlier payments at the national level.

Hospitals should monitor APC cost outlier payments for accuracy. If any unusual patterns arise, then compliance may also become an issue.

The high incidence of cost outliers noted in Case Study 5.33 may be quite appropriate. However, a high incidence should invoke a careful analysis to make certain that the charging mechanisms are appropriate. Cost outliers should be the exception, not the norm.

CASE STUDY 5.32   LENGTHY CYSTOSCOPIES

Most cystoscopies at the Apex Medical Center are generally routine and often are completed in less than 15 minutes. Today, Apex has a case that for various reasons has become complicated and takes 90 minutes to complete even though the proper coding is CPT 52000, cystourethroscopy. Apex charges by 15-minute time units at $1,000.00 per time unit. Thus, the basic charge for this service is $6,000.00. The APC payment for CPT 52000 is approximately $550.00. The Apex Medical Center's cost-to-charge ratio in this area is 0.50.

CASE STUDY 5.33   HIGH INCIDENT OF COST OUTLIERS

One of the reimbursement specialists at the Apex Medical Center routinely monitors cost outlier payments under APCs. This includes checking to make certain the cost outliers are paid and that the proper amount is paid. The specialist has noted that for cystoscopies, there is an unusually high incidence of cost outliers. In about 40% of the cases, an APC cost outlier is generated.

APC Grouper/Pricer

We have discussed a number of APC design and implementation parameters. Much of our discussion has really centered on the logic that is found in the APC grouper/pricer software. As you should realize at this point, to discuss all the logic that is programmed into the APC grouper and then the associated pricing system that actually calculates the overall APC payment would require a separate volume. While the logic is different, the complexity is on par with the MS-DRG grouper/pricer software.

As input to the APC grouper/pricer, we need to have the CPT code(s), HCPCS code(s), and any necessary modifiers. This information is sufficient to perform the grouping. Because there are geographical adjustments for determining the actual payment, there is some additional information that must be available to complete the pricing or payment calculation process.

Note that the biggest difference between MS-DRG grouping and APC grouping is that for MS-DRGs there is one—and only one—MS-DRG category that results from the grouping. For APCs there can be—and often are—multiple APC categories.

For our purposes we take a simple case and then show how it groups and is paid under APCs. Here are the services provided in an emergency department encounter:

1. Laboratory tests
2. X-ray of the right leg
3. Right leg fracture, no reduction, application of splint to the right leg
4. Laceration repair, 3.3-cm laceration right arm, simple
5. Laceration repair, left leg, 3.1-cm, intermediate

The laboratory tests will be paid outside of APCs through the clinical laboratory fee schedule. Also, there will be supplies that are charged but they will not enter into the coding process. Depending on the specific details in the documentation, we will have the following CPT/HCPCS codes and modifiers:

- Right leg fracture → 27780
- Laceration repair, right arm → 12002-59
- Laceration repair, left leg → 12032
- X-ray of the right leg → 73590
- ED E/M level → 99284-25

We assume that the geographic adjustment factor is 0.9889 for use in the 60%–40% calculation. Table 5.3 provides results of the grouping and pricing processes.

Table 5.3   APC Grouping Example

CPT/ HCPCS Code	APC	Status Indicator	Relative Weight	Payment Using $70.00 CF	Adjusted Payment Using 0.9889	Final Payment after Discounting
27780	0129	T	1.6000	$112.00	$111.25	$55.63
12002-59	0133	T	1.3300	$ 93.10	$92.48	$46.24
12032	0134	T	3.2000	$224.00	$222.51	$222.51
73590	0260	X	0.6600	$46.20	$45.89	$44.89
99284-25	0609	Q3	3.2400	$226.80	$225.29	$225.29

We are not quite finished. There are three status indicator T services, so we must apply discounting. APCs will pay 100% for the highest weighted service and then 50% for the other status indicator T services. This is shown in the rightmost column in Table 5.3. Note that the CPT codes 27780 and 73590 can have the "-LT" modifier attached, but this will not affect the grouping or pricing processes. The laceration repairs will not have either an "-LT" or "-RT" because the integumentary system does not have left- and right-paired organs except for the breasts.

As with MS-DRGs, you will not have to perform this calculation. The calculation will be performed by APC pricer software that will already have your geographic adjustment factor in place. To track reimbursement from your MAC, you will need to perform the grouping and pricing so that you know what to expect for reimbursement.

Also, we have not included the charges for these services. We would need the charges in order to calculate any possible cost outlier payment. In a case like this, any sort of a cost outlier would be unusual.

At this point you should be asking about the case-mix index that is so very useful in MS-DRGs or DRGs in general. Because the APC grouping process often groups to more than one APC category, the CMI used in DRGs is of little use in APCs. However, if you are fastidious and sum the total APC weight for each case (that is, encounter), then you can calculate the CMI the same way as for DRGs. Because a case is an encounter, all the weights for the potentially multiple APCs should be added together for the given case. The CMI can then be calculated based on the amalgamated weights from each case.

Deductibles and Copayments

Many healthcare payment systems have both deductibles and then copayments or coinsurance. For APCs, the deductible can vary and seems to be increasing over time. The typical range is $160.00 to $180.00. Now the two terms *copayment* and *coinsurance* are slightly different under the Medicare program:

- Copayment is the actual dollar amount.
- Coinsurance is the percentage of the payment that generates the copayment amount.

For APCs, the coinsurance is supposed to be at 20%, but at the time this text was prepared, the CMS had not yet achieved the goal of having the coinsurance be 20% in all cases. Also, the copayment amount for APCs is limited to the current inpatient deductible amount. Yes, this seems a rather strange limitation, but it means that in some cases the copayment amount is below the intended 20% coinsurance.

The Provider-Based Rule

The formalization of the provider-based rule (PBR) started at the same time APCs were implemented, namely with the April 7, 2000, *Federal Register*. While the two events are separate and distinct, there is a close relationship between hospital outpatient prospective payment and facilities that are provider based. The concept of hospital-based clinics pre-dates APCs, but there were already payment mechanisms in place for these hospital-based clinics that needed integration with APCs. The role of the Medicare physician fee schedule (MPFS) relative to these clinics was discussed in some detail in the companion text entitled *Fee Schedule Payment Systems*.

The main reference for the PBR in the Code of Federal Regulations (CFR) is at §413.65. During the time period from 2000 to the present, there have been tens of thousands of pages of discussions surrounding the PBR.* Also, the various directives from the CMS have morphed rather significantly over time and continue to change. For example, the whole issue of physician supervision became a contentious topic starting in 2008, and the change cycle has gone on into 2012. Consider Case Study 5.34.

The facts presented in Case Study 5.34 seem innocuous relative to any compliance issues. However, this is a provider-based operation paid under APCs. Starting in 2008, the CMS indicated that direct physician supervision was required for operations on campus as well as provider-based operations off-campus. Ostensibly, this requirement also applies to in-hospital provider-based operations. The question for Apex's infusion center is: Who is providing the direct physician supervision? This becomes a nontrivial question relative to immediate availability of the physician and the availability of the physician to take over care and alter the services being provided. Generally, a physician or qualified non-physician practitioner (NPP) can meet the supervisory requirements under the PBR. Only physicians can supervise diagnostic tests and services such as cardiac rehabilitation and pulmonary rehabilitation.

Case Study 5.34 illustrates only one of many issues that arise under the PBR. The most difficult aspect of this rule is with the definitions and terminology. You will see and hear all kinds

---

CASE STUDY 5.34   INFUSION CENTER ON CAMPUS

The Apex Medical Center has a nice, very active infusion center in a separate building on campus. There is a walkway connecting the infusion center to the hospital. Chemotherapy, blood transfusions, injection, infusion, hydration, and associated services are provided from 7:00 a.m. until 9:00 p.m. at night during the week. Specially trained nursing staff provides the services.

---

* See the Abbey & Abbey, Consultants, Inc. web site (www. APCNow.com) and click on PBR Information Toolkit.

of terminology used in different ways. The fundamental terminology with the PBR is *facility* or *organization*.

These two terms are not further defined in the PBR itself. You will also see words and phrases such as *entity, department, unit, cost center*, and the like. For our purposes we use the phrase *organizational unit*. An oversimplified operational rule to determine if an organizational unit is provider based is to determine whether a UB-04 claim form is filed for services in that organizational unit. For example, is the ED provider based? What about the radiology department? This list can be continued, but almost everything associated with a hospital, for which a UB-04 is filed, is provider based in some sense.

We have already entered the terminology challenge. For instance, we have already used the two phrases *hospital based* and *provider based*. If you are in a hospital setting, you can use these two phrases interchangeably. When the PBR was formalized starting in 2000, the CMS broadened the concept of "hospital –based" to include main providers that have provider agreements with the Medicare program. This certainly includes hospitals and can be extended to providers such as skilled nursing and home health, that is, facilities that have provider agreements with Medicare.

The four main concerns within the PBR are

1. Qualifying for provider-based status, including the need for attestations and determination requests
2. Prohibitions such as providing services under arrangement or entering into management contracts
3. Obligations such as EMTALA integration for off-campus provider-based clinics and notice of two copayments for provider-based clinics
4. Reporting any material changes that might affect provider-based status

Two questions immediately arise:

1. What are the requirements for being provider based?
2. Why would a hospital want operations such as provider-based clinics?

The second question is central to the topic of this text, mainly payment. This is discussed in greater detail in the next section of this chapter, but a short answer is that overall reimbursement from a provider-based clinic is significantly greater than the reimbursement for an equivalent freestanding clinic. Again we are ahead of ourselves with terminology because we have not defined provider-based clinics versus freestanding clinics. Freestanding clinics are typically owned and operated by physicians and, most importantly, they file only the 1500 professional claims and are paid at 100% under the Medicare physician fee schedule.

Provider-based clinics are part of a hospital, or possibly some other main provider, and claims are filed on both the 1500 for professional services and also on the UB-04 for technical services. In a facility setting, the professional component for physicians is reduced by the site-of-service differential contained in the MPFS. However, the combination of the reduced professional component along with the technical component payments is significantly greater than the single full payment for just the professional component.

The requirements for attaining provider-based status are significant. Note that each and every one of the criteria listed in the PBR must be attained. This situation is not a preponderance of meeting most of the requirements. The criteria first appeared in Program Memorandum A-96-7, and these criteria were slightly refined for use with formalizing the PBR. The basic criteria are

- Geographic proximity
- Integral and subordinate part
- Under common/licensure and accreditation
- Common ownership and control
- Day-to-day supervision
- Clinical services integration
- Held out to the public
- Financial integration

As you read through this list, you become aware that to have provider-based status, the facility or organization or situation must truly be part of the hospital (main provider). Each of these criteria can be expanded into rather significant discussions. We take a small sampling to give the reader a sense of how these criteria are applied.

1. *Geographic proximity:* When hospitals started developing provider-based clinics in the 1980s, CMS (then HCFA) became concerned because some of the off-campus clinics were located quite a distance from the hospital. Basically, the CMS wanted the clinics really close to the hospital, preferably not more than a few blocks. Congress did intervene and established a 35-mile default for meeting the geographic proximity requirement. Additionally, with the PBR itself, there are two ZIP code analyses that can be conducted to show that the given off-campus operation is truly in the same catchment area as the hospital. If all these tests fail, a hospital can still petition the CMS for special permission for an off-campus operation to be considered as meeting the criterion. Note that for operations on the hospital campus, there is little concern about geographic proximity.

2. *Clinical services integration:* While there are a number of requirements for integrating clinical services, one of them involves medical records. If a hospital has a provider-based facility or operation, then the medical records for that operation should be integrated into the hospital medical record system. For an operation inside the hospital, this is not much of an issue. As you move away from the hospital onto the campus in a separate building, then this requirement becomes more difficult. For off-campus operations, truly integrating the medical record system is a challenge. Luckily, technology can help significantly by having everything in a central computer site. Also, it appears that cross-referencing a remote set of records with the main hospital medical records meets this specific concern. Basically, anyone looking up a particular patient, either at the hospital or a remote provider-based site, should find that a portion of the medical record exists in more than one location.

3. *Held out to the public:* When individuals enter a provider-based operation, they should be fully aware that they have entered the hospital or main provider. For the hospital itself, this is not much of an issue. For a building on the campus, there should be some consideration that the signage for the building indicates that it is part of the hospital. The real issue here comes into play when you consider an off-campus operation. Great care must be taken to name the facility or operation such that an individual is fully aware that it is part of the hospital.

As you consider these three specific examples, you should realize that in being provider based, with a hospital as the main provider, everything should be established so that individuals fully recognize these facilities or operations as a part of the hospital.

**CASE STUDY 5.35   FREESTANDING CLINIC
CONVERTED TO PROVIDER BASED**

The Acme Medical Clinic is down the road about two blocks from the Apex Medical Center. Acme was founded by several family practice physicians and has been operating as a freestanding clinic for years. The physicians and the hospital have talked about the hospital acquiring the clinic and then hiring the physicians as employees under contracts. AMC's board has finally given approval for the hospital to purchase the clinic and hire the physicians.

Now we move on to the second question: Why would a hospital want to have provider-based operations? Some operations or departments are simply provider based by their very nature. The outpatient surgery or the radiology departments are typically inside the hospital and by their nature they are provider based. Keep in mind our overly simple operational test of filing a UB-04. The real interest lies in provider-based clinics either on-campus or off-campus. The reason for the interest is significantly increased reimbursement for provider-based clinics. Of course, hospitals may maintain that the monetary gain is secondary to the ability to provide higher-quality, integrated healthcare. Consider Case Study 5.35.

Acme, as a freestanding clinic, files claims only on the 1500 claim form for the professional component. For Medicare patients, CMS pays the full fee schedule amount from the Medicare physician fee schedule. When Apex acquires the clinic, a decision must be made: keep the clinic as a freestanding clinic or organize it as part of the hospital, that is, provider based. The hospital can elect to keep the clinic freestanding. From a coding and billing perspective, very little would change.

However, Apex can take the necessary steps, which can be rather significant, to make the clinic provider based. This would mean meeting all the criteria as enunciated in the PBR. The reason for going to all the trouble is that as provider based, two claims will be filed: a 1500 for the professional component and a UB-04 for the technical component. Because Acme is part of the hospital, when the 1500 claim form is filed, the place of service (POS) will be reported as hospital, outpatient. This is indicated by POS 22.* The POS will then cause the professional payment to be reduced to the facility-level payment within MPFS. This reduction in payment is called the site-of-service (SOS) differential. The justification is that if a technical component is separately paid, then the physician payment should be reduced because the physician's overhead expenses have been reduced.

In addition to the professional claim, the hospital will file a technical component claim on the UB-04. Because provider-based clinics provide outpatient services, payment for the technical component will fall under APCs. As we discuss in the next section, the combination of the two payments—a reduced physician payment along with a hospital payment—is significantly more than the single professional payment.

Provider-Based Clinics

Having briefly discussed the PBR, we can now focus on just provider-based clinics, how they are established, and how APCs along with the MPFS pay for services. Being provider based is a Medicare concept. When you move away from the Medicare program, these clinics are just

---

* For freestanding clinics, the POS is generally 11, physician's office.

like any other clinic. In limited cases, private third-party payers may recognize provider-based status to some degree. Thus, the process of filing two claim forms, or what we will call *split-billing*, can be limited only to Medicare or split-billing can be applied to all types of patients or applied to Medicare plus selected types of patients. While the whole point of split-billing is reimbursement enhancement, in theory, a provider-based clinic could file only a 1500 claim form. Of course, the site-of-service differential would still apply. Thus, the professional component payment would be reduced and there would be no technical component payment to offset the reduced professional payment.

First we address the rather technical issue of payment for provider-based clinics. We delimit our discussion to Medicare, in which payment is made for both the 1500 professional claim form and the UB-04 technical claim form. We use a simple example in Case Study 5.36 to illustrate the process:

The CPT coding for this case involves two CPT codes:

1. 99214: Level 4 E/M office visit, established patient
2. 11402: Excision, benign lesion 1.1 to 2.0 cm

For both MPFS and APCs, the "-25" modifier is needed on the E/M level to ensure separate payment because the E/M level was a separate, significantly identifiable service that went above and beyond the normal E/M that would have been provided only for removing the lesion.*

To calculate the professional payment, we need the relative values from MPFS and then a conversion factor. We will use simplified numbers because we are simply illustrating the process. We will use a conversion factor of $36.000 per relative value. The relative values from MPFS are broken down as follows:

1. Work component
2. Overhead component:
   a. Facility
   b. Non-facility
3. Medical malpractice

CASE STUDY 5.36   DERMATOLOGY PROVIDER-BASED CLINIC

The Apex Medical Center has the good fortune of having several provider-based clinics in several specialty areas. For dermatology, the hospital has three dermatologists and one plastic surgeon in a nice building on the hospital campus. Today, an elderly patient has been referred by a primary care physician for possible lesion removal. The dermatologist has seen the patient before, but it has been almost 3 years. The dermatologist performs a complete upper body integumentary examination for any possible abnormalities. Finding none, the dermatologist then removes a benign lesion 1.4 cm in diameter from the left arm.

---

* Note the discussion in the CPT/HCPCS section concerning NCCI policies involving E/M services provided with minor surgeries.

Table 5.4 MPFS Relative Value Units for Case Study 5.36

CPT	Work	PE Facility	PE Non-Facility	Malpractice	Total-Facility	Total Non-Facility
99214	1.50	1.00	1.50	0.10	2.60	3.10
11402	1.50	1.60	3.00	0.25	3.35	4.75

Note that there are two overhead components: one for service provided in a facility setting (provider based) and one for a non-facility (freestanding) setting. This difference is how the site-of-service differential is calculated. Table 5.4 provides the simplified RVUs (Relative Value Units) that we will use.

Now we can calculate the physician payment for both the freestanding and the facilities settings:

■ Freestanding (non-facility):
  – For 99214: 3.10 × $36.000 = $111.60
  – For 11402: 4.75 × $36.000 = $171.00
  – Total payment = $282.60
■ Provider-based (facility):
  – For 99214: 2.60 × $36.00 = $ 93.60
  – For 11402: 3.35 × $36.00 = $126.00
■ Total payment = $219.60

Thus, the physician payment has been reduced by $282.60 – $219.60 = $63.00. This is the site-of-service differential for the physician when services are provided in a facility setting that is provider based.

What about the APC payment? Here is the grouping and associated payments:

■ 99214 Maps to APC 0606 = $95.00
■ 11402 Maps to APC 0019 = $360.00
■ Total technical component payment = $475.00

Here are the final totals:

■ Service provided in a freestanding clinic: Total payment = $282.60
■ Service provided in a provider-based clinic: Total payment = $475.00 + $219.60 = $694.60

Through the provider-based clinic there is an increase in reimbursement of $694.60 – $282.60 = $412.00. This increase has occurred through a single encounter. Typically for E/M visits, the increases in reimbursement are more in the $50.00 to $70.00 range. However, even a moment's consideration will show that over thousands of visits, very large increases in payment can be garnered. This, among other reasons, is why hospitals consider developing provider-based clinics.

Next we look at three policy decisions that must be considered for provider-based clinics. Note that the three we discuss are among potentially hundreds of decisions that must be made.

1. Split billing
2. Fee schedules
3. Billing privileges

Split Billing: 1500 plus UB-04

Prior to the implementation of APCs and the formalization of the PBR, there was concern about hospital-based clinics being required to split-bill all patients if Medicare beneficiaries were being split-billed. Interestingly enough, in the April 7, 2000 *Federal Register*, there was a clear statement that hospitals could choose to split-bill Medicare only and/or optionally split-bill other third-party payers.[*] Thus, hospitals that establish provider-based clinics must make decisions as to whom they are going to split-bill. Some private third-party payers do recognize hospital-based clinics and will adjudicate both the professional and technical component claims. Consider Case Studies 5.37 and 5.38.

The results found in these two case studies would probably result in Apex not split-billing either third-party payer because there is not a great deal to gain. In the first example, Apex will probably generate greater payment but the increase will come at the consternation of patients who may well complain about the deductible. In the second case, the insurance company was wise enough to pay the same as it would to a freestanding clinic although the payment is split. Split-billing non-Medicare should be analyzed carefully relative to any gain versus disgruntled patients.

Embedded within this discussion of split-billing is that we have not considered the secondary payers. For Medicare beneficiaries who have one of the standard supplemental policies, there will be no additional out-of-pocket payments even with two separate claims and associated copayments, although this does not take into account any deductibles. What about other secondary payers? Or what if Medicare is secondary?

The answers to these questions quickly become complicated. One way to approach this is to split-bill Medicare primary only. For other situations, typically only the professional claim is filed

---

CASE STUDY 5.37   SPLIT BILLING NOT RECOGNIZED

The Apex Medical Center has several provider-based clinics and Apex is experimenting with split billing its larger private third-party payers. For one of the private payers, the two claim forms were adjudicated. The professional claim form was paid in full as if the clinic were free-standing. The technical component claim was not really recognized and the insurance company moved the billing to the patient's deductible.

CASE STUDY 5.38   SPLIT BILLING RECOGNIZED

Apex has been experimenting with split billing. One of Apex's larger private third-party payers does recognize provider-based status. Both the technical component claim and the professional claim were adjudicated and individually paid. However, the insurance company simply took the normal physician payment and split the payment between the physician and the hospital. The insurance company split the two payments using the same percentages as found in the MPFS for the services, that is, the normal site-of-service percentage reduction. Thus, this company paid no more than it would have paid to the physician; the overall payment was simply split.

---

[*] See 65 FR 18519.

at the full professional fee. There are still some lingering concerns because if Medicare is secondary, you will actually end up filing only the professional claim, but the Medicare claim will still have to report the POS as hospital, outpatient. Thus, the professional payment from Medicare's perspective would still be reduced.

The bottom-line is that hospitals do have to make some considered decisions about split-billing.

Establishing Fee Schedules

Regardless of which payers are split-billed, there is a significant question about establishing appropriate charges. For the Medicare program, there is the so-called *Medicare charging rule*. While the regulatory language surrounding this rule is quite complicated, an overly simplified version is that hospitals should not charge Medicare beneficiaries more than they charge other patients. So if we split-bill Medicare beneficiaries and we do not split-bill other types of patients, how can we be assured that the Medicare beneficiaries are charged the same, or possibly less, than the other patients? At issue is that in filing only a professional claim, we will use a physician professional fee schedule. When filing both professional and technical component claims, we will have separate fees for each claim. If we are not careful, the two fees in the split-billing may add up to more than the single physician fees.

One approach to this issue is to take the full physician set of charges (that is, the physician fee schedule) and split it into two parts: one for the physician charge and one for the hospital charge. If we split the full physician fee schedule, then the split-billing charges will be the same as the full physician fee schedule; that is, they will add up to the same amount. Consider Table 5.5.

If you study Table 5.5, you should find that the full physician fee amounts have been divided on a 60%–40% basis to generate the split physician and split hospital fees. Care must be exercised because we are dealing with two very different payment systems. The physician professional component is paid under a fee schedule so that the payment is the lesser of the charge or the fee schedule payment. Thus, the split physician fees must be higher than what MPFS will pay, that is, the reduced physician payment. APCs represent a PPS so that payment is fixed in advance regardless of what is charged. Thus for APCs, the fee charged can be below the amount that APCs will pay. However, be careful that the amount charged under APCs is at least as high as the copayment

Table 5.5 Split Fee Schedule for Provider-Based Clinic

CPT	Full Physician Fee Schedule Charge	Full Physician Payment Under MPFS	Split Physician Fee Charge	Reduced Physician Payment under MPFS	Split Hospital Fee Charge	Hospital Payment under APCs
99211	$50.00	$22.00	$30.00	$10.00	$20.00	$55.00
99212	$85.00	$43.00	$51.00	$28.00	$34.00	$80.00
99213	$140.00	$72.00	$84.00	$55.00	$56.00	$80.00
99214	$200.00	$110.00	$120.00	$85.00	$80.00	$100.00
99215	$260.00	$150.00	$156.00	$120.00	$104.00	$130.00

CASE STUDY 5.39   DIFFERENT E/M LEVELS

Sam, an elderly resident of Anywhere, USA, has presented to a family practice provider-based clinic. He is an established patient and has been having problems. Dr. Smith does a brief examination and then spends an hour counseling Sam. There is virtually no nursing involvement other than the use of the examination room.

---

amount. Note that the use of a 60%–40% split is arbitrary. You can use whatever split formula you want as long as the criteria mentioned above are attained.

With this type of split fee arrangement, if a non-Medicare patient presents, assuming you are not split-billing everyone, a single charge is made. For instance, for a level 4 E/M visit, the charge is $200.00. For a Medicare patient receiving a level 4 E/M visit, two charges are made—$120.00 for the physician and $80.00 for the hospital—which add up to the same $200.00. Thus, in this provider-based clinic setting, the same amount is being charged to both Medicare and non-Medicare patients.

As with many aspects of healthcare payment systems, there are some possible aberrations. The coding process, particularly for E/M levels, is different on the physician side relative to the hospital side. For professional coding, coding is based on what the physician does. On the hospital side, the coding is based on resource utilization. It is possible that two different E/M levels might occur in the split-billing arrangement. Note that this will not generally occur with medical or surgical procedures.

Review Case Study 5.39. While we do not have the actual documentation for this case study, the professional E/M will likely be coded at a level 5, that is, 99215, due to the length of the counseling time. On the hospital side, a mapping developed by the hospital will be used to determine the technical component E/M level.* Quite possibly, based on the information in the case study, this could easily be 99213. If Sam were a non-Medicare patient, the charge would be $260.00. As a Medicare patient, Sam will be charged $156.00 on the professional side and $56.00 on the hospital side for a total of $212.00. Luckily this charge to Sam is less than the charge to comparable non-Medicare patients. However, the converse of this particular case study can also occur.

The bottom-line is that hospitals must give careful consideration to how they develop the fee schedules for provider-based clinics and the associated split-billing process.

Billing Privileges

The third topic that we address is billing privileges. While billing privileges are a concern for private third-party payers, the greatest area of difficulty seems to occur with the Medicare program. For Medicare this involves the development, filing, and updating, as appropriate, of the CMS 855 forms. These are the Enrollment Application forms and there are five different forms:

    855-A – Part A
    855-B – Part B
    855-I – Individual
    855-0 – Ordering Referring

---

* In the April 7, 2000, *Federal Register*, the CMS directed hospitals to develop their own mappings of resources utilized and then to use the mappings to develop E/M levels. See 65 FR 18451.

CASE STUDY 5.40   CMS-855 FORMS AND CLINICS

Stanley is reviewing the roster of providers at the clinic that is due for conversion to provider based. There are five family practice physicians, two surgeons, three nurse practitioners, and two physician assistants. These healthcare providers will all become employees of the hospital. Stanley has been told that the hospital's CMS-855-A form will also need updating for the clinic as a new practice location.

      855-R – Reassignment
      855-S – DMEPOS

The most recent form is the 855-0 for ordering or referring physician or practitioner. The 855-R form is the shortest of the forms, while the others are much longer and may require attachments. Completing these forms and keeping them up-to-date can be a significant task. As hospitals develop provider-based clinics or convert freestanding clinics to provider based, the number of CMS-855 forms that must be considered can become overwhelming. Note that tied into this entire process are the National Provider Identifiers (NPIs). Let us join Stanley, who has been assigned the task of making certain that all the CMS-855 forms are in place in order to convert a freestanding clinic down the road into a provider-based clinic.

How many CMS-855 forms will Stanley need to consider? While we would need a little more information for a definitive answer, we can make some educated guesses:

■ For each physician/surgeon, there would be a CMS-855-I and a CMS-855-R.
■ For the clinic itself, there would be a CMS-855-B.
■ The hospital's CMS-855-A would need updating.
■ For the NPs, there would be a CMS-855-I and a CMS-855-R.
■ For the PAs, only a CMS-855-I would be needed.

This adds up to twenty-three different CMS-855 forms. Note that the PAs do not need a reassignment form because for PAs the employer is always paid. For the other physicians/practitioners, payment could be made directly to them but the reassignment form redirects payment to the hospital, that is, their employer. Handling this number of CMS-855 forms will be a significant task.

> **Note:** At the time this text was prepared, the CMS was implementing an electronic system so that the enrollment process and updating enrollment information could be performed electronically. *See* PECOS, the Medicare Provider Enrollment, Chain, and Ownership System (see https://pecos.cms.hhs.gov).

Special Situations

To complete our brief discussion of provider-based clinics, we can look at two special situations:

1. Specialty clinics
2. Provider-based clinical services

Specialty clinics abound at rural hospitals that are generally in smaller communities and do not have specialty physicians. Interestingly there are also hospitals in urban centers that also use this concept. The basic idea is that specialists from nearby metropolitan areas travel out to the smaller hospitals to provide services. Depending on circumstances, the specialist may come once a month or more often, as appropriate. The host hospital will typically schedule patients and provide clinical space for the visiting specialist. While clinic visits may be the main service provided, medical and surgical procedures are also sometimes provided in the clinic setting.

Relative to provider-based clinics, these specialty clinics may or may not be provider based. This is an organizational issue that must be established in the relationship between the hospital and the visiting specialists. While there are variations, the two fundamental approaches are

1. Establish as provider based
2. Establish as freestanding

For the freestanding version, the specialists contract with the hospital for the space, personnel support, supplies, and the like. There is a rental agreement and the rental amount must be well-documented as being at fair market value (FMV) for the resources provided. This means that the clinic is actually the physician's office and the normal professional component billing on the 1500 will be performed using a POS of 11, physician's office. The specialist receives full professional reimbursement under MPFS. The hospital does not file claims; payment to the hospital comes through the rental agreement.

The provider-based version involves the hospital billing a technical component and the physician billing a professional component. There is no rent paid by the specialist, the specialist simply comes and provides services. The physician will have to file the professional claim with a POS of 22, hospital, outpatient. Thus, the physician will receive a slightly reduced payment because of the site-of-service differential. However, because the physician is paying no rent, this payment reduction may be counterbalanced by paying no rent. The hospital will file a technical component claim on the UB-04 and, at least for Medicare, be paid under APCs.

Consider Case Study 5.41. There is nothing unusual about the arrangements described in Case Study 5.41. The hospital should establish a formal written contract with each of the physicians or physician groups that are participating in these arrangements. For the physicians paying rent, the contract should specify rent at FMV, and this amount should be reviewed at least annually or whenever there are any changes. Likewise, the physicians participating in the provider-based arrangement also need a contract. In the provider-based arrangement, the physician must fastidiously report POS 22, which drives the site-of-service reduction. Because the physicians are filing their own 1500 claim forms, the hospital will not necessarily know that the correct place of service is being reported. This requirement should be reflected in the contract. Interestingly enough,

---

CASE STUDY 5.41   SPECIALTY CLINICS

The Apex Medical Center has the good fortune of having ten different specialty physicians who hold specialty clinics once or sometimes twice a month. Six of the physicians have decided to pay rent and treat these specialty clinics as their own clinics, that is, freestanding. The other four have decided to participate with Apex in establishing their clinics as provider based.

the CMS has indicated that the hospital is responsible for the correct reporting of the POS even though the hospital may not develop and file the claim.*

The concept of *provider-based clinical services* illustrates a nuance in connection with provider-based clinics. Using the word *clinic* implies a recognizable separate entity or organizational structure. Also, at clinics there are generally two claim forms filed. There are also provider-based operations that do not require that two claims be filed. For instance, a hospital may establish an off-campus satellite radiology center. These satellite operations are typically extensions of the radiology department at the hospital and are established as provider based (i.e., file a UB-04 claim).

Keeping in mind that under a PPS like APCs, the basic idea is that if you do not code and bill for a service, there will never be any payment; there are situations in which nursing services are provided that are very similar to clinic services. These services are often provided by nursing staff, the location is typically some sort of outpatient service area, and the services are not directly codeable and thus they may be overlooked. Review Case Studies 5.42 and 5.43.

For both Case Studies 5.42 and 5.43, there is no service provided by a physician or qualified non-physician practitioner. However, both services are clinical services in a provider-based setting, and the services are not separately codeable; that is, there is no CPT or HCPCS code describing the service. However, resources have been consumed so that a claim should be filed. In both these cases, the answer is that an E/M service has been provided by nursing staff. For these types of services, which are often incidental services provided on an ad hoc basis, a technical component claim should be filed. E/M codes are generally developed based on a mapping, but most of these services can generally use a default level 1 E/M, namely 99211.

> *Note:* If these types of services are not coded and billed, there is an approximate loss of about $50.00. Under a PPS like APCs, if there is no coding and billing, there will never be any payment. Thus, recognizing circumstances such as the provider-based clinical services is important.

In summary, provider-based clinics have become a major topic for hospitals. While integration and the quality of care may be the purpose of establishing provider-based clinics, one of

---

CASE STUDY 5.42   IVIG SERVICES

Sarah is presenting to the infusion center at Apex for one of a series of intravenous immune globulin (IVIG) injections. However, she is not feeling well today. A nurse assesses Sarah and determines that she should not have the IVIG. Sarah is told to go home, rest, and then return the next day for the services.

CASE STUDY 5.43   CATHETER REMOVAL

It is 4:45 p.m. A patient is presenting to the Apex Medical Center's outpatient service area with a physician's order in hand. The patient has a catheter in place. The order indicates that the patient is to be voided. If there is more than 500 cc, then the catheter is to be left in place; otherwise the catheter is to be removed. The nurse performs the services and then, based on the orders, removes the catheter. The patient is then discharged home.

the attractive features is the ability to increase reimbursement under the Medicare program. The provider-based rule (PBR) is a complex rule that governs requirements for provider-based clinics. Note that the PBR really goes beyond the clinic context and actually applies to both inpatient and outpatient services within a hospital.

Ambulatory Surgical Centers

Ambulatory Surgical Centers (ASCs) represent a special designation under the Medicare program. Generally, outpatient surgical procedures are performed. Other private payers often recognize the concept of ASCs although there may or may not be any differentiation in payment relative to the same services provided in the hospital outpatient setting. There are also state licensing laws and accreditation requirements for these facilities. Some ASCs can be quite specialized, while others provide a broad array of surgical services. A group of ophthalmologists may establish an ASC to perform only cataract surgery. On the other hand, a hospital may establish an ASC on its campus to handle more routine surgical procedures.

Consider Case Study 5.44. In some cases there has been movement in converting ASCs into specialty hospitals. The reason for converting the ASC to a specialty hospital is to gain better reimbursement under APCs and increase the range of services so that payment can be gained from MS-DRGs.

For Medicare, ASCs are paid through a combination of a fee schedule, namely MPFS, and a prospective payment system for hospital outpatient services, APCs or Ambulatory Payment Classifications. This hybrid payment system started on January 1, 2008. Prior to this new system, ASCs were paid on a simple set of payment categories.

ASCs provide a wide range of surgical procedures. This can extend from fairly simple procedures to complex procedures requiring anesthesia. Some of the procedures performed in an ASC can also be provided in a medical office setting. Other, more complex surgical procedures fall outside the medical office realm and must be performed at an ASC or in a hospital setting, normally an outpatient setting.

ASC payment is a hybrid of APCs and MPFS. The overall formula for ASC reimbursement is as follows:

■ For ASC surgeries, payment is 65% of the APC payment
■ For office-based surgeries, payment is the lesser of:
  – 65% of the APC payment *or*
  – The non-facility PE RVU payment from the MPFS

CASE STUDY 5.44   ORTHOPEDIC ASC

Several of the orthopedic surgeons who are on the staff of the Apex Medical Center have established a very nice ASC right across the street from Apex. Orthopedic services are provided for Medicare patients as well as private payer patients. The ASC performs all and any orthopedic services that can legally be performed at the ASC. Now there is even talk about converting this ASC to a specialty, physician-owned hospital.

CASE STUDY 5.45   PILONIDAL CYSTS AT AN ASC

Among the surgeries being performed, one patient has a simple pilonidal cyst, CPT 10080, and another patient has a complex pilonidal cyst, CPT 10081. The services are successfully accomplished in both cases.

The ASC payment formula for Medicare represents a creative use of a part of the overall MPFS. Let us examine a case study to see how this formula works.

The question is: How is the ASC payment calculated? To illustrate consider Case Study 5.45. First of all, we need the payment that would be made under the APC system for hospital outpatient services. Table 5.6 shows the approximate payments and then 65% of that payment for the two codes.

Next, we need to calculate the MPFS payment using the non-facility RVUs. Table 5.7 gives us the approximate RVUs for these two codes.

Using $36.0000 as the conversion factor, then for 10080,

$$\$36.0000 \times 3.50 = \$126.00$$

and for 10081,

$$\$36.0000 \times 4.50 = \$162.00.$$

Thus, at the ASC, 10080 will be paid at $120.00 (i.e., 65% of APC payment) while 10081 will be paid at $162.00 (i.e., from the MPFS).

Considering our discussions about APCs in this chapter, why is there such a big difference between APC payments for 10080 (simple) and 10081 (complex)? The reason goes back to how the APC payments are determined. For these codes, the charges for 10081 must be significantly higher than for the 10080. This difference then drives the average costs and then these two services end up in very different APCs. Thus, the answer is that the payment is higher for 10081 because of coding and charge structures. However, where do you draw the line between simple and complex?

Table 5.6   APC Payments

CPT Code	APC Payment	65% of APC Payment
10080	$100.00	$65.00
10081	$900.00	$585.00

Table 5.7   RVUs under MPFS

CPT	Work	NonFacPE	FacPE	MedMal
10080	1.20	3.50	1.60	0.20
10081	2.50	4.50	2.00	0.45

Regardless of where and how you draw the line, having a 900% increase in reimbursement for the complex versus the simple is questionable at best.

Today there is a great deal of activity with ASCs. Hospitals often own and operate ASCs, and sometimes ASCs, if properly located, are converted into extensions of the hospital outpatient surgery department in order to gain full APC payment.

Payment System Interfaces for APCs

Payment systems meet each other in some obvious circumstances and also in more subtle ways. Thus, different payment systems must interface in some way. Actually, the very first case study in this chapter, Case Study 5.1—*Splinting in the Emergency Department*, involves a payment system interface. In that case study, the physical therapy services would normally be paid under the MPFS. However, in that case study, the splinting services really did fall under APCs and would be paid through APCs. However, correct coding and billing, and thus payment, depend on not using the –GP modifier.

Previously in this chapter we discussed two of the many interfaces for APCs, namely

1. Provider-based clinics
2. Ambulatory surgical centers

In both cases, the interface was between APCs and MPFS. Now let us take a simple Case Study namely, 5.46, that illustrates a less obvious interface, this time with MS-DRGs.

This case study appears innocuous. Sam needs the surgery and his physician has decided to perform the service on an inpatient basis and payment for the hospital will be made by MS-DRGs. However, this same procedure can be performed on an outpatient basis with payment coming from APCs. Now if APCs interface smoothly to MS-DRGs, there should not be too much difference in payment between APCs and MS-DRGs. If there is not too much difference, then there will be no incentive to provide the service in one setting versus the other. Considering this service along with hundreds of other services that can be provided in one setting versus another, a smooth interface is really needed.

Unfortunately, many of these procedures gain much more reimbursement under MS-DRGs than under APCs. This becomes a payment issue and auditors will want to check for the medical necessity of performing this type of procedure as an inpatient versus an outpatient.

Skilled nursing services have their own prospective payment system that we will briefly discuss in the next chapter. Outpatient services with payment under APCs often have to interface with residents from skilled nursing facilities. Review Case Study 5.47.

So what is unusual about this case study? The problem with the situation described in the case study is that HBO therapy is included under the SNF PPS through consolidated billing. Thus, when patients from the SNF are brought over to the hospital for HBO services, the payment to the hospital does not come through APCs; the service must be paid by the SNF to the hospital because the service

---

CASE STUDY 5.46   SURGICAL SERVICE OUTPATIENT VERSUS INPATIENT

Sam needs to have carotid stent placement. His physician has decided to perform this procedure on an inpatient basis even though Sam is otherwise in pretty good health.

CASE STUDY 5.47   HYPERBARIC OXYGEN THERAPY

The Apex Medical Center has decided to establish an HBO (hyperbaric oxygen) service using an outside firm. This is a provider-based operation and most of the services are for outpatients. The physicians in the community are quite excited because they have elderly patients in skilled nursing homes that can benefit from this service.

CASE STUDY 5.48   ER SERVICES WITH EVENTUAL INPATIENT ADMISSION

Sam has been brought to the Apex Medical Center's ED suffering from chest pains and weakness. A thorough assessment is made and Sam in placed in the chest pain protocol and placed in observation. After several hours in observation, Sam is getting worse and he is then admitted as an inpatient for further services.

in included in the SNF payment. Most likely in this situation, there will be a damper on patients from an SNF going to have HBO therapy. This case study is an example of a coverage interface.

Another interface between APCs and MS-DRGs occurs at the front-end of an inpatient admission. This is through the MS-DRG 3-day pre-admission or 3-day payment window.

Normally the ED and observation services would be coded and billed on an outpatient basis and be paid under APCs. However, with the MS-DRG pre-admission or payment window, the charges for these services will be included in the inpatient billing (see Case Study 5.48). This window is discussed in Chapter 4 and circumstances can become rather convoluted.

In Case Study 5.49, the patient was not admitted to Apex as an inpatient. Thus, all the services provided will be coded, billed, and reimbursement will come from APCs. Presuming that the patient is admitted to the other hospital, whatever ER services are provided at the receiving hospital will be bundled into the inpatient admission at the receiving hospital.

The way in which different payment systems come together can become complicated, and careful analysis is often needed. APCs represent a prime example. There can be coverage issues, different payments depending on location of service, and medical necessity needs correlated against the acuity level of the facility, just to name a few. For APCs, the most intricate interface is with the MPFS relative to provider-based clinics.

CASE STUDY 5.49   ER SERVICES WHERE A TRANSFER OCCURS

An elderly patient has been brought to Apex's ED after an accident. The patient reports multiple symptoms, including chest pain and difficulty breathing along with lacerations and a fractured leg. In the ER the patient is carefully worked up. The lacerations are all repaired, x-rays show a nondisplaced fracture, which is splinted. The chest pain and difficult breathing worsen, and the decision is to transfer the patient to a larger hospital that can provide more comprehensive care.

APCs and the *Federal Register* Process

CMS uses the standard National Public Rulemaking (NPRM) process to update APCs each calendar year. As with other Medicare-developed payment systems, various rules and regulations are included in a system of manuals that are updated through transmittals involving change requests (CRs). Each year in the May through July timeframe, the CMS issues a proposed set of changes for APCs and then on or about November 1st of each calendar year, the final rules and regulations through the *Federal Register* are released for implementation on January 1st.

Here is a typical time sequence for the *Federal Register* issuances for APCs:

> July 15th: Proposed *Federal Register* issued
> August 15th: End of the 60-day comment period
> November 1st: Final *Federal Register* issued
> January 1st: Final rules go into effect

For APCs, the final *Federal Register* entries are often issued well into November and sometimes even early December. This leaves little time for proper preparation. When CMS submits a *Federal Register* entry, the *examination copy* will often be available several weeks before the official copy. This does assist hospitals in obtaining the needed information closer to the November 1st date.

These *Federal Register* entries can, and often do, involve hundreds of pages of discussions on various topics involving APCs and related topics such as the provider-based rule (PBR) and ambulatory surgical centers (ASCs). Hospital personnel who want to keep up-to-date with APCs must be extremely careful to follow exactly what is included in these APC updated *Federal Registers*. Sometimes important, relevant information may also be in the *Federal Registers* that updates both MS-DRGs and the Medicare physician fee schedule (MPFS).

The NPRM process is used to update the *Code of Federal Regulations* or the CFR. Much of the discussion in a *Federal Register* entry is called the preamble. The actual changes to the CFR are in a much shorter section at the end of the *Federal Register* entry. In terms of guidance for the Medicare program, the CFR language, which is often fairly brief, is used to develop the extensive CMS manual system. These manuals are updated through transmittals that are frequently issued throughout the year. Even more informal guidance is provided through Q&As on the CMS website and other documents that are irregularly issued. There is also guidance that is issued by the Medicare Administrative Contractors (MACs).

Quality Reporting and Compliance for APCs

APCs represent one of the most complicated payment systems ever developed. As a result, both quality reporting and compliance are major issues. As with other healthcare payment systems, quality reporting along with possible payment reductions is rapidly becoming the norm.

Compliance issues for APCs number well into the hundreds.* Most of the issues result from incorrect coding that includes the improper use of modifiers. The two modifiers that create most of the problems are the "-25" and "-59" modifiers. As with MS-DRGs, the coding cannot be any better than the underlying documentation so that documentation becomes an issue. Add in the complexity of physician supervision under the provider-based rule and we have yet another compliance concern.

---

* See, for instance, the *APC Integrity Program* developed by Abbey & Abbey, Consultants, Inc.

CASE STUDY 5.50 INPATIENT ADMISSION SWITCHED TO OUTPATIENT OBSERVATION

Sarah was admitted to the hospital on Thursday evening. She is recovering nicely and it is now Saturday morning. Utilization review has been assessing the reasons for the admission. The attending physician has been contacted and everyone agrees that this should have been an observation case, not an inpatient admission.

CASE STUDY 5.51 INFUSIONS DURING OBSERVATION SERVICES

Coding and billing staff at Apex are concerned about billing for hydrations and infusions while the patient is in observation. There is confusion about whether the observation hours during which hydrations and infusions occur should be subtracted from the overall number of observation hours.

CASE STUDY 5.52 RADIATION ONCOLOGY AND PHYSICIAN SUPERVISION

The Apex Medical Center has a nice radiation oncology program with two radiation oncologists employed by the hospital. The physicians' offices are located in a very nice medical office building right across the parking lot from the hospital. The physicians will see patients in the office while radiation services are being provided at the hospital by specially trained technicians.

Case Study 5.50 illustrates a compliance issue than spans both MS-DRGs and APCs. The proper way to address the situation in this case study can become somewhat complicated. What if the attending physician states that an observation admission was intended from the beginning and that a clerical error has been made to classify this as an inpatient admission? Otherwise, Condition Code 44 must be considered and the billing significantly altered.

At issue in Case Study 5.51 is the proper definition of the phrase *active monitoring*. If the hydration or infusions require active monitoring, then the hours of hydration and/or infusion should be subtracted from the hours reported for observation services. However, a very precise definition of active monitoring is needed.

For Case Study 5.52, the issue of immediate availability of the radiation oncologists has been raised. Only a radiation oncologist could alter the course of treatment and thus it appears that they must be immediately available to the hospital area where the radiation treatments are actually provided. What would you suggest that Apex do to maintain proper compliance?

Of particular concern for APC compliance are the recovery audit contractors (RACs). This is an extensive audit program that has been developed by the CMS to address overpayments and, theoretically, underpayments.[*]

---

[*] See Dr. Abbey's text entitled *The Medicare Recovery Audit Contractor Program: A Survival Guide for Healthcare Providers*, published by CRC Press, 2010, ISBN=978-1-4398-2100-8.

Summary and Conclusion

APCs are the most complicated PPS used today. This statement is subjective; but given all the features and breadth of coverage along with the ongoing rate of change from year to year, the level of detail and intertwining complexities is formidable. There are variations of APCs. APGs were a precursor to APCs, and these two PPSs share many common features while exhibiting some startling differences.

APCs have been designed and developed by the Medicare program as an outpatient prospective payment system. Some services, notably physical, occupational, and speech therapy services, are not covered by APCs. Coverage can become complex with APCs. There is a series of status indicators that helps define the complex grouping logic that is used to group to the various APC categories.

The unit of service is an encounter. While the concept of an encounter seems intuitively simple, in application there can be difficulties in precisely defining what constitutes an encounter. Similarly, the unit of payment is also based on the encounter. As with other PPSs, there is a great deal of bundling with items such as inexpensive supplies and pharmacy items being packaged. The packaging concept for APCs is a multilevel process often indicated by the use of status indicator N that signifies no payment...well, no separate payment. Some of the bundling actually occurs at the hospital chargemaster level through rules and regulations governing what can and cannot be charged separately.

APCs borrow from the Medicare physician fee schedule in that multiple surgical procedures are discounted. If multiple surgical procedures are provided, then the highest paying procedure is paid at 100% and the lesser paying procedures are discounted to 50%.

The classification of services provided and items rendered for patient care consists of the CPT and HCPCS coding systems along with an extensive array of modifiers. Some modifiers affect payment while others are informational only. Coding guidelines for outpatient CPT and HCPCS coding are still being developed. The national correct coding initiative edits and policies have also been brought over to the hospital outpatient side. Unfortunately, some of these edits and policies are not easily adaptable to hospital outpatient coding. For APCs, the simple mantra is "no code – no payment." Unless services are coded there will never be any payment under APCs. For complex coding areas, professional coding staff is essential.

As with other prospective payment systems, APCs have both a grouper and a pricer. Typically, these two programs are integrated into a single grouper/pricer program. For a hospital to know what payment is to be made, the hospital must acquire its own grouper/pricer. The case-mix index that is so useful for MS-DRGs is much less used because when grouping under APCs, multiple categories can, and most often are generated. The fact that multiple APC groups are generated also affects the statistical calculations for annually recalibrating the APC weights.

APCs are intimately involved with hospital-based clinics. These clinics come under the general provider-based rule that involves additional complications. The economic incentive for provider-based clinics is that two claims are filed: one for the professional component and one for the technical component. The professional claim is filed on the 1500 claim form and then payment, on a reduced basis, is made under the Medicare physician fee schedule. The technical claim is filed on the UB-04 and then paid under APCs. The combination of a reduced physician payment along with the hospital payment can be significantly greater than that generated at a freestanding clinic using only the 1500 claim form.

Chapter 6

Other Prospective Payment Systems

Introduction

MS-DRGs and APCs are both extremely complex prospective payment systems. Both systems have been modified and customized for other third-party payers. In this chapter we examine several other prospective payment systems, starting with Medicare-developed systems that address different types of healthcare providers. We complete the chapter with two extended case studies addressing how private third-party payers can use the PPSs developed by Medicare.

In all our discussions, keep in mind the key features of any PPS. This includes coverage, classification system, bundling of services, grouping, payment, and special features.

Notes:
1. Several of the PPSs discussed below use what are called HIPPS codes. HIPPS is an acronym for Health Insurance Prospective Payment System. These are five position alphanumeric codes used for PPSs that use a case-mix developed from a patient assessment instrument of some sort. The case-mix groups represent specific sets of patient characteristics. These HIPPS codes go onto the UB-04 or electronic equivalent and typically indicate the results of grouping or establishing the case-mix for a particular case. In each of the areas that use HIPPS codes, we briefly look at the format, and thus the content, of these HIPPS codes.
2. All the Medicare PPSs discussed in this chapter are routinely updated through the *Federal Register* process. While these *Federal Register* entries may not be as extensive as with MS-DRGs or APCs, they are still quite significant and require careful study. The usual process of proposing changes and then finalizing changes is used.

Skilled Nursing Facilities (SNFs)

Skilled nursing services abound in several different organizational settings. Traditionally, skilled nursing services were provided at freestanding SNF facilities. With greater degrees of integration, skilled nursing services may be more closely related to hospitals. There are also nursing homes that do not provide the acuity of services found in SNFs. In some cases, a facility may have both skilled beds and just nursing home beds. There are other levels of care, such as assisted living. Some facilities will have a full range of accommodations to meet varying levels of needs on the part of the patients, who are often called residents.

The Balanced Budget Act of 1997 (BBA 1997) mandated the establishment of a case-mix prospective payment system for SNFs. For cost reporting periods beginning on or after July 1, 1998, the SNFs were converted from cost based to the new PPS. Payments are based on a per-diem basis. Payment rates are adjusted for the case mix and for geographic purposes. The costs for furnishing SNF services include routine, ancillary, and capital costs.

> *Note:* The case-mix reference is to a more general concept than the case-mix index found in MS-DRGs. Case mix in this care simply refers to establishing a classification system based on a representative mix of cases. The classification system is intended to establish acuity and service levels. These acuity levels can then be used to develop the actual payment levels.

SNF services can be provided in independent skilled nursing facilities, in provider-based skilled nursing facilities, distinct part skilled nursing, or for rural areas what are called swing beds. Swing beds allow hospitals to use their beds as either a regular inpatient bed or as a skilled nursing bed. As you might imagine, there are numerous rules, regulations, and conditions of participation relative to providing skilled nursing services under the Medicare program.

On the payment side, the SNF PPS is used for virtually all skilled nursing service with the exception of critical access hospitals (CAHs), which are paid on a cost basis.

Coverage

Coverage for skilled nursing services is complex and sometimes frustrating. There are two levels:

1. Coverage for the SNF stay itself
2. Coverage of specific services under the SNF payment

CASE STUDY 6.1   OBSERVATION FOLLOWED BY INPATIENT FOLLOWED BY SKILLED NURSING

Sarah was brought to the Apex Medical Center's ED suffering from cough, congestion, fever, and general weakness. Her attending physician placed her in an observation bed and started intravenous antibiotics. She slowly improved and after 2 days in observation she was admitted to the hospital. After 2 days as an inpatient, she was much improved but she really needed skilled nursing services for a week or so. She was taken to the local nursing facility where she recovered nicely and was discharged home.

The basic facts in Case Study 6.2 are not uncommon, and this is a modified version of Case Study 4.24. As discussed with MS-DRGs, there is a great deal of emphasis on short-stay inpatient admissions such that physicians and hospitals are very sensitive to using observation in lieu of an inappropriate inpatient admission. In this case, Sarah needed inpatient care but she was in the hospital, as an inpatient, for only 2 days. This means that she did not achieve the 3-day inpatient qualifying stay for the SNF services to be covered. Thus, in this case, Sarah would have to pay for the SNF services.

Coverage of specific services is a major issue with SNF services. There is the concept of *consolidated billing*. The acronym SNF-CB is sometimes used.[*] As with other PPSs, most services provided during a covered SNF stay are bundled; that is, the complete package of care goes into the SNF PPS payment. In Case Studies 3.6 and 5.47, the provision of hyperbaric oxygen (HBO) for SNF patients is presented. HBO therapy is part of the SNF package of services under consolidated billing.

Instead of trying to list everything that is included through consolidated billing, it is easier to list those services that are not included. Here is a brief listing:

- Physician professional services
- Dialysis services
- Ambulance services
- Intensive or emergent services
- Chemotherapy and chemotherapy drugs
- Radioisotope services
- Customized prosthetics

This is only a general listing. When billing SNF services, a great deal of study must be undertaken to understand what is, and what is not, a part of consolidated billing. The bundling requirements under consolidated billing change from year to year so that both SNFs and other healthcare providers that might be affected must study the latest updates.

The circumstances described in Case Study 6.2 are quite typical. This is an emergent service that does not fall under the SNF-CB. The ambulance services will be covered and paid under the Medicare Ambulance Fee Schedule, and the services in the ED will be paid to Apex under APCs and the Clinical Laboratory Fee Schedule. However, note that for HBO services, the ambulance trips to and from Apex will not be covered separately but are part of the SNF-CB.

Case Study 6.3 presents a very technical issue with SNFs and other facility settings, including hospitals. The SNF-MS PPS pays for all services that are provided incident-to those of a

---

CASE STUDY 6.2   SNF RESIDENT ED VISIT

A resident at the Summit SNF has taken a tumble and sustained two lacerations. An ambulance brings the resident to the Apex Medical Center's ED. The patient is examined, lab tests performed, x-rays taken for possible fractures, and even a CAT scan performed to check for a possible stroke. The only injuries are the two lacerations that are repaired and the ambulance takes the patient back to Summit.

---

[*] See the CMS website: http://www.cms.gov/SNFConsolidatedBilling/ for further information.

**CASE STUDY 6.3   PHYSICIAN AND NURSE
PRACTITIONER VISITING AN SNF**

Dr. Smith from the Acme Medical Clinic goes to the Summit SNF once a month. Today he is bringing a nurse practitioner to assist him with several residents. After a busy day, Dr. Smith and the NP return to the clinic. Dr. Smith tells the billing staff to bill all the services in his name because the NP was working under his direct supervision.

physician. A physician can only bill professionally for those services that he or she personally provides in a facility setting. In Case Study 6.3, the NP's services are part of the SNF payment because they are incident to those of the physician. A better arrangement is to have the physician and NP separately bill for the services that they each provided. There will be a difference in payment because for Medicare the NP will receive only 85% of what the physician will receive (i.e., 100% of the MPFS). If the physician were to bill for the NP services, then the physician would receive 100%.

A physician must order SNF services so that there is a certification and recertification process. The issue of medical necessity for SNF services is an ongoing challenge.

Coverage for skilled nursing services under the SNF-PPS becomes fairly complicated. There are special requirements for SNF coverage, and there are significant delimitations on how long coverage can be provided. Keep in mind that the hallmark of PPSs in general is bundling and that the SNF-PPS is certainly no exception.

Classification and Grouping

The SNF PPS does not really use a coding system as such. What is used is a rather extensive instrument called the Minimum Data Set (MDS) and the Resident Assessment Instrument (RAI). This is a data set that must be filled out by nursing staff, and the intent of this instrument is to establish an acuity level for the skilled nursing services that actually comprises the case-mix process. These are RUGs (Resource Utilization Groups). The basic idea is that the information from the MDS/RAI process groups to a particular RUG from which payment can be calculated. The number of RUGs varies according to the version of RUGs that is currently in use. A typical number is in the 50 to 70 group range.

A study of the RUGs requires significant effort. Here we simply illustrate one of the RUGs in generic form. This will be enough to give you a basic idea of how RUGs classify services.

Low Rehabilitation Plus Extensive Services—RUG Category is RLX=RLX:
    Rehabilitation therapy for a minimum of 45 minutes/week
    AND
    3 days of any combination of three rehab disciplines
    AND
    Nursing rehabilitation 6 days/week, two services
    AND
    IV feeding in past 7 days
    OR
    IV medications, suctioning, tracheotomy care, or ventilator/respirator in past 14 days

AND
ADL score of 7 or more

ADL is an acronym for Activities of Daily Living. Also, we need to know what constitutes nursing rehabilitation services. They are

- Passive and/or active ROM (range of motion)
- Amputation/prosthesis care training
- Split or brace assistance
- Dressing or grooming training
- Eating or swallowing training
- Transfer training
- Bed mobility and/or walking training
- Communication training
- Scheduled toileting plan and/or bladder retraining program

As should be fairly evident with a single example such as this, developing the data that drive the RUG assignment is extremely important and becomes quite detailed very quickly.

SNF Payment

The SNF-PPS has a grouper program that takes into account all the variables, including geographic adjustments. Continuing our single RUG category of RLX, here are some approximate numbers that go into the overall calculation:

Nursing component: $480.00
Therapy component: 35.00
Non-case mix component: 80.00
Labor-related portion: 360.00
Non-labor-related portion: 155.00
Total rate: 595.00

In the data above, the total rate is the national payment; the geographic adjustment has not yet been calculated, but the labor versus non-labor split has been indicated.

When filing SNF claims, the HIPPS coding system is used. Here is the data layout:

- 1st, 2nd, and 3rd positions: RUG case-mix group (e.g., the RLX in our example)
- 4th and 5th positions: Assessment indicator – reason and timeframe for completing the MDS

SNF Issues

As you should be able to discern, the SNF-PPS is rather complicated. While it does not approach the complexity of MS-DRGs and APCs, this PPS does require extremely careful use, particularly the minimum data set and the resident assessment instrument. In particular, nursing staff must be carefully trained to fully understand how the whole process of data driving the RUG assignment and then the payment really works, as well the impact that those developing the data can have on final reimbursement.

CASE STUDY 6.4 SNF-BASED CLINIC

The Summit nursing facility has grown over the past 10 years. There is now a sizeable skilled nursing population along with an ever-growing nursing home and even assisted living. Summit is now considering establishing its own clinic and hiring physicians to mainly serve the nursing facility population. Currently, Summit has already hired two nurse practitioners, although there is no professional billing for their services.

There are aspects of the SNF-PPS that we have not discussed. For instance, there are HIPPS codes (that is, Health Insurance PPS codes) that are used on the UB-04 claim form to indicate the rate or case-mix rate information. There are also numerous compliance issues that government auditors, including the RACs (Recovery Audit Contractors), often review for possible overpayments. Also, there are issues concerning gaining billing privileges and the CMS-855 forms along with all the documentation concerning physician certification and recertification.

In concluding our brief discussion of the SNF-PPS, let us consider a different kind of issue that relates to the provider-based clinics we discussed in Chapter 5 on APCs.

Consider Case Study 6.4. Summit will need to pursue with some care the development and use of an SNF-based clinic. Under the provider-based rule, an entity that has a provider agreement with the Medicare program can establish a clinic just as do hospitals. The big questions will involve how to properly code and bill for services, what happens if a physician leaves the clinic and goes into the skilled nursing portion of the facility, and the economic advantages or disadvantages of such an arrangement.

Home Health

Home health services are growing at a rapid rate. Particularly as the Medicare population ages and the baby boom generation matures, the retired elderly population is often adamant about staying in their own homes as long as possible. There is an increasing range of home health services, including more advanced levels such as home health infusion therapy, sometimes referred to as sub-acute home health care. Also, home health can be short term with just a few visits, or this level of care can be provided for years with multiple visits each week.

As with other prospective payment systems, the HH-PPS has some unusual characteristics. The services that must be addressed by the HH-PPS include periodic nursing visits, home health aide visits, physical therapy visits, and the like. The concept of being *homebound* is important for home health services. Fundamentally, for an individual to qualify for home health services, he or she is supposed to be homebound, but just what does this mean?

Coverage

As with skilled nursing services, home health services involve two different kinds of coverage issues:

1. Coverage for providing home health services
2. Coverage of specific services under the home health payment

CASE STUDY 6.5   HOMEBOUND QUALIFICATIONS

Samantha is now well into her nineties. She can no longer walk with a cane. She is able, for brief periods, to use a walker. Her preferred method of getting around is a wheelchair. She lives alone in her home of many years. The only time she leaves her home is to go to the doctor, the dentist, and bi-weekly visits to the beauty parlor. She has even given up going to church.

As with skilled nursing, consolidated billing is used, but the consolidated billing for home health is much simpler than for skilled nursing. Nursing service, home health aide services, physical therapy, and speech therapy services are all covered. Routine and nonroutine supplies are included, as are medical social services. Generally, DME is not paid through the HH-PPS. Emergency services, physician visits, outpatient procedures, and the like are all separate. Obviously, hospital inpatient services require careful coordination of payments so that the Medicare program is not double-paying for services.

Now the question of qualifying for coverage rapidly becomes a medical necessity issue. A physician must order the home health services. An assessment, typically by a home health nurse, must be made to determine if the needs of the individual meet the criteria for home health services to apply. As mentioned above, being homebound, that is, mobility criteria, is one of the issues that must be addressed through the assessment process.

Now, the question posed in Case Study 6.5 is whether or not Samantha meets the homebound criteria in order to qualify for home health coverage. Obviously, there is a great deal of detail missing in this brief case study. The real information must be developed through the home health nurse's assessment. This process will use the patient assessment instrument.

Unit of Service/Unit of Payment

The HH-PPS uses a 60-day episode-of-care for payment purposes. For practical purposes, the unit of payment (i.e., 60-days) is also the unit of service, but there are multiple services within this 60-day period.

Consider Case Study 6.6. Stanley will probably do a combination of individual visits and then also look at a small sampling or 60-day episode-of-care cases. Keep in mind that over 60 days, there can easily be twenty-five individual visits from different healthcare providers under the home health umbrella.

Note that in Case Study 6.7 the OIG agent did not pick the 60-day episode-of-care as a case. Rather, individual visits were selected. In this case the home health agency will need to produce

CASE STUDY 6.6   AUDITING HOME HEALTH SERVICES

Stanley, a health care consultant, has been asked to conduct a study for a home health agency in Anywhere, USA. Because of the way services are provided, Stanley is concerned about how to obtain an appropriate sampling of cases. Should the cases be picked at the individual visit level, or should the cases be picked based on 60-day episodes-of-care?

CASE STUDY 6.7   OIG VISIT TO A HOME HEALTH AGENCY

An OIG agent has arrived in Anywhere, USA to conduct a probe audit at the home health agency. Apparently there have been some complaints about over-billing. The OIG agent has selected thirty individual visits by nurses. The specific visits are all for different patients and they go back up to 3 years.

---

documentation for each of the visits. The OIG agent may also contact the individual patients to confirm that the nurse did visit on the indicated dates of service.

Classification/Grouping

The classification system used by the HH-PPS is driven by a patient assessment form, namely the OASIS assessment form. OASIS is an acronym for Outcome and Assessment Information Set. This is an extensive form that requires a significant amount of time to complete. Typically, a nurse will complete this form at the time of the initial assessment and/or whenever updating is needed based on the patient's condition. The OASIS gathers information concerning the patient's medical condition and needed medical and therapy services.

The information from the OASIS is then mapped or grouped into the Home Health Resource Groups (HHRGs). There are approximately 150 different HHRGs. The groups represent the different levels of acuity for home health services or what is called the case mix to calculate the home health payment.

Home Health Payment

There is a single base rate payment amount for a 60-day episode-of-care. While the rate changes every year, a typical figure might in the $2,400.00 range. Of course, it is not quite that simple! Case Studies, 6.8, 6.9, and 6.10 illustrate some of the challenges:

As these three case studies illustrate, using a 60-day period requires that several unusual circumstances be addressed, at least for payment purposes. The home health services may be for a very limited period of time, in which case some sort of inlier adjustment should be made. Fairly frequently there will be less than 60 days of utilization. How do we account for this? Also, the patient's status may change, either by improving or by deteriorating. How will this be handled?

As with most other PPSs, the HH-PPS has a pricer program that can take all these variables into account. One variable not yet mentioned is that payments are geographically adjusted just as in all other Medicare PPSs. Other variables that must be considered are

---

CASE STUDY 6.8   HOME HEALTHCARE LIMITED TIME PERIOD

Sarah is back home after an inpatient stay and then an SNF stay with a pressure fracture of the back. She is doing reasonably well. Home health services have been established with a nursing visit twice a week, physical therapy twice a week, and a home health aide visiting three times a week. However, after only a week, she falls, fractures her hip, and is taken to the hospital.

CASE STUDY 6.9 HOME HEALTH LESS THAN 60 DAYS

Sam has returned home after a hospital stay. Only limited home health services are being provided. A nurse visits once a week and a home health aide also visits once a week. After 4 weeks, Sam has recovered to the point that he is ambulating quite well and home health services are no longer needed.

CASE STUDY 6.10 HOME HEALTH CHANGE IN STATUS

An elderly Medicare beneficiary has been receiving home health services for some time. The patient did develop an infection, which has been treated on an outpatient basis, but clearly the patient's health status has changed at least for the time being. The physician orders additional home health services.

- Low utilization payment adjustments (LUPAs)
- Partial episode payment (PEP) adjustments
- Significant change in condition (SCIC) adjustments
- Outlier payments

   Note: As with other Medicare PPSs, there are ongoing changes, some of which do become political at times. If you are a healthcare provider using the HH-PPS, then watch carefully for changes in rules, regulations, payment rates, cost-of-living updates, and the like.

The HIPPS coding system is used for home health services. Here is the data layout:

   1st Position: A numeric value representing the Grouping step
   2nd Position: Alphabetic representing the Clinical domain
   3rd Position: Alphabetic representing Functional domain
   4th Position: Alphabetic representing the Service domain
   5th Position: Supply groups

   The Grouping step relates to early versus late episodes-of-care. Clinical, functional and service data provide information for proper payment. The supply group is interesting because payment can be made for one of six different severity levels of supplies. Keep in mind that supplies must be carefully identified for those that are routine versus those that qualify for separate payment.[*] Here is a generalized set of payment levels that must, of course, be geographically adjusted and these change every year.

Base Episode-of-Care - $2,400.00	Medical Supplies
LUPA add-on - $100.00	Severity Level 1 - $ 15.00
LUPA visit rate - $55.00 Home Health Aide	Severity Level 2 - $ 55.00

---

[*] See routine versus non-routine supplies discussed with APCs.

Medical social services - $195.00	Severity Level 3 - $150.00
Occupational therapy - $135.00	Severity Level 4 - $225.00
Physical therapy - $135.00	Severity Level 5 - $330.00
Skilled Nursing - $120.00	Severity Level 6 - $600.00
Speech language pathology - $140.00	

Long-Term Care Hospitals (LTCHs)

Long-term care hospitals have a separate payment system under the Medicare program. Actually, LTCHs use a spinoff of MS-DRGs. The acronyms become a little complicated. The LTCH prospective payment system is termed the LTC-PPS and uses MS-LTCH-DRGs as the base for a modified DRG payment system. The LTC-PPS is correlated with MS-DRGs so that all the updates, payment rates, recalibration, rebasing, and other updating activities actually appear in the *Federal Register* entries that are devoted to MS-DRGs. Many of the features from MS-DRGs carry over, at least in concept. For instance, the statistical calculations for recalibration of the MS-LTCH-DRGs use the same formula as MS-DRGs, but the base claims data come from LTCHs. There is also a cost outlier to provide additional payment for unusually expensive cases.

Note: You may also see the terms "Long-term acute care hospital" utilized.

Coverage

The LTCH designation under the Medicare program applies to acute care hospitals that also meet a number of other criteria. The main criterion is that there is an average length of stay of 25 days. As the name implies, these are hospitals that treat patients requiring longer stays due to extensive comorbidities and/or complications. These hospitals are often developed in conjunction with a short-term acute care hospital. Consider Case Study 6.11.

While this is just an idea, a great deal of research will be needed. For instance, is there a patient population that can sustain this model? Will it be difficult to obtain the LTCH designation? Is there a financial advantage in having an LTCH for these cases? This same model can be considered for satellite operation, that is, having a satellite campus. This sometimes arises when two hospitals merge and the short-term acute care services are all moved to the main campus. The satellite campus might better support an LTCH.

CASE STUDY 6.11   LTCH INSIDE AN ACUTE CARE HOSPITAL

A large metropolitan hospital has encountered a challenge. The hospital is having more and more patients who are quite sick with multiple disease processes. These patients are requiring a month or more of care in order to properly recover. The idea has arisen that part of the acute care hospital space, the third and fourth floors, be dedicated to such patients and that a hospital-within-a-hospital be established with an LTCH designation.

> ### CASE STUDY 6.12   TRANSFER TO LTCH
>
> Sam has been at the Apex Medical Center for 10 days. The MS-DRG to which his services group has a GMLOS of 8 days. Sam has several rather severe comorbidities. There is an LTCH in the area that can better address Sam's needs on a longer-term basis. Sam is transferred, remains at the LTCH for 6 weeks, and is discharged home under a home health plan of care.

Whenever there is a condition such as an average length-of-stay of 25 days, the whole issue of counting days suddenly becomes important. This is a Medicare designation, so does the 25-day length-of-stay apply only to Medicare? Or can other types of patients be counted in the calculation?

Based on the discussion in Chapter 4, you should start to ask yourself questions about what carries over from MS-DRGs to the LTC-PPS. For instance, in Case Study 6.12 the transfer in this case is from a PPS hospital to a PPS hospital. Thus, the normal transfer rules apply. In this case, for Apex, Sam exceeded the GMLOS of 8 days so that there is no reduction in payment for Apex. Sam is eventually discharged to a home health plan of care. Does the MS-DRG post-acute care transfer rule apply to LTCHs?

Classification and Grouping for LTCHs

The LTCH-PPS uses exactly the same MDCs and DRGs as those used for MS-DRGs. The overall grouping process uses ICD-10 diagnosis and procedure codes. Thus, coding for the LTCH-PPS is essentially the same. However, the data used to generate the relative weights and GMLOS are from LTCHs, and thus the weights and the LOS data are quite different. Look at Table 6.1. The MS-LTC-DRG weights are much closer to 1.0000. This makes some sense because the development of the weights is based, loosely, on a 25-day stay. Also, the GMLOS for the MS-LTC-DRGs is significantly longer, as would be expected for the types of services being provided. The general expectation of GMLOS would be in the 25-or-more-day range. The SSO (Short Stay Outlier)

Table 6.1   MS-LTCH DRG versus MS-DRGs

MS-LTC-DRG	Base MS-LTC-DRG	MS-LTC Weight	MS-DRG Weight	MS-LTC DRG Geometric Mean Length-of-Stay (GMLOS)	MS-DRG Geometric Mean Length-of-Stay (GMLOS)	Short Stay Outlier (SSO) Threshold
326	326	1.7000	5.9000	37.0	13.0	30.8
327	326	0.8000	2.8000	25.0	7.0	20.8
328	326	0.6000	1.4000	22.0	3.0	18.3
391	391	0.9500	1.2000	23.0	4.0	19.2
392	391	0.6000	0.7000	19.0	2.8	15.8

threshold is something new relative to the other PPSs that we have discussed. While this involves a payment calculation, we do look at this in this section of the text.

Given the 25-day stay requirement, what happens if the patient is in the LTCH for a period shorter than the GMLOS? Well, there should probably be a reduction in payment. While this is mathematically an outlier, for healthcare payment purposes, this may be referred to as an inlier. So how is the SSO threshold calculated? The formula is to take 5/6th of the GMLOS as the SSO threshold. This means that potentially there will be a reimbursement decrease if the patient is not in the LTCH at least for a period of time that is 5/6th of the normal stay (i.e., GMLOS).

The formula, or more correctly the algorithm, used to calculate the SSO payment is quite convoluted. For those of you who like a challenge, here is the algorithm:

The SSO payment is the lowest of:
The full MS-LTC-DRG payment,
120% of the MS-LTC-DRG per-diem payment,
100% of the cost of the case using provider-specific CCR,
A blend of:
The IPPS (MS-DRG) calculated as a per diem and capped at the full IPPS MS-DRG amount, and
120% of the MS-LTC-DRG per-diem amount.

Clearly, this calculation will be left to the MS-LTC-DRG pricer software.

MS-LTC-DRG Pricer

The pricer for the LTCH-PPS is a modified form of the MS-DRG pricer. What is needed is the conversion factor or base rate for the LTCH-PPS. The base rate is generally in the $40,000.00 to $42,000.00 range. This base rate, as with the other data with the LTCH-PPS, varies each year and is generally increased by some sort of cost-of-living adjustment. There is also the geographic adjustment, as with other Medicare payment systems.

There are cost outliers. The cost outlier threshold is in the $20,000.00 range. This means that a given case would need to have costs that are greater than $20,000.00 to even be considered for additional payment. There is the usual labor versus non-labor adjustment process, and the wage index is still used as in MS-DRGs. The labor versus non-labor ratio is in the 75% to 25% range.

Other Features for the LTCH-PPS

As with other Medicare PPSs, quality and quality reporting is an issue that continues to develop. For LTCHs, issues such as urinary catheter associated urinary tract infections and pressure ulcers are of concern. The present-on-admission (POA) indicator and possible reimbursement reductions by eliminating certain diagnoses from the grouping process is an issue.

The bottom-line is that the LTCH-PPS is an interesting spinoff of MS-DRGs. This payment system has been developed to address a specific type of service and associated service providers. Note that in studying the MS-LTC-DRGs, the data upon which the weights are calculated are really quite minimal. Whereas MS-DRGs have hundreds of millions of claims, MS-LTC-DRGs may have only thousands of claims that are used for the calculations.

Also, by the very nature of LTCHs, there are payment system interfaces that do come into play. In some situations, services provided by an LTCH may be similar to those provided by skilled nursing or an inpatient rehabilitation facility. Thus, the questions arise: Are there any payment incentives to provide the same services in one type of facility versus another?

Inpatient Rehabilitation Facilities

The IRF-PPS provides reimbursement for hospitals and hospital units that can meet certain requirements under the Medicare program. If the requirements are met, then the hospital falls under the IRF-PPS. As with skilled nursing and home health, the whole process of classification and grouping is driven by a rather extensive patient assessment instrument called the IRF-PAI. The IRF must have grouper software to process the specific data elements from the PAI to obtain a specific HIPPS code. The appropriate HIPPS code is placed on the UB-04 to gain reimbursement.

The two main issues for IRFs are

1. Qualifying
2. The Patient Assessment Instrument (PAI)

An IRF provides services only in certain circumstances. Here are some examples of the types of conditions that require intensive rehabilitation services:

■ Stroke
■ Spinal code injury
■ Congenital deformity
■ Amputation
■ Major multiple trauma
■ Hip fracture
■ Brain injury
■ Burns

This list is not exhaustive and other criteria may apply. Let us join Sarah in Case Study 6.13.

Now the big question is whether or not Sarah qualifies to goes to the IRF unit. Because she had bilateral knee replacement and she is older than 85 years, she may qualify.

For a hospital or hospital unit to be classified as an IRF, the qualified services must represent a preponderance of the services provided. This is called the *compliance percentage threshold*. In other words, to be classified as an IRF, most of the services provided to patients must fall within those services delineated by the Medicare program. See the partial list above. If the IRF fails to

CASE STUDY 6.13—BILATERAL KNEE REPLACEMENT

Sarah has finally agreed to have knee replacement on both sides. She goes to the Apex Medical Center where the surgical procedure is performed and things go well. She is in the hospital for 5 days and then she needs to move to either a skilled nursing facility or to the inpatient rehabilitation unit of the hospital.

meet this compliance percentage threshold, then the IRF will fall back into the regular IPPS payment process.

The second major issue for IRFs is the proper use of the IRF-PAI. The patient assessment instrument is not particularly long, but great care must be taken in completing the form with proper information. ICD-10 coding is required so that competent coding staff must be utilized. Here are some brief examples of the type of data collected:

- Medical needs:
  - Comatose
  - Delirious
  - Swallowing status:
    - Regular food
    - Modified Food
    - Parenteral feeding
- Functional modifiers:
  - Bladder assistance/accidents
  - Bowel assistance/accidents
- Self-care
- Locomotion

The IRFs use HIPPS codes. Here is the layout:

1st Position: Comorbidity tier
2nd, 3rd, 4th, and 5th Positions: Case-mix group

Inpatient Psychiatric Facilities (IPFs)

Hospitals may have an inpatient psychiatric unit or an entire hospital may be devoted to inpatient psychiatric services. As you might imagine, there is a special PPS that is used to reimburse IPFs. Basically, IPFs are exempt from the IPPS, and the IPF PPS provides for a per diem payment rate. This daily payment amount is adjusted when the final calculation is made. We have been calling the process of calculating the payment a pricer.

Now the MS-DRG grouper is used for IPFs. So the grouping process consists of coding a case through ICD-10 codes.* The psychiatric cases group to one of seventeen allowed MS-DRG categories or groups. MS-DRG payment is not calculated. For IPF payment, everything revolves around the base rate, which is adjusted to determine the overall per-diem payment. The base rate is adjusted each year, basically for cost-of-living increases. The base rate runs in the $700.00 range.

Here is a brief synopsis of the flow for pricing:

- Base rate, which is
  - Adjusted for geographic factors (76%–24% labor to non-labor via wage index)
  - Adjusted for facility factors (geographic adjustments)
  - Adjusted for patient or PPS factors (*see* MS-DRG categories)

---

* See also, DSM-IV codes (Diagnostic and Statistical Manual of Mental Disorders).

    – Adjusted for variable per-diem factors

    – Checked for addition of services outside the base rate

■ Checked for possibility of cost outlier

As should be expected after studying other PPSs, there are a number of idiosyncrasies with the IPF PPS. Case Studies 6.14, 6.15, and 6.16 illustrate some of these unusual characteristics.

In Case Study 6.15 the fundamental question is: Can the hospital charge separately for the ER visit and the laceration repair. The answer is no. Once the inpatient admission, in this case to an IPF, has commenced, services such as those with the emergency department are part of the IRF payment. The good news is that the payment calculation does allow for some additional payment for ER services under certain circumstances. Other extra payment may be made for rural locations and teaching situations.

ECT services are paid separately from the per-diem payment for IPFs. This is a part of the pricer program with an extra payment being added in for each ECT service.

As with other PPSs that we have discussed, the issue in Case Study 6.16 is whether this is simply an interrupted stay or a true discharge with a new admission. For IPFs, a 3-day rule is used. If the patient is re-admitted within 3 days of a discharge, then it is simply an interrupted stay.

We have discussed only some of the payment issues for IPFs from the perspective of the IPF-PPS. This PPS is unusual in that a per-diem base rate is the main unit of payment. This per-diem base rate goes through a number of adjustments before final payment is made. Note that there are many coverage issues for Medicare beneficiaries in terms of how long services can be provided. Also, the typical deductibles and copayment issues are present.

CASE STUDY 6.14   ER UTILIZATION WHILE IN IPF

Sydney has been having some problems and he is admitted to the distinct part inpatient psychiatric unit on Monday morning. Later that day, he injuries himself, apparently an accident from a fall, sustaining several lacerations. He is taken to the emergency department where the lacerations are repaired and he returns to the IPF.

CASE STUDY 6.15   ECT SERVICES

One of the physicians at the Apex Medical Center performs ECT (electro-convulsive therapy), including patients at the distinct part IPF. This is a relatively expensive service and there is concern that this service may simply be part of the IPF base rate.

CASE STUDY 6.16   INTERRUPTED STAY VERSUS DISCHARGE

On Monday morning, Sydney is finally being discharged from the IPF. Several family members pick him up and take him home. However, on Wednesday, after being taken to the emergency department at Apex, he is readmitted to the IPF unit.

End-Stage Renal Dialysis (ESRD)

The last Medicare PPS that we discuss is for outpatient ESRD. This is a relatively new PPS. The 4-year transitional process of full implementation started on January 1, 2011. This PPS literally pays for just one service, namely dialysis. Of course, healthcare payment is never that simple. The dialysis service along with certain pharmaceuticals, laboratory tests, and supplies are included into the dialysis payment. Other pharmaceuticals and supplies are paid outside the ESRD PPS payment. Thus, the ESRD PPS has consolidated billing just as is found in the SNF PPS, although on a much simpler basis. The bundling of these additional items also addresses one of the key features of a PPS; that is, there is significant bundling.

These outpatient services are generally provided at Medicare-certified dialysis facilities. Even in modest-sized communities, it is not unusual to have freestanding facilities or facilities that are part of an integrated delivery system, although they are organizationally independent. ESRD-certified facilities may also provide dialysis services for hospital patients under contract with the hospital.

Dialysis services can be provided in a patient's home under certain circumstances. For home dialysis services, there is a choice. The patient may elect to have the ESRD-certified facility provide the services; this is Method I. The facility is paid the same amount as they would if the patient came to the facility. As usual, there is a deductible and coinsurance of 20% for Medicare.

The patient may also choose Method II, in which case the supplies and equipment are provided by a DME (durable medical equipment) supplier and are paid under the DMEPOS fee schedule. The DME supplier must accept assignment for the Medicare program. Deductibles and copayments are still present. Home or self-dialysis training is necessary.

The classification system is trivial because we are dealing with a single service, dialysis, for which there will be a bundled payment. However, there is still a grouping process that used a case-mix approach. The elements that determine the case mix include

- Age Range:
  - <18 years
  - 18–44 years
  - 45–59 years
  - 60–69 years
  - 70–79 years
  - ≥80 years
- Body surface area (BSA)
- Body mass index (BMI)
- Pediatric status
- Selected comorbidities

Additionally, as with virtually all Medicare PPSs, there is a geographic adjustment using the wage index for a given geographic area. For unusually resource-intensive cases, there is even a cost outlier that is available. There are even payment adjustments for low-volume facilities.

As mentioned, there is consolidated billing. The main challenge here is to determine what additional supplies, pharmacy items, and tests are outside the consolidated billing and thus outside inclusion in what is called the base rate, which is the basic PPS payment amount. Those items not included are

- Physician's professional services
- Separately billable laboratory services
- Separately billable drugs
- Blood and blood products
- Bad debt

This is one of the simplest prospective payment systems that provides payment for a single service. Even with this system, there are complexities. There is a case-mix adjustment that affects the final payment and there is also a consolidated billing feature. All the key elements are present for a PPS, albeit somewhat simplified in certain cases.

Private Third-Party Payer Utilization of PPSs

In preceding chapters we discussed MS-DRGs for IPPS and APCs for OPPS. Previously in this chapter we briefly reviewed several other PPSs for home health, skilled nursing, rehabilitation, psychiatric, dialysis services, and long-term care hospitals. During the past 25 years, the state Medicare program has been quite busy developing and refining various PPSs. Note that the Medicaid program also sometimes uses prospective payment, generally based on what the Medicare program uses.

Private third-party payers can and do use PPSs as developed by the Medicare program. In almost every instance, the private payer will make modifications to the existing framework developed by Medicare and even modified systems utilized by other private payers. The discussion of any specific implementation can fill a separate manual.

Thus, we will discuss private payer utilization of PPSs using two extended case studies. The first case study is from the perspective of the Apogee Health System. In the second case study, we join the financial analysts and actuaries at the Maximus Insurance Company.

For the Apogee Health System here is the rundown of the proposed changes from this TPP:

- Inpatient: MS-DRGs with a 20% increase above the Medicare payment rate
- Outpatient: An enhanced form of APGs using local incidence and charge data
- Home Health: HH-PPS with a 25% increase above the Medicare payment rate
- Skilled Nursing: RUGs classification with a 15% increase above the Medicare payment rate

While Case Study 6.17 is provided only for educational purposes, there are times when healthcare providers are faced with major changes; the number and magnitude of changes in this case study is significant. For this case, three of the four payment areas are utilizing well-known PPSs

---

CASE STUDY 6.17   PROPOSED USE OF PROSPECTIVE PAYMENT

The Apogee Health System now consists of three hospitals, along with a wide variety of clinics, nursing facilities, and home health. There is one major private third-party payer (TPP) that represents nearly 40% of the revenue stream. The TPP is in the process of converting payments from a percentage of charges payment system to several modified prospective payment systems. Currently, the percentage of charges payment level is 85%.

developed by the Medicare program. For outpatient services, the new payment process is utilizing an outpatient prospective payment system that is not known. Our first analysis is the APG system being utilized and then we will return to the other three PPSs for further analysis. For our purposes, we designate the new APG system as N-APGs.

For the N-APG system, the following steps should be addressed:

1. Understand the N-APG system.
2. Assess the financial impact of this new payment process.
3. Assess the operational impact of the new payment system.
4. Study any peripheral issues such as patient relations, physician relations, and interface issues.

First, the N-APG system must be examined and studied. In our previous discussions, a template has been provided and can be used as a systematic way to analyze a given PPS. Here are the main components:

- Coverage
- Unit of service and unit of payment
- Classification system
- Grouping process
- Payment calculation

So for the N-APG system, the coverage of services must be identified, including any services or items excluded from payment. For instance, APCs do not cover physical therapy and occupational therapy. So what about N-APGs? Also, what about laboratory? Is this included in N-APGs, or is it separated out for separate payment on some other basis. Durable medical equipment may also be an issue relative to coverage or non-coverage.

Also, there may be requirements for preauthorizations to obtain coverage for a particular service such as surgeries and special oncology services. There may even be some delimitation on who can provide the services (e.g., physicians versus practitioners) in order for coverage to apply.[*]

The unit of service and unit of payment, if different, must be determined. For virtually all hospital outpatient prospective payment systems, the unit of service is the same as the unit of payment which is an encounter. The concept of an encounter and the many possible variations for implementing this concept has been previously discussed; see Chapter 5. How the encounter is established in N-APGs can have a significant impact operationally and also affect the N-APG grouping process. For instance, if a 3-day window of service is used, then there may be specific claims filing requirements relative to having all services in the 3-day window on the same claim.

The typical classification system for outpatient prospective payment involves CPT and HCPCS. However, ICD-10 could also be used to some extent. For instance, for the E/M levels, the diagnosis codes could be used to drive the proper E/M level payment. Both CPT and HCPCS are extensive code sets, and numerous coding guidelines are necessary to ensure proper use of the codes and associated modifiers. Thus, the question of what coding guidelines are to be used is quite appropriate. In addition to impacting the overall payment for services, there could also be operational impacts through the need to provide special training for coding staff.

---

[*] While the Medicare program has recognized many non-physician practitioners for payment purposes, private third-party payers may or may not recognize any given non-physician practitioner classification.

The grouper/pricer for N-APGs should be acquired and testing for selected cases should be undertaken. While the grouper/pricer will be needed to assess financial impacts, there is also the concern about how cases group. Are there edits? If so, how many edits? How were the edits developed? What about modifier utilization? Also, is there discounting for surgeries or other services? In general, what kind of bundling is involved in the N-APGs?

Continuing with the pricer, are there any geographical adjustments? What about any sort of cost outlier or cost inlier? Care should be taken to see if there are any other unusual logic constructs within the grouper/pricer. For instance, is there any sort of global surgical package? What about pre-operative and post-operative encounters?

After studying the critical elements of N-APGs, a careful assessment of the financial impact for the N-APG system must be considered. There are two basic approaches to take:

1. Process a historical file of claims through the N-APG grouper/pricer to see what N-APGs would pay for these historical claims.
2. Develop specific sets of cases that represent either a general case mix or sets of services that are specific to selected service areas.

With either approach, Apogee financial analysts will have to develop sets of claims that meet any special requirements for coding and claims filing that might exist within N-APGs. In some sense these sets of claims can provide a benchmark for analysis.

One fairly tractable area is the emergency department. It is not difficult to generate a set of, say, fifty cases that can then be processed through the N-APG grouper/pricer to see how payments are being made. The payment amounts under N-APGs and the previous payment process can then be compared. Another area that will be of interest is the catheterization laboratory where coronary and vascular catheterizations are performed. Also, any clinics that are owned or operated by the hospital are of interest. A key question for N-APGs will be how this system does or does not address the whole provider-based clinic issue.

If this approach is pursued for other service areas, then virtually all the outpatient areas covered by N-APGs will be addressed. If significant reductions in payments are found, Apogee may need to further negotiate the contracts for the use of N-APGs.

The historical approach is probably the most accurate way to determine possible financial impact. If a set of claims over a 6-month time period can be developed and then processed through the N-APG grouper/pricer, a comparison of reimbursement under the new and old approaches can be compared. As with the mix-of-cases approach, the claims themselves may need modification for any special coding and billing requirements under N-APGs.

The third step is to consider operational impacts. Interestingly, there may be some very real changes that must be considered. Certainly there may be some coding and billing requirements that must be used that may not have been necessary in the previous percentage of charges payment system. For instance, there may be modifiers that must now be used. New edits will probably be put into place. The chargemasters at the hospital may also need updating and changes implemented. For instance, some items such as expensive supplies and devices may be paid on a cost pass-through basis, but, by contract, the charge can only be 20% above acquisition cost.

Utilization review may also become involved due to frequency limitations on certain services. Certainly there will be increased edits relative to certain services in the N-APGs. Keep in mind that Apogee is changing from a percentage-of-charges contract to prospective payment.

Percentage-of-charges contracts are generally very straightforward. Under PPSs of any type, there will be more delimitation for coding, billing, and associated utilization of services.

The fourth area for consideration is patient relations, physician relations, and any other possible concerns. On the patient side, the process of informing and educating patients is really the responsibility of the insurance company implementing the new payment mechanisms. In reality, patients will often have questions and want answers at the time services are provided or certainly after they receive their explanation of benefits (EOBs). For the Apogee Health System this means that system personnel must be fully trained and ready to address questions.

Throughout this text the extremely important role of documentation is discussed. In moving to a PPS of any type, physician behavior relative to documentation, among other issues, is vitally important. Thus, Apogee will need to work through the medical staff organizations at the different system providers to develop proper training and acclimation to the new PPS payment processes being used. Another indirect issue is how the N-APGs will interface to other payment processes provided under this insurance contract.

In addition to the grouping logic, the Apogee analysts will want to consider how the relative weights were calculated for N-APGs and then also how the payment rate was determined. Note that in the case study local claims data were used to develop this system. Thus, the weights and associated payment rate may be vastly different from any other APC or APG payment system. Because local claims data are being used, the volume of data for certain N-APG categories may be minimal. Are all the weights within a reasonable range? If some categories are well outside what appears normal, then this should be questioned.

Now that the major issues relative to changing to the N-APGs have been discussed, consideration must be given to the other changes for inpatient, home health, and skilled nursing. Fortunately these service areas will be moving to payment based on well-known and generally refined PPSs from the Medicare program. Many of the operational impacts will be mitigated because the same PPSs or very similar PPSs are being used for Medicare beneficiaries.

One question that must be addressed for each of PPSs is whether or not there are any modifications that have been made. For instance, the insurance company may be using MS-DRGs and then paying 20% above, but certain services such as neonatal and pediatrics may be broken out in some fashion. There may even be some sort of modification, such as that discussed with the TRICARE MS-DRGs. In the skilled nursing area, there may be changes in what is included in the consolidated billing. For instance, the insurance company may have decided to pay for hyperbaric oxygen therapy separately. For home health, there may be some sort of special arrangements for physical and occupational therapy.

The second major concern for these well-established PPSs will be the financial impact. As discussed above with the N-APGs, a historical analysis can be performed or a model may be developed that reflects the mix of cases provided in the given service area. Apogee will want to have a very good idea of how overall reimbursement will be affected for the inpatient, home health, and skilled nursing areas.

In summary for Case Study 6.17, throughout this text a template has been developed to understand prospective payment systems. This template can be used as a tool to assess and analyze any given PPS. For this case study there are several different PPSs. For the Apogee Health System, one of the new payment systems is N-APGs. We have discussed the application of the template to this new system in order for Apogee to understand what is happening. Also, if necessary, revising the contract may be necessary if the financial projections show significantly different payment levels from the current percentage-of-charges contract.

**CASE STUDY 6.18   MAXIMUS INSURANCE
COMPANY UTILIZATION OF PPSS**

Maximus has been growing at a fairly rapid pace. Marketing has begun in two additional states. The time has come to gain more control over expenditures to hospitals, clinics, physicians, and other healthcare providers. The financial analysts at Maximus are looking at making changes in the following areas:

- Inpatient: Currently a per-diem surgery/per-diem medical; move to inpatient PPS of some sort.
- Outpatient: Currently a percentage of charges; move to some form of APCs.
- Home Health: Currently a flat rate nursing visit/flat rate home health aide visit – other services at charges; this is a low-volume area, but cost containment with some sort of packaged approach is desired, particularly with supplies.
- Skilled Nursing: Currently a per diem; this area is growing and cost containment is desired.

Switching gears, Case Study 6.18 represents a different perspective is now considered. This time, the perspective is that of an insurance company considering prospective payment as a way to better control their costs, that is, the amount that is paid out to healthcare providers for patients covered by the insurance company.

As with the Apogee Health System case study, some sort of systematic approach is needed in order for Maximus to develop and implement prospective payment systems.

For inpatient services, Maximus is using a per-diem payment approach for inpatient services and is differentiating medical cases from surgical cases. Actually, Maximus is already using a very simplified prospective payment system. Maximus has probably established a per-diem payment rate for each of the two types of services, that is, inpatient medical and inpatient surgical. Thus, payments are fixed in advance. The classification is just the two types of services and the grouping uses the type of service (i.e., surgical versus medical). Obviously this is a very simplified prospective payment system.

The issue for Maximus is how to move to a much more detailed and robust inpatient prospective payment system so that costs can be contained while still being able to negotiate contracts with healthcare providers. Certainly, Maximus is not in a position to develop from scratch a full-blown inpatient prospective payment system. The current two-level system could easily be enhanced to more categories, such as using the MDCs from various DRG systems. The MDCs could then better differentiate the payments for the inpatient services.

On the inpatient side, the next step would be to consider piggybacking on an already existent DRG system such as the Medicare MS-DRGs. Perhaps a payment rate of 35% above the MS-DRG payment might be used. This way, all the hard work for developing a PPS has been accomplished. The coding, grouping, and payment processes are already in place. Most likely, Maximus will want to make changes. Perhaps only the operating cost reimbursement will be provided, but not the capital. Also, there may not be recognition of any of the Medicare special designations.

Basically, if a current DRG system is used for piggybacking, the analyst at Maximus will need to go through the entire template that we have discussed for PPSs in general and then special features that are endemic to inpatient DRG systems.

For outpatient services, Maximus will need to go through an analysis similar to that discussed with the N-APGs in Case Study 6.17. Maximus will need to consider some sort of grouping system to better categorize the outpatient services. Most likely this will entail adopting the classifications from an existing APC or APG payment system. While there are multiple grouping and payment issues, the biggest concern will probably be the relative weights for any system that Maximus might adopt. The question here is whether or not Maximus would like to use its own claims experience in developing the weights versus using an already established system. If Maximus decides to use its own claims data, then several years of claims data will need careful analysis even after the specific APC/APG implementation has been selected.

Whatever the case, Maximus will need to carefully consider a move from a percentage-of-charges to a full-blown outpatient prospective payment system. An intermediate step in this type of progression would be to adopt an APC/APG system and then increase the conversion factor or simply pay a percentage above the payment rate calculated from the given APC/APG system. This will give Maximus the time that is needed to fully assess various options, including moving to using their own claims to develop the relative weights.

For home health services, with the information contained in the case study, Maximus may have some time to fully explore any options that might exist. Currently, this is a low volume area that is growing. The HH-PPS developed by the Medicare program does provide for acuity of care differentiation. The HH-PPS is driven by a patient assessment instrument called OASIS that can easily be adopted by Maximus along with the publicly available grouping software that takes the patient assessment data and converts it into a HIPPS code. The main decisions that Maximus will need to make involve peripheral considerations such as separate payment for unusual supplies and the overall payment rate. For Maximus this may be one of the easier systems to quickly adopt with some modifications.

Skilled nursing will be a bigger challenge for Maximus. To better delineate services, some sort of acuity classification is needed. The Medicare SNF-PPS will certainly provide such an acuity classification through the RUGs. This is a data-driven system using the patient assessment process involving the minimum data set. Certainly for Maximus, the use of the minimum data set and the various groups under RUGs will be attractive. Also, as the Medicare program updates the RUGs, Maximus can also update as appropriate.

For the Medicare program, there is the process of consolidated billing. While Maximus will need to consider payment rates, an easy approach would be to simply use a percentage increase about the Medicare rate. Also, the various rules for consolidated billing must be addressed. Thus, the analysts at Maximus will need to carefully go through the various consolidated billing requirements to determine which of these requirements should be retained and/or if any new requirements should be put into place.

The analysts and actuaries at the Maximus Insurance Company can certainly consider piggybacking on the different PPSs that have been developed by the Medicare program. Careful analysis will be needed along with extensive financial projections. Typically, a number of features will be changed with some new features added. For Maximus, a regional company, to actually develop a new PPS from the ground up would be overly burdensome and such an investment is unlikely.

In summary, for Maximus, many of the same concerns surrounding PPSs are very much the same as for healthcare providers. The perspective is the opposite; healthcare providers receive payments while Maximus is concerned about making payments. Fortunately for Maximus and other private third-party payers, there is an ever-increasing number of PPSs that have been developed by the Medicare program.

Summary and Conclusion

We have considered a number of other PPSs in this chapter. The SNF-PPS and the HH-PPS are both rather complex systems that are data driven through some sort of patient assessment instrument. For these two payment systems, the actual grouping is performed by the healthcare provider with appropriate software provided through Medicare. The grouping process generates a code that indicates the acuity and level of services being provided. It is this code that actually drives the actual payment for a unit of service. For home health services, the HH-PPS pays on a 60-day payment unit. Skilled nursing is on a per-diem arrangement. Coverage through medical necessity is a key issue for both skilled nursing and home health services. One of the interesting concepts for home health is that of being homebound.

Long-Term Care Hospitals (LTCHs) have a relatively new PPS, the LTC-PPS using MS-LTC-DRGs. This PPS is a rather major modification of MS-DRGs. While the grouping of cases to a specific MS-DRG remains essentially the same, the development of weights and associated payment levels is quite different. While the level of services for LTCHs may be essentially the same as for short-term acute care hospitals, the emphasis is on longer-term care generally centered around 25 days.

Inpatient psychiatric hospitals and inpatient rehabilitation hospitals now also have their own prospective payment systems. The terms used are typically *inpatient psychiatric facilities* and *inpatient rehabilitation facilities.* Often these types of services are provided in distinct part units of other hospitals. Both types of providers have rather unique PPSs under Medicare. For instance, for psychiatric payment there is a per-diem national base rate. The pricing process for this base rate actually constitutes most of what would ordinarily be grouping in other PPSs.

Additionally, the use of PPSs by private third-party payers has been illustrated by two extended case studies. The variations of PPSs used by private third-party payers are numerous and are typically developed on a contractual basis. Private third-party payers often piggyback on Medicare PPSs. A healthcare payer must make numerous decisions and analyze possible changes when adopting a specific PPS.

For healthcare providers that are paid through a modified PPS, there are also considerations that must be made. This text offers a simple template for this type of analysis, including

■ Coverage
■ Unit of service and unit of payment
■ Classification system
■ Grouping process
■ Payment calculation

Conclusion and Endnote

Prospective payment systems are complex. Well, at least they can be complex. If the range of services is extensive, such as hospital inpatient or hospital outpatient services, then extreme complexity is almost assured. Hospital inpatient services cover a broad spectrum of medical and surgical services. Hospital outpatient services represent an even broader diversity of services. Thus, the prospective payment systems for hospital inpatient (i.e., MS-DRGs) and hospital outpatient services (i.e., APCs) are quite detailed with convoluted grouping logic. In recent years there has even been a split between short-term acute care hospitals and long-term care hospitals with a separate prospective payment process for long-term care hospitals (i.e., MS-LTC-DRGs).

If the range of services addressed is significantly delimited, then the degree of complexity can be reduced. For example, the end-stage renal dialysis prospective payment system is basically a bundling of dialysis and associated supplies and care. This system uses a case-mix adjustment with just a few factors to determine the case-mix that then adjusts the payment for these external factors. Ostensibly, this system is more basic because there is really only a single service that is covered by the payment process.

Prospective payment is characterized by significant bundling. PPSs are different from fee schedule payment systems in that payment is not the lesser of the charges or the fee schedule payment amount. Under a PPS, payment is made regardless of the charges made. Under PPS, charges are still important, but only on a more global basis. For some PPSs, the charges for services are converted to costs using a cost reporting process. The cost data are then statistically analyzed to generate relative values for services within a classification system and then payment is calculated.

The number of PPSs is increasing, particularly under the Medicare program. Additionally, private payers also use prospective payment often by modifying Medicare PPSs. The principles remain the same; the specific implementations may be quite different.

To understand prospective payment systems, you need some sort of systematic way to study these payment systems. A template to look at the standard features within any PPS has been provided for your use. Keep in mind that certain features within the template may be exaggerated for one system and then minimized in another system. Thus, two systems may appear very different and still be properly classified as prospective payment systems.

Be certain to enjoy your studies of healthcare payment systems. They are in a state of constant change and will only become more complex over time.

Duane C. Abbey, Ph.D.
Duane@aaciweb.com
www.aaciweb.com

Appendix A: Case Studies

Chapter 1 Case Studies

Case Study 1.1—*Emergency Department Visit Involving Finger Splint*—An individual has presented to a hospital's emergency department after twisting his right index finger. The ER physician performs a general examination to make certain there are no other problems except for the twisted finger. The physician examines the finger. Routine laboratory tests are performed just for safety. Based on x-rays, there is no fracture, only a sprain, and a finger splint is applied to protect the finger during the healing process. The patient is discharged home with a supply of analgesics for pain control.

Case Study 1.2—*Medicare Plus a Percentage*—The Maximus Insurance Company (MIC) provides healthcare insurance. Payments must be made for hospital inpatient services. To simplify the process, MIC has decided to simply reimburse hospitals whatever Medicare pays through APCs plus 25%.

Case Study 1.3—*Medicare Supplemental Insurance*—Sydney has been on Medicare for about 10 years. He uses Medicare traditional and then has a supplemental policy. Sydney has been very pleased because when he goes to his primary care physician or even a specialist, he does not have to pay anything out of pocket.

Case Study 1.4—*Spouse with Group Health Plan*—Stephen is fortunate enough to have a spouse who is still working and he is covered under a group health insurance plan. He has Medicare as secondary. When he goes to the doctor or has services at the hospital, he often receives multiple documents explaining benefits and payments and sometimes he must pay some of the bill.

Chapter 2 Case Studies

Case Study 2.1—*Clinical Nurse Specialist versus Nurse Practitioner*—The Apex Medical Center (AMC) employs a clinical nurse specialist (CNS) who is devoted to oncology services. The CNS works closely with specialty physicians in providing oncology services. Apex has decided not to file professional claims for the CNS. However, there is a nurse practitioner (NP) who works in two different provider-based clinics and Apex has decided to file professional claims for the NP.

Case Study 2.2—*Freestanding Clinic inside the Apex Medical Center*—A new internal medicine physician has come to Anywhere, USA. The physician wants to start an independent practice. The Apex Medical Center offers to rent space to the new physician, including nursing and clerical staff. A suite of offices and examination rooms are provided on the third floor of the hospital.

Case Study 2.3—*Hospital-Owned and -Operated Clinics*—The Apex Medical Center has acquired two different family practice clinics, both of which are about 20 miles away in opposite directions. Apex decides to operate one of the clinics as provider-based by filing two different claims, one for the professional and one for the technical component. Due to competitive pressures, the other clinic is operated as a freestanding clinic and files only the 1500 form.

Case Study 2.4—*Orthopedic Specialty Hospital*—The Apex Medical Center is a general short-term, acute care hospital. Two years ago, a specialty hospital addressing only certain types of orthopedic surgeries was established about 2 miles down the road. The specialty hospital does not have an emergency department (ED). Apex views the specialty hospital as siphoning off the more common orthopedic services such as knee replacements and hip repairs that are being performed at the specialty hospital.

Case Study 2.5—*Per-Diem Payment for Inpatient Services*—The Apex Medical Center is reviewing a contract with a private insurance company. The payment methodology for inpatient services is quite simple. There is a per-diem payment rate for medical cases and another higher payment rate for surgical cases.

Case Study 2.6—*LTCH inside a Short-Term Acute Care Hospital*—A large metropolitan hospital has discovered that it has numerous long-term patients, some staying for up to 2 months or even longer in some cases. Better reimbursement as an LTCH appears to offer a solution. As a result, the hospital is reorganizing one floor of the hospital to accommodate a hospital-within-a-hospital. The new hospital will be an LTCH actually inside the short-term, acute care hospital.

Case Study 2.7—*Apogee Healthcare System*—The Apex Medical Center has been invited to join the Apogee Healthcare System. Currently, Apogee has three hospitals in the region along with half a dozen skilled nursing facilities, eight home health agencies, two dozen physician clinics, and a reference laboratory. One of the attractions of joining Apogee is that there are sophisticated billing processes that can be used by Apex.

Case Study 2.8—*Competing DME Suppliers*—Anywhere, USA has the distinction of having nearly a dozen DME suppliers in the immediate area. The Apex Medical Center has attempted to use selected DME suppliers but the competition is so fierce that Apex has decided to become a DME supplier itself in order to avoid complaints from local suppliers.

Case Study 2.9—*PEN Therapy at a Nursing Facility*—Anywhere, USA has a nursing facility that provides skilled nursing and also lower acuity level nursing services. There are several patients who need PEN (parenteral enteral nutrition) therapy. All of these patients are Medicare patients. Most of them are in skilled nursing but two of them are simply in nursing beds.

Case Study 2.10—*Private Pay Home Health Services*—The Apex Medical Center has established a home health service as a part of its integrated services strategy. Most of the patients are Medicare beneficiaries, and payment is made through the Medicare home health PPS. However, there is increasing difficulty in qualifying patients for these services under the Medicare program. As a result, there are requests for these services on a private basis with direct payment from the patients.

Case Study 2.11—*IDTF Billing for Radiology Services*—Anywhere, USA has an IDTF across town from the Apex Medical Center. Due to its location, many patients and physicians find that it is convenient to use. In some cases, physicians near the IDTF simply use it as a place to have radiology services provided. The ordering physician may elect to bill for the professional interpretation while the IDTF bills only for the technical component. In other cases, a radiologist at the IDTF interprets the test so that the IDTF bills for the total component, that is, both the professional and technical components.

Case Study 2.12—*IDTF Acquired by Apex and Converted to Provider Based*—The Apex Medical Center has decided to purchase the IDTF that is located across town. (See Case Study 2.11.) The hospital takes the necessary steps to convert this into a hospital-based facility. This means that the radiology services are now provided as an extension of the radiology department of the hospital.

Case Study 2.13—*ASC across the Street*—A group of surgeons has decided to establish an ASC right across the street from the Apex Medical Center. A wide variety of less complicated surgical services are provided at the ASC. The ASC opens at 6:00 a.m., 6 days a week, and closes promptly at 5:00 p.m. each day.

Case Study 2.14—*Cataract Surgery ASC*—Anywhere, USA has the distinction of having a specialized ASC in the community. While this is not a metropolitan area, there are a sizeable number of retirees on Medicare. This ASC specializes in one, and only one, surgery, namely cataract surgery with IOL (intraocular lens) implantation. While there is a single ophthalmologist, there are three operating bays that have plate glass windows so that friends and relatives of the patient can observe the operation. Also, the ASC has several small buses that will go out, pick up, and then return the patients after the surgery.

Chapter 3 Case Studies

Case Study 3.1—*Payments Less than Costs*—A financial analyst at the Apex Medical Center has been analyzing the payments received for inpatient services under a specific PPS. Apparently there are several categories that pay significantly below the associated costs for the services. This is occurring with several different types of ophthalmic surgical services.

Case Study 3.2—*New Technology Pacemakers*—The Apex Medical Center has had the good fortune of having two specialized cardiologists join the medical staff. Both of these physicians are now scheduling significant numbers of pacemaker implantations. Most of these services are performed outpatient. A major third-party payer makes a single, bundled payment for both the surgical service and the pacemaker device itself. Unfortunately, new high-tech pacemakers are being used that cost well above the outpatient prospective payment system payment.

Case Study 3.3—*Cataract Surgery*—There is an ophthalmologist who is on the medical staff of the Apex Medical Center. The ophthalmologist is working with the surgical staff at Apex in order to dedicate 2 days a week for only cataract surgeries. A time period of 20 minutes is allotted for each surgery and four different operating suites will be required. This way there will be quick throughput of the patients and thus both the ophthalmologist and the hospital will be more efficient and thus increase the reimbursement amounts received.

Case Study 3.4—*Nursing Staff Levels*—The Summit Nursing Facility is located in Anywhere, USA, down the street from the Apex Medical Center. To optimize reimbursement by lowering costs, Summit is considering reducing the number of registered nurses and using less-expensive medical workers.

Case Study 3.5—*Self-Administrable Drugs*—Two weeks ago, Sarah went to the Apex Medical Center's Emergency Department late in the evening with a headache and significant nasal congestion. While she was diagnosed with sinusitis, she was given a decongestant and a pain medication, both in tablet form, along with prescriptions for additional pharmacy items. Today, Sarah has received a bill from the hospital for the self-administrable drugs. Apparently, she must pay for the tablets she took at the hospital.

Case Study 3.6—*HBO Therapy*—The Summit Nursing Facility has a number of elderly residents who are Medicare beneficiaries. The Apex Medical Center is now offering hyperbaric oxygen therapy treatments. Several of the nursing facility patients need HBO to address some rather severe wounds and their physicians are prescribing such services.

Case Study 3.7—*Splinting Services*—Sam, an elderly retired rancher, has presented to the Apex Medical Center's ED with a badly sprained right elbow. The ED is unusually busy with several accident cases. The ER physician calls physical therapy to have a PT come to the ED to fabricate and apply a splint for Sam.

Case Study 3.8—*Two ED Visits on the Same Day*—Sam has been having a difficult day. In the morning he presents to the Apex Medical Center's ED complaining of abdominal pain. A diagnosis of indigestion is made and medication prescribed, after which he goes home. While at home he has a slight fall and in the afternoon comes back to the ED with a minor laceration.

Case Study 3.9—*Pre-Surgery Clinic*—The Apex Medical Center has established a clinic to handle assessments for patients who are scheduled for surgery, both inpatient and outpatient. From the day before surgery on out to 2 weeks prior to surgery, patients come to the clinic and are assessed by a nurse, laboratory and radiology tests are provided, a pre-surgery history and physical are made by a practitioner if not already performed, and an anesthesiologist makes an assessment as well.

Case Study 3.10—*Outpatient Surgery Claim*—Sylvia is auditing a claim that has been developed for an outpatient surgical case. This claim will be paid under a hospital outpatient PPS and she is checking to see how this will group. Here are the main charges on the claim:

- 14 Pharmaceutical items
- Surgical room charge/code for first procedure

- Surgical room charge/code for second procedure
- Pre-surgical room charge
- Recovery charge
- Post-recovery room charge
- Anesthesia
- 27 Supply items

The grouping process shows that there are only two payable categories. The pricer software indicates that the more extensive surgery is paid at 100% but the lesser surgery is paid at only 75%.

Case Study 3.11—*Separately Paid Fluoroscopy*—One of the private third-party payers for the Apex Medical Center uses a PPS for hospital outpatient services. A question has arisen concerning the way that fluoroscopy services are being bundled. For some cases there is separate payment for the fluoroscopy and in other cases the payment is bundled into some other service. The billing personnel at AMC have not been able to determine the logic for bundling (or not) the fluoroscopy services.

Case Study 3.12—*Preponderance of Complicated Cases*—A large regional hospital has the good fortune of having several well-recognized specialists in urology and nephrology. As a result, there are many cystoscopy procedures performed at the hospital. However, a significant preponderance of the cases is complex and takes longer than usual. Because of the larger number of complex cases, the averaged payment under one of the PPSs being used is generating payments that are well below the costs of providing the services.

Case Study 3.13—*Skewed CCRs*—The Chief Financial Officer (CFO) at the Apex Medical Center is reviewing the CCRs from the current cost report and it is noted that some of the CCRs are rather strange. Here is a small sample of the CCRs:

Operating Room	0.65374
Recovery Room	1.10045
Delivery & Labor Room	0.92834
Ultrasound	0.55641
Laboratory	0.66730
IV Therapy	0.88452
Respiratory Therapy	0.45885
Physical Therapy	0.87043
Observation	0.34650
Emergency Room	1.05478

Case Study 3.14—*Pricing Drug-Eluting Stents*—The service area personnel in the catheterization laboratory are setting the charges for the expensive drug-eluting stents that are used with coronary catheterization. Because these are expensive items, they are being marked up only 10% as per the tiered pricing formula for supply items and devices.

Chapter 4 Case Studies

Case Study 4.1—*Patient Transferred to Another Hospital*—Stephen, an elderly resident of Anywhere, USA, has been at the Apex Medical Center since he was admitted on Tuesday. It is now Thursday and he is being transferred by ambulance to another hospital. He remains in the second hospital until Monday, when he is discharged.

Case Study 4.2—*Same Day Admit and Discharge*—Sarah presented to the Apex Medical Center's ED not feeling well. She was admitted as an inpatient at 7:30 a.m. Infusion therapy was provided and by 4:00 p.m. she was more than ready to go home. Her attending physician discharged her at 7:00 p.m.

Case Study 4.3—*Admit Followed Shortly by Discharge*—A patient was admitted as an inpatient at 11:00 p.m. on Tuesday evening. First thing Thursday morning, the patient was discharged at 7:00 a.m.

Case Study 4.4—*Declining Case Mix Index*—The CFO at the Apex Medical Center has been tracking the CMI on a weekly basis and has noted that it is slowly decreasing and has been doing so over the past several years. An outside consulting firm has also been tracking this decline and has informed the CFO that the coding staff at Apex is incorrectly undercoding cases and their incompetence is causing the decline.

Case Study 4.5—*Elderly Patient with Pneumonia*—Sally has been admitted to the hospital with cough, congestion, slight fever, and she is not feeling well. The physician documents a diagnosis of pneumonia and proceeds to provide intravenous antibiotics. Oxygen is provided because the oxygen saturation is low. While there are other services provided, there are no other real diagnoses documented. Sylvia, an inpatient coder, is reviewing the case. For some reason the physician did not have tests to identify the organism causing the pneumonia. Also, according to the documentation, Sally appeared dehydrated but there is no diagnosis.

Case Study 4.6—*Equally Valid Principal Diagnoses*—Sylvia is working on a rather extensive medical case. A patient was in the hospital for 15 days and had a number of problems. After studying the documentation and performing the diagnosis coding, there are two distinctly different diagnosis codes that appear equally responsible for occasioning the admission of the patient.

Case Study 4.7—*Physician Documents Acute Respiratory Distress*—Sylvia is working on an admission of an elderly lady who apparently had a stroke. She was in the hospital for 5 days and had a very complete workup, including an MRI. There was a specialty consult along with other services. Right in the middle of all the documentation, the physician documents acute respiratory failure. However, nothing else appears in the record relating to this diagnosis.

Case Study 4.8—*Transfer to Higher Level of Care*—Sam has been in the hospital for 2 days with an unusual respiratory condition. His condition has been diagnosed as needing a higher level of care. He is taken by ambulance to a larger hospital where he completes his recovery over the course of 6 days.

Case Study 4.9—*Inpatient Leaves against Medical Advice*—Stephen has been admitted to the Apex Medical Center for care. He is rather disgruntled and after lunch on the second day, he leaves. Unfortunately, later the same day, he is taken by family members to another hospital about 60 miles down the road where he is admitted and stays for 5 days.

Case Study 4.10—*Discharge to Skilled Nursing*—Sam has been at the Apex Medical Center recovering from an illness. He has been in the hospital for 5 days and the physician determines that he can be discharged and placed in a skilled nursing home to complete his recovery.

Case Study 4.11—*Patient Returns Just after Being Discharged*—Steve has been in the hospital for 4 days and he is ready to go home. Family members pick him up after he has been discharged from the hospital. However, in driving some 40 miles back to his home, he has a significant relapse. He is driven back to the hospital, proceeds through the emergency department, and his attending physician decides to readmit him.

Case Study 4.12—*Patient Discharged and Admitted to Different Hospital*—Sydney has been at the Apex Medical Center for the past 5 days. He is cleared for discharge and family members have picked him up to go home. The trip takes an hour and a half and about 70 miles down the road Sydney is obviously not doing well. His family members decide to take him to a nearby hospital. He is assessed and then admitted to the hospital.

Case Study 4.13—*MRI at Another Hospital*—Sam has been admitted to the Apex Medical Center. His physicians have determined that he needs immediate MRI (magnetic resonance imaging) service. Unfortunately, Apex's MRI equipment is temporarily down. Sam is put in an ambulance and driven 60 miles to another hospital. The test is performed and Sam is brought back by ambulance.

Case Study 4.14—*Coding without the Discharge Summary*—Several physicians at the Apex Medical Center are notorious for completing the discharge summary documentation. These summaries can become lengthy because they review the overall case and then list all the diagnoses and any procedures that were performed. Due to the need for developing the claims on a timely basis, coding staff go ahead and code the case without the discharge summary.

Case Study 4.15—*Sequencing Codes from the Discharge Summary*—During a recent inpatient audit at the Apex Medical Center, the auditor noted that for two of the coding staff, the sequencing of the diagnosis and procedure codes was always the same as the physician listed in the discharge summary. The first diagnosis automatically became the principal diagnosis and then the other codes were reported in the same order as the physician listed the diagnoses and procedures.

Case Study 4.16—*Freestanding Clinic Network*—The Apex Medical Center has four provider-based clinics and five freestanding physician clinics. The freestanding clinics are 25 to 50 miles from the hospital, while the provider-based clinics are right in Anywhere, USA. Some of the outlying freestanding clinics have stand-alone laboratories and basic radiology services.

Case Study 4.17—*Hospital System*—The Pinnacle Health System owns two separate hospitals located about 30 miles apart. The system also owns twenty-five clinics in the general catchment area of the two hospitals. These clinics are all freestanding. There is a separate clinic organization owned by the system that operates these clinics.

Case Study 4.18—*Related Therapeutic Services*—On Monday afternoon, Sam goes to one of the Apex Medical Center's freestanding clinics complaining of fever, cough, and some congestion. He is examined by a nurse practitioner (NP) who makes an assessment, runs laboratory tests, and takes chest x-rays. The nurse practitioner briefly confers with a physician and then provides Sam with a prescription for a course of antibiotics and sends him home to rest. The claim for these services will be under the supervising physician's name. On Wednesday, a neighbor brings Sam to the hospital and he is admitted with pneumonia.

Case Study 4.19—*Pre-Admission and Post-Admission Window*—Sandra, the director of patient financial services at Apex, is grappling with a difficult situation. One of their major insurance companies is using a modified form of DRGs and has now implemented 10-day pre-admission and 10-day post-discharge windows. While it is difficult to even determine what should be bundled, now they have wait about 2 weeks after discharge before the claim can be developed and filed.

Case Study 4.20—*Delayed Transfer to Skilled Nursing*—Sandra, the director of patient financial services, is reviewing a claim. Sam was in the hospital for several days and then discharged home. The claim was filed with home as the discharge status. However, Sandra has become aware that Sam went to a skilled nursing home 2 days after he was discharged.

Case Study 4.21—*Pressure Ulcers on Admission*—Stephen is a long-term resident of a nursing facility. He has been transported by ambulance to the Apex Medical Center's ED. He is suffering from what appears to be pneumonia and his condition is deteriorating. He is rushed through the ED to an inpatient bed. Unfortunately, he has several pressure ulcers that are developing and this is not noted during the admission. He is in the hospital for 12 days and significant efforts are involved in not only taking care of the pneumonia, but also addressing the pressure ulcers.

Case Study 4.22—*Short-Stay Admission Changed to Observation*—Early in the week, an elderly patient was started on a diuretic and instructed to take extra potassium supplements. On Friday morning, the individual was brought to the ED suffering from a life-threatening potassium deficiency. The patient was started on intravenous potassium and admitted to the hospital. By mid-afternoon the patient was feeling quite well and laboratory tests indicated that the electrolytic imbalance was corrected. Utilization review intervened just as the physician was discharging the patient. The physician agreed that this should have been an observation case and the physician wrote an order for observation, which, in this case, lasted for 1 hour.

Case Study 4.23—*Knee Replacements and 3-Day Stays*—Sydney, the Chief Compliance Officer at the Apex Medical Center, has requested a computer run of Medicare beneficiaries over the past 6 months who have had a unilateral knee replacement and who then went on to skilled nursing for recovery. Sydney is amazed to find that there were 408 such cases and that 371 of the cases involved exactly a 3-day stay, nine cases involved just a 2-day stay, and the other twenty-eight cases involved more than a 3-day stay.

Case Study 4.24—*Observation Followed by Inpatient Admission Followed by Skilled Nursing*—The medical staff at the Apex Medical Center has become sensitive to admitting patients for possible short stays. Instead, observation is being ordered and then, if necessary, an inpatient admission can be made after the observation. One of the physicians is concerned because a patient was in observation for 2 days and is now in the hospital as an inpatient for 2 days. The patient is now ready to go to skilled nursing to complete his recovery. However, the necessary 3-day stay has not been met, so the skilled nursing services are not covered. The physician is very concerned about this situation.

Chapter 5 Case Studies

Case Study 5.1—*Splinting in the Emergency Department*—The ED at the Apex Medical Center is quite busy today. One of the ER physicians has requested that a PT come to the ED to fabricate and apply a splint for a dislocated elbow. The PT provides the services and then returns to the Therapies Department at AMC.

Case Study 5.2—*3-Day Window of Service — Surgery*—On Monday, Sarah went to one of Apex Medical Center's hospital-based clinics. In this case she saw a gastroenterologist concerning a colonoscopy. On Wednesday, she went to Apex to have a colonoscopy performed.

Case Study 5.3—*Multiple Visits within 3-Day Window*—Sally has not been feeling well. On Tuesday evening she goes to the Apex Medical Center's ED where several diagnostic tests are performed but no definitive diagnosis can be made. She is given a mild analgesic for pain. On Thursday she goes to one of Apex's clinics and is examined by a family practice physician. Further tests are ordered. On Saturday evening, Sally presents to the ED in significant distress. She is taken to an operating room where an appendectomy is performed on an urgent basis.

Case Study 5.4—*Multiple Lacerations*—While visiting a friend, Sally inadvertently crashed through a plate glass doorway. She was not seriously injured, but she did sustain several lacerations. There was a deep laceration on the left forearm, several minor lacerations on the other arm, and five lacerations on the legs.

Case Study 5.5—*ER Visit*—On Saturday mornings, Sam washes his car. Unfortunately, on this Saturday morning he cuts his hand on the windshield wiper blade. A neighbor takes Sam to the Apex Medical Center's ED where Sam is examined and his laceration is repaired using two sutures and some wound adhesive. Sam's neighbor returns him home.

Case Study 5.6—*Outpatient Surgery*—Sarah has presented to the Apex Medical Center at 8:00 a.m. for an elective outpatient surgery. She is taken to the pre-operative room where she changes clothes and receives some preliminary medications. She is taken to surgery, anesthesia is induced, and the operation is performed. Recovery only takes 3 hours and she then returns to the post-operative room, which is the same as the pre-operative room. She relaxes for several hours and then returns home.

Case Study 5.7—*Blood Transfusions*—Sally has been having some very real difficulties with anemia. Her family practice physician sees her at 9:00 a.m. and her physician orders the transfusion of a unit of blood over at the hospital. By late afternoon, Sarah is still not feeling quite right and she again goes to see her physician, who then orders that a second transfusion be performed over at the hospital. The second unit is transferred and Sally is feeling much better and goes on home.

Case Study 5.8—*ER Followed with Observation*—On Thursday evening, Sam has been having some chest pains. His daughter-in-law takes him to the ED at the Apex Medical Center. A thorough workup is performed, including a battery of laboratory and radiology tests. A definitive diagnosis cannot be made. A cardiologist is called in and a decision is made to place Sam in observation. Sam stays in observation until Saturday afternoon, at which time he is discharged home.

Case Study 5.9—*Second ER Visit*—It is now Saturday afternoon and Sam, from Case Study 5.5, is relaxing at home after his laceration repair. Now he is beginning to have some abdominal pains and he finally decides to go to the Apex Medical Center's ED for the second time in a day. Luckily, after a fairly complete workup including diagnostic radiology and ultrasound, Sam apparently has a mild case of gastroenteritis. He is given a prescription and sent home.

Case Study 5.10—*ER Visit Requiring a CAT Scan*—Sandy has been brought to the Apex Medical Center's ED. She suffered a fall and has several minor injuries. During the workup by the ER physician, the ER physician determines that a CAT scan should be performed. Unfortunately, Apex's CAT scanner is down for repairs. Sandy is carefully bundled into an ambulance, which then transports her to another hospital about 45 miles away. A CAT scan is performed and Sandy is brought back and placed in observation for 2 days before being discharged home.

Case Study 5.11—*Surgical Code Correlation Audit*—The Chief Compliance Officer at the Apex Medical Center has become aware that because they now have a new regional MAC (Medicare Administrative Contractor), the MAC can easily compare the codes on the physician's 1500 claim form and the hospital's UB-04 claim form. With the cooperation of several surgeons, 100 cases have been selected to see if the physicians' surgical codes are the same as the hospital's surgical codes. Surprisingly, the audit shows that there were twenty cases in which the codes were different.

Case Study 5.12—*Laceration on the Arm*—Sam has presented to the Apex Medical Center's Urgent Care Clinic that is located about a mile from the main hospital. Sam was gardening when he suffered a laceration on the left forearm about 3.0 cm in length. The wound is not deep but needs attention. The nurse does a general assessment, thoroughly cleanses the wound, and obtains a suture tray. One of the physicians comes in, examines the wound, sutures the wound, and also uses a skin adhesive. The nurse applies a dressing and instructs Sam to return immediately if there are any problems. Otherwise he is to return in a week to have the sutures examined for removal.

Case Study 5.13—*Vascular Catheterization on of Both Legs*—A lower extremity revascularization procedure is being performed on Sam. Conscious sedation is used, the surgeon using a femoral puncture of the left leg. Both legs are addressed. In the right leg, a stent is placed. In the left leg, a balloon angioplasty is able to open an artery. A vascular plug is placed and Sam goes to recovery.

Case Study 5.14—*Laceration Repairs in the ED*—Susan was out riding her bicycle when there was a slight mishap. She is not seriously injured; she has a laceration (3.0 cm) on the left arm and another deeper laceration (3.2 cm) on her right arm. Upon presentation to the ED, she is triaged and then seen by an ER physician who performs a general examination. After the general examination, the two lacerations are examined. The left arm requires a simple laceration repair while the right arm requires an intermediate closure. The nurse applies dressings and gives Susan the discharge instructions to return to the ED in a week to have the sutures removed or to come back immediately if there are any problems.

Case Study 5.15—*Return to ED for Suture Removal*—Susan, from Case Study 5.14, is now returning to the Apex Medical Center's ED to have her sutures removed. It has been 6 days and the lacerations are pretty well healed. The nurse encounters Susan and determines that the medical condition with which Susan is presenting is not an emergency. The nurse obtains a tray. One of the ER physicians briefly examines the wounds and orders the nurse to remove the sutures. The nurse completes the work and sends Susan on her way.

Case Study 5.16—*Uncomplicated Fractured Rib*—Sam is presenting to the ED after he fell off his horse. Other than some bruises and a contusion, he is complaining of some upper chest pain. Laboratory tests are run and x-rays taken. He is diagnosed with a simple fracture of one rib that is uncomplicated. He is provided with an analgesic, educated on how to delimit activities until the rib can heal, and then he is discharged home.

Case Study 5.17—*Extended Outpatient Surgical Procedure*—Sam has presented to the outpatient surgery unit of the Apex Medical Center. An outpatient hernia repair is scheduled. However, as the procedure progresses, a much more extensive procedure must be performed. Sam goes to recovery and after 7 hours is placed in observation. He is discharged after 2 days of observation. Coding staff at Apex are now coding the case and realize that the actual procedure performed is on the CMS inpatient-only list.

Case Study 5.18—*Injections during Surgery*—The billing personnel at the Apex Medical Center are concerned about proper billing for injections before surgery. For some patients, the surgeon will order a pre-surgery antibiotic injection. These injections are performed only when medically necessary and are not a routine part of the surgery itself.

Case Study 5.19—*Drug-Eluting Stents*—The Apex Medical Center is performing more and more coronary catheterization services using the more expensive drug-eluting stents. The financial analysts at the hospital cannot understand why the payments for the drug-eluting stent placements do not pay for the full difference between regular stenting and drug-eluting stenting.

Case Study 5.20—*Direct Observation Admission*—Sam has not been feeling well. His daughter-in-law takes him to the doctor's office. After a thorough examination, the physician decides that Sam should go into observation over at the hospital. The physician writes an order and Sam is taken to the hospital where he is place in an observation bed after a nursing assessment.

Case Study 5.21—*Observation Admission from a Provider-Based Clinic*—Sarah has made it to one of the Apex Medical Center's provider-based clinics. The clinic is located in a medical office building right next to the hospital. After a thorough workup, the physician decides that Sarah should be taken over to the hospital and placed in an observation bed. Hospital personnel, via a wheelchair, move Sarah to the hospital along with the clinical record showing the physician's assessment and order for observation.

Case Study 5.22—*Chest Pains with a Minor Laceration*—Sam has been having some chest pains and his son takes him to the ED at the Apex Medical Center. Upon exiting the car, Sam does sustain a minor laceration on his hand. In the ED, a fairly complete workup is performed and he is placed under the chest pain protocol. The laceration on his hand is repaired and he is in observation for 2 days and then released home.

Case Study 5.23—*Multiple Surgeries – ED*—Steve, a Medicare beneficiary, has been driven to the ED at Apex. He was in an accident and hurt his right leg and suffered a laceration on the left forearm. In the ED, Steve is assessed, x-rays are taken, and laboratory services are provided. There is a nondisplaced fracture of the right leg and the laceration on the forearm is sutured. A cast is applied to the leg to address the fracture.

Case Study 5.24—*Multiple Surgeries—Colonoscopy*– Sarah is presenting to the Apex Medical Center to have a routine colonoscopy. This is her fifth colonoscopy. Under conscious sedation, the colonoscopy proceeds fairly smoothly. There are two polyps removed by the snare technique. There are also four small polyps removed using the cold biopsy forceps. Samples of the polyps are forwarded to pathology. She is awakened and recovers within 2 hours, at which point she is taken home by her daughter.

Case Study 5.25—*Post Outpatient Surgery Observation*—An elderly patient has presented to the hospital for an outpatient surgical procedure. The surgery proceeds according to plan and the patient is taken to recovery. The patient recovers very slowly with nausea and discomfort. After 6 hours, the surgeon orders the patient taken to observation where the patient spends the night and discharge occurs mid-morning.

Case Study 5.26—*Pre-Surgery Clinic*—To better care for surgery patients, the Apex Medical Center has established a pre-surgery clinic. Surgeons send patients to this clinic several days before the scheduled surgery. A nurse performs a thorough assessment, radiology and laboratory services are provided, and the anesthesiologist examines the patient and completes the anesthesia question- naire. The patient is also given detailed instructions on where and when to report, along with what should be expected.

Case Study 5.27—*Pre-Surgery History and Physical Examination*—The Apex Medical Center performs a high volume with a wide variety of outpatient surgical procedures. A problem has been encountered that patients sometimes present for surgery without a pre-surgery history and physi- cal (H&P) or an H&P that is not current. The hospital has hired a Nurse Practitioner (NP) who is in the operative areas in the mornings to perform or update H&Ps so that surgery can take place.

Case Study 5.28—*Return to Operating Room*—An elderly patient presented to the Apex Medical Center for an outpatient surgical procedure. The procedure took longer than usual and the patient had difficulty in recovery. The patient was placed in observation. The next day the patient was examined and the surgeon determined that the operation must be performed again. The patient was returned to the operating room and the surgery was successfully performed. The patient remained in observation for 2 days and was discharged.

Case Study 5.29—*E/M Visit with Laboratory and X-ray*—Sarah has awakened with a stuffy nose and sore throat. She calls the Acme Medical Clinic only to find that her primary care physi- cian is out of town and the clinic personnel direct her to go to the ED at Apex. She presents, is screened, and then sees a physician. A chest x-ray and laboratory tests are run, as well as a brief examination. She is sent home with several prescriptions.

Case Study 5.30—*Coronary Catheterization Laboratory*—Sam has presented to the Apex Medical Center's Catheterization Laboratory. He has been having some chest pains and associated problems. Using conscious sedation, through a left femoral puncture, the catheter is advanced to the heart, diagnostic tests are performed, and a drug-eluting stent is placed using an angioplasty balloon. Additionally, an atherectomy is performed on a different coronary artery. Upon withdrawing the catheter down through the aorta, the physician performs nonselective angiography at the renal level and then also performs bilateral lower extremity angiography with the catheter located at the aortic bifurcation. A vascular plug is deployed for closure.

Case Study 5.31—*Autologous Blood Salvage* *—Sally is having an operative procedure performed. The operation itself takes about an hour and during the operation, any blood that is lost is being collected, processed, and infused back into Sally. The operation goes smoothly; Sally is taken to recovery and is sent home 6 hours later.

Case Study 5.32—*Lengthy Cystoscopies*—Most cystoscopies at the Apex Medical Center are generally routine and often are completed in less than 15 minutes. Today, Apex has a case that for various reasons has become complicated and takes 90 minutes to complete even though the proper coding is CPT 52000, cystourethroscopy. Apex charges by 15-minute time units at $1,000.00 per time unit. Thus, the basic charge for this service is $6,000.00. The APC payment for CPT 52000 is approximately $550.00. The Apex Medical Center's cost-to-charge ratio in this area is 0.50.

Case Study 5.33—*High Incident of Cost Outliers*—One of the reimbursement specialists at the Apex Medical Center routinely monitors cost outlier payments under APCs. This includes checking to make certain the cost outliers are paid and that the proper amount is paid. The specialist has noted that for cystoscopies, there is an unusually high incidence of cost outliers. In about 40% of the cases, an APC cost outlier is generated.

Case Study 5.34—*Infusion Center on Campus*—The Apex Medical Center has a nice, very active infusion center in a separate building on campus. There is a walkway connecting the infusion center to the hospital. Chemotherapy, blood transfusions, injection, infusion, hydration, and associated services are provided from 7:00 a.m. until 9:00 p.m. at night during the week. Specially trained nursing staff provides the services.

Case Study 5.35—*Freestanding Clinic Converted to Provider Based*—The Acme Medical Clinic is down the road about two blocks from the Apex Medical Center. Acme was founded by several family practice physicians and has been operating as a freestanding clinic for years. The physicians and the hospital have talked about the hospital acquiring the clinic and then hiring the physicians as employees under contracts. AMC's board has finally given approval for the hospital to purchase the clinic and hire the physicians.

Case Study 5.36—*Dermatology Provider-Based Clinic*—The Apex Medical Center has the good fortune of having several provider-based clinics in several specialty areas. For dermatology, the hospital has three dermatologists and one plastic surgeon in a nice building on the hospital campus. Today, an elderly patient has been referred by a primary care physician for possible lesion removal. The dermatologist has seen the patient before, but it has been almost 3 years. The dermatologist performs a complete upper body integumentary examination for any possible abnormali-

---

* See CPT code 89861.

ties. Finding none, the dermatologist then removes a benign lesion 1.4 cm in diameter from the left arm.

Case Study 5.37—*Split Billing Not Recognized*—The Apex Medical Center has several provider-based clinics and Apex is experimenting with split billing its larger private third-party payers. For one of the private payers, the two claim forms were adjudicated. The professional claim form was paid in full as if the clinic were freestanding. The technical component claim was not really recognized and the insurance company moved the billing to the patient's deductible.

Case Study 5.38—*Split Billing Recognized*—Apex has been experimenting with split billing. One of Apex's larger private third-party payers does recognize provider-based status. Both the technical component claim and the professional claim were adjudicated and individually paid. However, the insurance company simply took the normal physician payment and split the payment between the physician and the hospital. The insurance company split the two payments using the same percentages as found in the MPFS for the services, that is, the normal site-of-service percentage reduction. Thus, this company paid no more than it would have paid to the physician; the overall payment was simply split.

Case Study 5.39—*Different E/M Levels*—Sam, an elderly resident of Anywhere, USA, has presented to a family practice provider-based clinic. He is an established patient and has been having problems. Dr. Smith does a brief examination and then spends an hour counseling Sam. There is virtually no nursing involvement other than the use of the examination room.

Case Study 5.40 —*CMS-855 Forms and Clinics*—Stanley is reviewing the roster of providers at the clinic that is due for conversion to provider based. There are five family practice physicians, two surgeons, three nurse practitioners, and two physician assistants. These healthcare providers will all become employees of the hospital. Stanley has been told that the hospital's CMS-855-A form will also need updating for the clinic as a new practice location.

Case Study 5.41—*Specialty Clinics*—The Apex Medical Center has the good fortune of having ten different specialty physicians who hold specialty clinics once or sometimes twice a month. Six of the physicians have decided to pay rent and treat these specialty clinics as their own clinics, that is, freestanding. The other four have decided to participate with Apex in establishing their clinics as provider based.

Case Study 5.42—*IVIG Services*—Sarah is presenting to the infusion center at Apex for one of a series of intravenous immune globulin (IVIG) injections. However, she is not feeling well today. A nurse assesses Sarah and determines that she should not have the IVIG. Sarah is told to go home, rest, and then return the next day for the services.

Case Study 5.43—*Catheter Removal*—It is 4:45 p.m. A patient is presenting to the Apex Medical Center's outpatient service area with a physician's order in hand. The patient has a catheter in place. The order indicates that the patient is to be voided. If there is more than 500 cc, then the catheter is to be left in place; otherwise the catheter is to be removed. The nurse performs the services and then, based on the orders, removes the catheter. The patient is then discharged home.

Case Study 5.44—*Orthopedic ASC*—Several of the orthopedic surgeons who are on the staff of the Apex Medical Center have established a very nice ASC right across the street from Apex. Orthopedic services are provided for Medicare patients as well as private payer patients. The ASC performs all and any orthopedic services that can legally be performed at the ASC. Now there is even talk about converting this ASC to a specialty, physician-owned hospital.

Case Study 5.45—*Pilonidal Cysts at an ASC*—Among the surgeries being performed, one patient has a simple pilonidal cyst, CPT 10080, and another patient has a complex pilonidal cyst, CPT 10081. The services are successfully accomplished in both cases.

Case Study 5.46—*Surgical Service Outpatient versus Inpatient*—Sam needs to have carotid stent placement. His physician has decided to perform this procedure on an inpatient basis even though Sam is otherwise in pretty good health.

Case Study 5.47—*Hyperbaric Oxygen Therapy*—The Apex Medical Center has decided to establish an HBO (hyperbaric oxygen) service using an outside firm. This is a provider-based operation and most of the services are for outpatients. The physicians in the community are quite excited because they have elderly patients in skilled nursing homes that can benefit from this service.

Case Study 5.48—*ER Services with Eventual Inpatient Admission*—Sam has been brought to the Apex Medical Center's ED suffering from chest pains and weakness. A thorough assessment is made and Sam in placed in the chest pain protocol and placed in observation. After several hours in observation, Sam is getting worse and he is then admitted as an inpatient for further services.

Case Study 5.49—*ER Services Where a Transfer Occurs*—An elderly patient has been brought to Apex's ED after an accident. The patient reports multiple symptoms, including chest pain and difficulty breathing along with lacerations and a fractured leg. In the ER the patient is carefully worked up. The lacerations are all repaired, x-rays show a nondisplaced fracture, which is splinted. The chest pain and difficult breathing worsen, and the decision is to transfer the patient to a larger hospital that can provide more comprehensive care.

Case Study 5.50—*Inpatient Admission Switched to Outpatient Observation*—Sarah was admitted to the hospital on Thursday evening. She is recovering nicely and it is now Saturday morning. Utilization review has been assessing the reasons for the admission. The attending physician has been contacted and everyone agrees that this should have been an observation case, not an inpatient admission.

Case Study 5.51—*Infusions during Observation Services*—Coding and billing staff at Apex are concerned about billing for hydrations and infusions while the patient is in observation. There is confusion about whether the observation hours during hydrations and infusions should be subtracted from the overall number of observation hours.

Case Study 5.52—*Radiation Oncology and Physician Supervision*—The Apex Medical Center has a nice radiation oncology program with two radiation oncologists employed by the hospital. The physicians' offices are located in a very nice medical office building right across the parking lot from the hospital. The physicians will see patients in the office while radiation services are being provided at the hospital by specially trained technicians.

Chapter 6 Case Studies

Case Study 6.1—*Observation Followed by Inpatient Followed by Skilled Nursing*—Sarah was brought to the Apex Medical Center's ED suffering from cough, congestion, fever, and general weakness. Her attending physician placed her in an observation bed and started intravenous antibiotics. She slowly improved and after 2 days in observation she was admitted to the hospital. After 2 days as an inpatient, she was much improved but she really needed skilled nursing services for a week or so. She was taken to the local nursing facility where she recovered nicely and was discharged home.

Case Study 6.2—*SNF Resident ED Visit*—A resident at the Summit SNF has taken a tumble and sustained two lacerations. An ambulance brings the resident to the Apex Medical Center's ED. The patient is examined, lab tests performed, x-rays taken for possible fractures, and even a CAT scan given to check for a possible stroke. The only injuries are the two lacerations that are repaired and the ambulance takes the patient back to Summit.

Case Study 6.3—*Physician and Nurse Practitioner Visiting an SNF*—Dr. Smith from the Acme Medical Clinic goes to the Summit SNF once a month. Today he is bringing a nurse practitioner to assist him with several residents. After a busy day, Dr. Smith and the NP return to the clinic. Dr. Smith tells the billing staff to bill all the services in his name because the NP was working under his direct supervision.

Case Study 6.4—*SNF-Based Clinic*—The Summit nursing facility has grown over the past 10 years. There is now a sizeable skilled nursing population along with an ever-growing nursing home and even assisted living. Summit is now considering establishing its own clinic and hiring physicians to mainly serve the nursing facility population. Currently, Summit has already hired two nurse practitioners, although there is no professional billing for their services.

Case Study 6.5—*Homebound Qualifications*—Samantha is now well into her nineties. She can no longer walk with a cane. She is able, for brief periods, to use a walker. Her preferred method of getting around is a wheelchair. She lives alone in her home of many years. The only time she leaves her home is to go to the doctor, the dentist, and bi-weekly visits to the beauty parlor. She has given up even going to church.

Case Study 6.6—*Auditing Home Health Services*—Stanley, a health care consultant, has been asked to conduct a study for a home health agency in Anywhere, USA. Because of the way services are provided, Stanley is concerned about how to obtain an appropriate sampling of cases. Should the cases be picked at the individual visit level, or should the cases be picked based on 60-day episodes-of-care?

Case Study 6.7—*OIG Visit to a Home Health Agency*—An OIG agent has arrived in Anywhere, USA to conduct a probe audit at the home health agency. Apparently there have been some complaints about over-billing. The OIG agent has selected thirty individual visits by nurses. The specific visits are all for different patients and they go back up to 3 years.

Case Study 6.8—*Home Healthcare Limited Time Period*—Sarah is back home after an inpatient stay and then an SNF stay with a pressure fracture of the back. She is doing reasonably well. Home health services have been established with a nursing visit twice a week, physical therapy twice a week, and a home health aide visiting three times a week. However, after only a week, she falls, fractures her hip, and is taken to the hospital.

Case Study 6.9—*Home Health Less than 60 days*—Sam has returned home after a hospital stay. Only limited home health services are being provided. A nurse visits once a week and a home health aide also visits once a week. After 4 weeks, Sam has recovered to the point that he is ambulating quite well and home health services are no longer needed.

Case Study 6.10—*Home Health Change in Status*—An elderly Medicare beneficiary has been receiving home health services for some time. The patient did develop an infection, which has been treated on an outpatient basis, but clearly the patient's health status has changed at least for the time being. The physician orders additional home health services.

Case Study 6.11—*LTCH inside an Acute Care Hospital*—A large metropolitan hospital has encountered a challenge. The hospital is having more and more patients who are quite sick with multiple disease processes. These patients are requiring a month or more of care in order to properly recover. The idea has arisen that part of the acute care hospital space, the third and fourth floors, be dedicated to such patients and that a hospital-within-a-hospital be established with an LTCH designation.

Case Study 6.12—*Transfer to LTCH*—Sam has been at the Apex Medical Center for 10 days. The MS-DRG to which his services group has a GMLOS of 8 days. Sam has several rather severe comorbidities. There is an LTCH in the area that can better address Sam's needs on a longer-term basis. Sam is transferred, remains at the LTCH for 6 weeks, and is discharged home under a home health plan of care.

Case Study 6.13—*Bilateral Knee Replacement*—Sarah has finally agreed to have knee replacement on both sides. She goes to the Apex Medical Center where the surgical procedure is performed and things go well. She is in the hospital for 5 days and then she needs to move to either a skilled nursing facility or to the inpatient rehabilitation unit of the hospital.

Case Study 6.14—*ER Utilization while in IPF*—Sydney has been having some problems and he is admitted to the distinct part inpatient psychiatric unit on Monday morning. Later that day, he injuries himself, apparently an accident from a fall, sustaining several lacerations. He is taken to the emergency department where the lacerations are repaired and he returns to the IPF.

Case Study 6.15—*ECT Services*—One of the physicians at the Apex Medical Center performs ECT (electro-convulsive therapy), including patients at the distinct part IPF. This is a relatively expensive service and there is concern that this service may simply be part of the IPF base rate.

Case Study 6.16—*Interrupted Stay versus Discharge*—On Monday morning, Sydney is finally being discharged from the IPF. Several family members pick him up and take him home. However, on Wednesday, after being taken to the emergency department at Apex, he is readmitted to the IPF unit.

Case Study 6.17—*Proposed Use of Prospective Payment*—The Apogee Health System now consists of three hospitals, along with a wide variety of clinics, nursing facilities, and home health.

There is one major private third-party payer (TPP) that represents nearly 40% of the revenue stream. The TPP is in the process of converting payments from a percentage of charges payment system to several modified prospective payment systems. Currently, the percentage of charges payment level is 85%.

Here is the rundown:

■ Inpatient: MS-DRGs with a 20% increase above the Medicare payment rate
■ Outpatient: An enhanced form of APGs using local incidence and charge data
■ Home Health: HH-PPS with a 25% increase above the Medicare payment rate
■ Skilled Nursing: RUGs classification with a 15% increase above the Medicare payment rate

Case Study 6.18—*Maximus Insurance Company Utilization of PPSs*—Maximus has been growing at a fairly rapid pace. Marketing has begun in two additional states. The time has come to gain more control over expenditures to hospitals, clinics, physicians, and other healthcare providers. The financial analysts at Maximus are looking at making changes in the following areas:

■ Inpatient: Currently a per-diem surgery/per-diem medical; move to inpatient PPS of some sort.
■ Outpatient: Currently a percentage of charges; move to some form of APCs.
■ Home Health: Currently a flat rate nursing visit/flat rate home health aide visit – other services at charges; this is a low-volume area, but cost containment with some sort of packaged approach is desired, particularly with supplies.
■ Skilled Nursing: Currently a per diem; this area is growing and cost containment is desired.

Appendix B: Acronyms

The following is a list of the more common acronyms used in connection with healthcare payment systems. New acronyms and terminology seem to arise almost every day.

1500: Professional Claim Form (See CMS-1500)
6σ: Six Sigma (see Quality Improvement Techniques)
AAHAM: American Association of Healthcare Administrative Management
A/P: Accounts Payable
A/R: Accounts Receivable
AA: Anesthesia Assistant
ABC: Activity-Based Costing
ABN: Advance Beneficiary Notice (see also NONC, HINNC)
ACC: Ambulatory Care Center
ACEP: American College of Emergency Physicians
ACHE: American College of Healthcare Executives
ACO: Accountable Care Organization
ACS: Ambulatory Care Services
ADA: Americans with Disabilities Act
AFS: Ambulance Fee Schedule
AGPAM: American Guild of Patient Account Managers (see AAHAM)
AHA: American Hospital Association
AHIMA: American Health Information Management Association
ALJ: Administrative Law Judge
ALOS: Average Length-of-Stay
AMA: American Medical Association, or American Management Association
AMC: Apex Medical Center, or Acme Medical Clinic
AMLOS: Arithmetic Mean Length of Stay
AO: Advisory Opinion
AOAA: American Osteopathic Association Accreditation
APC(s): Ambulatory Payment Classification(s)
AP-DRG(s): All Patient DRG(s)
APG(s): Ambulatory Patient Group(s)
APR-DRG(s): All Patient Refined DRG(s)
ASC: Ambulatory Surgery Center
ASCII: American Standard Code for Information Interchange
ASF: Ambulatory Surgical Facility

AVGs: Ambulatory Visit Groups
BBA: Balanced Budget Act (of 1997)
BBRA: Balanced Budget Refinement Act (of 1999)
BIPA: Beneficiary Improvement and Protection Act (of 2000)
BLS: Bureau of Labor Statistics
BPR: Business Process Reengineering
CA-DRGs: Consolidated Severity-Adjusted DRGs
CAH: Critical Access Hospital
CAP: Capitated Ambulatory Plan
CBA: Cost Benefit Analysis
CBR: Coding, Billing, and Reimbursement
CBRCO: CBR Compliance Officer
CC (computer): Carbon Copy
CC: Coding Clinic
CC: Complication and Comorbidity
CCI: Correct Coding Initiative (see also NCII)
CCO: Chief Compliance Officer
CCR: Cost-to-Charge Ratio
CCs: Complications or Comorbidities
CCU: Critical Care Unit
CDM: Charge Description Master (see generic term: CM, Charge Master)
CENT: Certified Enterostomal Nurse Therapist
CEUs: Continuing Education Units
CF: Conversion Factor
CFO: Chief Financial Officer
CfP(s): Condition(s) for Payment (see 42 CFR §424)
CFR: *Code of the Federal Register*
CHAMPUS: Civilian Health & Medical Program of the Uniformed Services
CHAMPVA: Civilian Health & Medical Program of the Veterans Administration
CHC: Community Health Center
CHCP: Coordinated Home Health Program
CIA: Corporate Integrity Agreement (see also Settlement Agreement)
CIO: Chief Information Officer
CIS: Computer Information System
CLFS: Clinical Laboratory Fee Schedule
CM: Charge Master
CMI: Case Mix Index
CMP: Competitive Medical Plan
CMS: Center for Medicare and Medicaid Services
CMS-1450: UB-04 claim form as used by Medicare
CMS-1500: 1500 claim form as used by Medicare
CMS-855: Forms used to gain billing privileges for Medicare
CMS+AP-DRGs: CMS DRGs modified for AP-DRGs logic
CNP: Certified Nurse Practitioner
CNS: Clinical Nurse Specialist
CON: Certificate of Need
COO: Chief Operating Officer

CoPs: Conditions of Participations
CP: Clinical Psychologist
CPI: Consumer Price Index
CPI-U: Consumer Price Index - Urban
CPT: Current Procedural Terminology (currently CPT-4, anticipated to go to CPT-5)
CQI: Continuous Quality Improvement
CRNA: Certified Registered Nurse Anesthetist
CS-DRGs: Consolidated Severity-Adjusted DRGs
CSF: Critical Success Factor
CSW: Clinical Social Worker
CT: Computer Tomographic
CVIR : Cardiovascular Interventional Radiology
CWF: Common Working File
DBMS: Data Base Management System
DED: Dedicated Emergency Department (see EMTALA)
DHHS: Department of Health & Human Services
DME: Durable Medical Equipment
DMEPOS: DME, Prosthetics, Orthotics, Supplies
DMERC: Durable Medical Equipment Regional Carrier (see CMS MACs)
DNS: Domain Name System (Internet)
DOD: Department of Defense (see Electronic Shredding Standards)
DOJ: Department of Justice
DP: Data Processing
DRA: Deficit Reduction Act (of 2005)
DRG: Diagnosis Related Group(s) (see AP-DRGs, APR-DRGs, SR-DRGs, CA-DRGs, MS-DRGs)
DSH: Disproportionate Share Hospital
E/M: Evaluation and Management
EBCDIC (computer): Extended Binary Coded Decimal Information Code
ECG: Electrocardiogram
ED: Emergency Department
EDI: Electronic Data Interchange
EEO: Equal Employment Opportunity
EEOC: Equal Employment Opportunity Commission
EGHP: Employer Group Health Plan
EHR: Electronic Health Record
EKG: See ECG. German for Elektrokardiogramm
E/M: Evaluation and Management
EMC: Electronic Medial Claim
EMG: Electromyography
EMI: Encounter Mix Index
EMTALA: Emergency Medical Treatment and Labor Act
EOB: Explanation of Benefits
EOMB: Eplanation of Medicare Benefits
EPA: Environmental Protection Agency
EPC(s): Event-Driven Process Chain(s)
EPO: Exclusive Provider Organization
ER: Emergency Room (see also Emergency Department)

ERISA: Employment Retirement Income Security Act
ESRD: End-Stage Renal Disease
FAC: Freestanding Ambulatory Care
FAQs: Frequently Asked Questions
FBI: Federal Bureau of Investigation
FDA: Food and Drug Administration
FEC: Freestanding Emergency Center
FFS: Fee for Service
FFY: Federal Fiscal Year
FI: Fiscal Intermediary
FL: Form Locator (see UB-04)
FLSA: Fair Labor Standards Act
FMR: Focused Medical Review
FMV: Fair Market Value
FQHC: Federally Qualified Health Center
FR: *Federal Register*
FRGs: Functional Related Groups
FRNA: First Registered Nurse Assistant
FTC: Federal Trade Commission
FTP: File Transfer Protocol (Internet)
FY: Fiscal Year
GAF: Geographic Adjustment Factor
GAO: Government Accountability Office
GI: Gastrointestinal
GMLOS: Geometric Mean Length-of-Stay
GPCI: Geographic Practice Cost Index
GPO: Government Printing Office
GSP: Global Surgical Package
H&P: History and Physical
HBO: Hyperbaric Oxygen
HCFA: Health Care Financing Administration (now CMS)
HCO: Health Care Organization
HCPCS: Healthcare Common Procedure Coding System (previously HCFA's Common
     Procedure Coding System)
HFMA: Healthcare Financial Management Association
HHA: Home Health Agency
HHMCO: Home Health Managed Care Organization
HH-PPS: Home Health Prospective Payment System
HHRG: Home Health Resource Group
HHS: Health and Human Services
HICN: Health Insurance Claim Number
HIM: Health Information Management (see also Medical Records)
HIPAA: Health Insurance Portability and Accountability Act (of 1996)
HIPAA TSC: HIPAA Transaction Standard/Standard Code Set
HMO: Health Maintenance Organization
HPSA: Health Personnel Shortage Area
HSC-DRGs: Health System Consultants Refined DRGs

HTML: HyperText Markup Language (Internet)
HTTP: HyperText Transfer Protocol (Internet)
HURA: Health Underserved Rural Area
HwH: Hospital-within-a-Hospital
I & D: Incision and Drainage
ICD-9-CM: International Classification of Diseases, 9th Revision, Clinical Modification
ICD-10-CM: International Classification of Diseases, 10th Revision, Clinical Modification (replacement for ICD-9-CM, Volumes 1 and 2)
ICD-10-PCS: ICD-10 Procedure Coding System (replacement for ICD-9-CM, Volume 3)
ICD-11-CM: International Classification of Diseases, 11th Revision, Clinical Modification
ICD-11-PCS: ICD-11 Procedure Coding System
ICU: Intensive Care Unit
IDS: Integrated Delivery System
IG: Inspector General
IME: Indirect Medical Education
IOL: Intraocular Lens
IP: Inpatient
IPA: Independent Practice Arrangement/Association
IPF: Inpatient Psychiatric Facility
IPPS: Inpatient Prospective Payment System
IR: Interventional Radiology
IRF: Inpatient Rehabilitation Facility
IRS: Internal Revenue Service
IS: Information Systems
ISP: Internet Service Provider
IV: Intravenous
IVIG: Intravenous Immune Globulin
JCAHO: Joint Commission on Accreditation of Healthcare Organizations
KSAPCs: Knowledge, Skills, Abilities and Personal Characteristics
LCC: Lesser of Costs or Charges
LCD: Local Coverage Decision (see also LMRP)
LLC: Limited Liability Company
LLP: Limited Liability Partnership
LMRP: Local Medical Review Policy
LOS: Length-of-Stay (see AMLOS, GMLOS, and ALOS)
LTCH: Long-Term Care Hospital (see also Long-Term Acute Care Hospital)
LTCH-PPS: LTCH Prospective Payment System
LTRH: Long-Term Rehabilitation Hospital
LUPA: Low Utilization Payment Adjustments
MA: Medicare Advantage
MA: Medical Assistance
MAC: Medicare Administrative Contractor
MAC: Monitored Anesthesia Care
MCC(s): Major Complication(s) or Comorbidity(ies)
MCE: Medicare Code Editor
MCO: Managed Care Organization
MDA: M.D. Anesthesiologist

MDC: Major Diagnostic Category
MDH: Medicare Dependent Hospital
M-DRGs: Medicare DRGs (DRGs used from FY1984 to FY2008 by Medicare)
MDS: Minimum Data Set
MedPAC: Medicare Payment Advisory Council
MEI: Medicare Economic Index
MFS: Medicare Fee Schedule (see also MPFS)
MIS: Management Information System
MMA: Medicare Modernization Act (of 2003)
MM-APS-DRGs: Medicare Modification All Payer Severity DRGs
Modem (computer): MODulator-DEModulator
MOG: Medicare Outpatient Grouping
MPFS: Medicare Physician Fee Schedule
MRI: Magnetic Resonance Imaging
MSA: Metropolitan Statistical Area
MS-DOS (computer): Microsoft Disk Operating System
MS-DRGs: Medicare Severity DRGs (CMS established in 2007)
MS-LTC-DRGs: Medicare Severity Long-Term Care DRGs
MSO: Medical Staff Organization
MSOP: Market-Service-Organization-Payment
MSP: Medicare Secondary Payer
MUA: Medically Underserved Area
MUE: Medically Unlikely Edit
MVPS: Medicare Volume Performance Standard
NCCI: National Correct Coding Initiative
NCD: National Coverage Decision
NCQA: National Committee for Quality Assurance
NCQHC: National Committee for Quality Health Care
NF: Nursing Facility
NP: Nurse Practitioner (some variation; for instance, ARNP – Advanced Registered Nurse Practitioner)
NPP: Non-Physician Provider/Practitioner
NM: Nurse Midwife
NSC: National Supplier Clearinghouse
NTIOL: New Technology Intraocular Lens
NTIS: National Technical Information Service
NUBC: National Uniform Billing Committee
OASIS: Outcome and Assessment Information Set
OBRA: Omnibus Reconciliation Act
OCE: Outpatient Code Editor
OIG: Office of the Inspector General (see HHS)
OMB: Office of Management and Budget
OP: Outpatient
OPPS: Outpatient Prospective Payment System
OPR: Outpatient Payment Reform
OR: Operating Room
OSCAR: Online Survey Certification and Reporting (System)

OT: Occupational Therapy or Therapists
OTA: Occupational Therapists Assistant
P&P: Policy and Procedure
PA: Physician's Assistant
PACT: Post Acute Care Transfer
PAI: Patient Assessment Instrument
PAM(s): Patient Accounts Manager(s)
PBD: Provider Based Department
PBR(s): Provider-Based Rule(s) (see 42 CFR §413.65)
PE: Practice Expense
PECOS: Provider Enrollment, Chain, and Ownership System
PEN: Parenteral Enteral Nutrition
PEP: Partial Episode Payment
PERL: Practical Extraction and Reporting Language (Internet)
PET: Positron Emission Tomography
PFS: Patient Financial Services
PHO: Physician Hospital Organization
PMPM: Per Member Per Month
POA: Present on Admission
POS: Place of Service
POS: Point of Service
PPA: Preferred Provider Arrangement
PPO: Preferred Provider Organization
PPP: Point-to-Point Protocol (Internet)
PPR: Physician Payment Reform
PPS: Prospective Payment System
PRB: Provider Review Board
PRM: Provider Reimbursement Manual
PRO: Peer Review Organization
ProPAC: Prospective Payment Assessment Commission
PS&E: Provider Statistical and Reimbursement (Report)
PSN: Provider Service Network
PSO: Provider Service Organization
PT: Physical Therapy or Physical Therapist
PTA: Physical Therapy Assistant
QA: Quality Assurance
QFD: Quality Function Deployment
RAC: Recovery Audit Contractor
RAPs: Resident Assessment Protocols
RAT-STATS: See OIG Statistical Software
RBRVS: Resource-Based Relative Value Scale
RC: Revenue Code (see also RCC)
RCC: Revenue Center Code (from the UB-04 Manual)
RFI: Request For Information
RFP: Request For Proposal
RFQ: Request For Quotation
RHC: Rural Health Clinic

RM: Risk Management
RN: Registered Nurse
RRC: Rural Referral Center
RUGs: Resource Utilization Groups
RVS: Relative Value System
RVU: Relative Value Unit
RY: Rate Year
S&I: Supervision and Interpretation
SAD: Self-Administrable Drug
SCH: Sole Community Hospital
SCIC: Significant Change in Condition
SDS: Same-Day Surgery
SFY: State Fiscal Year
SGML: Standardized General Markup Language (Internet)
SI: Status Indicator
SLIP: Serial Line IP Protocol (Internet)
SLP: Speech Language Pathology (see also ST)
SMI: Service Mix Index
SMTP: Simple Mail Transfer Protocol (Internet e-mail)
SNF: Skilled Nursing Facility
SNF-CB: SNF Consolidated Billing
SOC: Standard of Care
SR-DRGs: Severity Refined DRGs (HCFA proposed in 1994)
Sol-DRGs: Solucient Refined DRGs
SOS: Site of Service
ST: Speech Therapy (see also SLP)
SUBC: State Uniform Billing Committee
TLAs: Three-Letter Acronyms
TPA: Third-Party Administrator
TPP: Third-Party Payer
TQD: Total Quality Deployment
TQM: Total Quality Management
TSC: Transaction Standard/Standard Code Set (see HIPAA)
UB-04: Universal Billing Form – 2004 (previously UB-92)
UCR: Usual, Customary, Reasonable
UHC: University Health System Consortium
UHDDS: Uniform Hospital Discharge Data Set
UPIN: Unique Physician Identification Number
UNIX: Not an acronym, but a play on the word "eunuch" (computer)
UR: Utilization Review
URL: Uniform Resource Locator (Internet address)
USC: United States Code
VDP: Voluntary Disclosure Program
VSR: Value Stream Reinvention
W-2 form: Tax withholding form
WWW (Internet): World Wide Web
XML (Internet): eXtensible Markup Language

Index